THE WAR ON HEALTH

Satan's Agenda † God's Victory

I0541882

Printed in the United States of America
ISBN 978-1-95843-424-6 (paperback)
ISBN 978-1-95843-425-3 (ebook)
LCCN: 2022911806

Education; Health; Self-Help

MainSpring Books
5901 W. Century Blvd Suite 750
Los Angeles, CA, US, 90045
www.mainspringbooks.com

How to Take Back Your Health & Fulfill Your Destiny

THE WAR ON HEALTH

Satan's Agenda † God's Victory

Dr. Gail M. Davis
written by Jennifer Gumienny

ENDORSEMENTS

"What Dr. Gail has written will not only give you a new perspective on health and wellness but open your mind to many revelations God has provided about the root causes of illness and disease. Allow yourself to be enlightened, encouraged, and transformed by the words you are about to digest in this book on Real Health with Real Truth. In every generation there are leaders, innovators and forerunners who blaze trails. They endure the persecution, the friction, and the hardship that comes with being at the tip of the spear. As a friend and fellow warrior in the realm of the Spirit, Dr. Gail Davis embodies all of these things in the health and wellness world. Are you ready for the ride of your life? Turn the page and get ready to blast off."

John Jubilee
Founder - John Jubilee Transformations LLC., dba Energized Health

"In her book "*The War on Health*" Dr. Gail masterfully weaves the "seen" and "unseen" realms together for a panoramic view of how science and scripture go hand in hand to reveal God's plan for our physical and spiritual health and wholeness. She fearlessly uses her own life experiences and the eternal truths of the word of God to lead the way for the reader to follow. Her book is not only informative and encouraging but also a step-by-step guide to living the life God has intended for us to live."

Lisa Makowski
Pastor - Anthem Church

"Dr. Davis has brought into light the best ways of taking care of our body; God's ways. She has also shared her personal journey which is very encouraging. I highly recommend it."

Grace Khoo
Founder - Living Keys Studio

"If you are serious about taking control of your health, then this book is for you. War on Health exposes the truth about the root causes of poor health, while equipping the reader with knowledge and wisdom from God's Word. This book will change the way you approach your mental, spiritual and physical health. It's not just a book, it's a valuable resource that you will want to refer to again and again."

Patrice and Gina Tsague
Founders - Nehemiah Project International Ministries, Inc.

"Gail, you are a woman of God! *The War on Health* has inspired me to fight! Thank you for sharing your personal journey guided by the Holy Spirit to open up our minds to our destiny and identity of Spirit, Soul and Body made in the image and likeness of God. This book is for everyone desiring God's truth on healthy living. It will transform your life and give you victory."

Glenn Repple
Founder & Managing Partner - Repple Wealth Group

"*The War on Health* brings a fresh revelation of wisdom to chew on. Each chapter is meticulously laid out, and Dr. Gail's expertise rings loud and clear through each section. She so clearly articulates both the spiritual and natural effects of food and medication on the body, soul, and spirit. This book could not have been written at a more perfect time. I know this book will cause many spiritual eyes to be opened to the truth, and people will begin to shift their perspective and change what they are feeding on. This book is a game changer. Definitely a download from Adonai!"

Deborah Coates
Intercessor - Apostolic Intercessors Network

"War on Health - Satan's Agenda, God's Victory, by Dr. Gail Davis is a spirit filled and heart-felt book that you would want to share with every person you come in contact with. It envelopes truth, wisdom, health, and most of all the love of God and our redeemer Jesus Christ. While reading the book, I was able to further appreciate the contents shared on our physical bodies and ways in which we can improve on our health through lifestyle behaviors and modifications. This book is beyond complete in the ways in which it provides significance in the understanding of spirit, soul, and body. You are not only in for a fulfilling read but an unimaginably blessed and improved life. Feed your spirit, soul, and body in this page turner. I just can't wait to share this gift with my family, patients, and friends."

Dr. Juanita Cox ND, CNS®, LDN,BSc.
Founder - The Velma B. Cox Foundation for Type II Diabetes & Amp;
High Blood Pressure, Naturopathic Doctor, Certified Nutrition
Specialist®, Dietitian-Nutritionist

"Too many people are experiencing the frustrations of sickness and suffering. The search for a better sense of conscious well-being and relief from debilitating illnesses is intense. *The War on Health* by Dr. Gail M. Davis is absolutely superb! It is both inspirational and informational with very practical, love filled, God-centric and prayerfully rich affirmations to help a broad spectrum of audiences. Being a responsible steward of our bodies, is to understand how the body works and the vital role personal responsibility plays in our health and wellness experience. When sickness comes it is essential that we employ time-honored principles that, in cooperation with both natural and spiritual laws, will build up and restore the whole person – BODY, MIND AND SPIRIT.

The War on Health is a must read for anyone looking for a powerful and practical approach for applying God's original medicine for achieving outrageous health and vitality for their whole person - leading to both temporal and eternal victory.

What a blessing!!!"

Elisa Sharps, ND. PhD
Executive Director - International Institute of Original Medicine (IIOM)

"Dr. Gail Davis' manuscript comes just in time as we seek sustained health during this season of crisis. Her book is both an amazing testimony of healing and an accurate road map which guides us into personal health and well-being!"

Rev. Dr. Sheryl L. Price
Founder - His Hands Ministries Fellowship Inc. and Aligned for His Glory Network

"In the book "War on Health", Dr. Gail pours out her heart on health and faith and how they coincide together for a healthier, more abundant life. You see her passion for Jesus, our Messiah, and the importance of how our body is a temple unto the Lord. Dr. Gail will take you on a new journey of thinking outside the box. She will challenge you to think about your choices, and the consequences they will have on your life. In the world we live in today, her message could not be more timely. As the pages unfold, you will begin to see different paths you can take for a healthier lifestyle. I pray that this book will encourage people to stop and think about what they put into their bodies and look deeper at the root causes of underlying health issues."

Kilee Adley
Owner - KLA Medical

"I was honored to be asked to write an endorsement for my sister's second book, *The War on Health*. Being a physician (an Anesthesiologist for over 20 years), all I have known and practiced is mainstream medicine. Nutrition has never been a real part of the medical curriculum. Growing up with a sister who knows her purpose has had its pro's and con's! I will admit that reading this book has opened my eyes to REAL TRUTH that she has been telling me all along. I thank God that I am no longer in the dark! I am so thankful that my sister was brave enough to print the truth. I can honestly say that myself and my family have stayed well through the pandemic because of her knowledge. The medical profession needs this book!"

Kara Davis-Conliffe MD
Anesthesiologist - Independent Contractor

"Dr. Gail Davis has not only written a much-needed manuscript for us as unhealthy people but took a very simple concept like eating and thinking right, which can literally save thousands of lives, to make us pay close attention to how we care for the only body we have. She tells us of her own healing after spending a lot of money seeking answers when going from doctor to doctor. Dr. Gail's illness caused her to examine her lifestyle very closely, what she was eating, thoughts she was entertaining, and toxic words she was speaking over herself. She acknowledges being well on her way to destroying her own body/ temple but soon discovered a deeper revelation of God's principles in His Word on caring for her temple.

Dr. Gail reiterates the significance of understanding our authentic identities, leading to a broader understanding of the importance of what we eat. Because we are a three-part being - mind, spirit, and body - we must learn how to maintain a healthy presence here on earth. She makes the brain-gut connection a simple solution for the lay person. What we eat affects our brain, which affects our mental, emotional, and physical state.

Throughout *War on Health*, Dr. Gail discusses the importance of giving the Holy Spirit free reign to teach the reader truths so we can eliminate the free radicals of erroneous eating, stress, anxiety, fear, worry, anger, resentment, unforgiveness, and whatever other toxins and contaminates we give access to run rampant in our bodies and minds. When we change our eating and thinking habits, we literally change our lives. We often go outside the mandate of the purpose of the temple which is to host the Kingdom resident on the inside of us.

I am not only thrilled this book is finally being made available to the world, but equally excited to call Dr. Gail a friend, someone who does not mind sharing God's truths. I believe this is a book in pursuit of discovery, particularly as the reader steps into his/her true authentic identity."

Gayle Rogers, PhD.
Founder - Forever Free/Apostolic Coaching for Empowerment

DISCLAIMER

The information in this book is intended to provide helpful information and general knowledge to the reader. This book is not meant to be used as a substitute for the medical advice of a licensed physician, nor should it be used to treat or diagnose any medical condition or emergency treatment.

Please keep in mind that all of the opinions expressed throughout the book are part of my personal experiences. These are the insights and the Biblical perspectives that God revealed to me through my own healing journey. He will also guide you. I am not responsible for your healing - it is only God who heals. From the foundation of an intimate love relationship, God the Father will lead you. I was commissioned by God to sow my testimony and knowledge on the pages of this book, and my hope is that these insights will bear fruit in your life, as you apply them, and follow His leadership.

Although some dietary changes are recommended, they may not be suitable for everyone, so a health care provider should be part of your decision making. Please DO NOT use this information to diagnose or develop a treatment plan for a health problem or disease without consulting a qualified healthcare professional.

Only you can be responsible for your own health and safety. You are a testimony in the making because someone else is waiting and needs to hear your story - how God led you into healing!

TABLE OF CONTENTS

ACKNOWLEDGMENTS AND DEDICATION

This book is dedicated to my Lord and Savior, Jesus Christ, for giving me the creative idea to transform a powerpoint presentation into a book. Thank you, Lord, for giving me the motivation to write, not only my story, but also the courage to expose the truth and give your people hope. Thank you, Lord, for sharing Your heart with me and giving me Your passion to see people set free. You are truly the God of Love.

I want to thank my parents, James and Connie Davis for always supporting me, believing in me and encouraging me. You both are a blessing in my life and I treasure you.

Thank you to the reader's panel and Tammi Wenzig, my editor, for your contribution. All of your time, effort, and suggestions are greatly appreciated.

Special thanks to Nehemiah Publishing for overseeing the initial publishing phase and partnering with my vision. Thank you Poh Sim and your design team for your exceptional photos and amazing creativity.

I would also like to thank MainSpring Publishing for overseeing the final publishing phase and marketing strategies. Your professionalism and invaluable insight has been outstanding. I look forward to working with you on future projects.

Lastly, a BIG thank you to my writer, Jennifer Gumienny. It was so easy working with you. God knew what he was doing when He sent you to me. You were hand-picked by Almighty God and have been such a blessing in my life. I could never have done this without you.

PREFACE

One of my desires in writing this book is that more people would see the truth. The media tells us all sorts of reports about what is best for our health which seems to change every month! How do you actually know what is good for you? People everywhere are struggling with persistent health issues: poor digestion, brain fog, migraines, high blood pressure, weight issues, heart disease, cancer and many more. What is going on? This rise in illness isn't just physical, as mental health issues like anxiety, suicidal thoughts and depression are more common than ever. And no one seems to have a cure! Where do we turn for answers?

I have good news for you. There's a simple answer: turn to the One from whom all wisdom originated; to the Spirit of truth. Jesus promised:

*"When the Spirit of truth comes, **He will guide you** into all truth"* John 16:13 NLT.

*"Then you will know the truth, and **the truth will set you free**"* John 8:32 NIV.

God wants to help you. He is the God of all wisdom, and all knowledge. He is the only One that knows your unique makeup, and what your body, soul, and spirit need to function optimally.

And He wants to have a personal relationship with you. A relationship filled with ongoing communication so that He can instruct you how to get well and stay well. His invitation is real:

"You will seek me and find me when you seek me with all your heart" Jeremiah 29:13 NIV.

When my body began to break down. I went to so many doctors, spent so much money, and no one seemed to know what was really going on. So I turned to God and He helped me. Now, I wish I had done that from the very beginning! He literally led me to the wisdom that I needed to turn my health around.

This book is written to encourage you to turn to God first. Though I will share some of the key things I learned about health and nutrition, my primary motive in writing this book is to inspire you to engage with God on your own journey towards health. I have some wisdom, but He has all wisdom and knows specifically what you need to walk in wholeness. Another reality is that we have a common enemy. One who seeks to steal, kill, and destroy the abundant life that God wants to give us (Jn. 10:10). I hope to expose some of the fear tactics and deception running rampant in the healthcare industry. The enemy of our souls wants to rob us of what is rightfully ours, and he is prowling around the food and pharmaceutical industry in America promoting fear and blindness. I hope this book serves to open your eyes to his strategies so you aren't duped the way I was! The more we understand his tactics, the more clear-minded we become in our lifestyle choices.

God is good and He wants His children to live free from illness. This is part of our spiritual inheritance. He has created you with a divine destiny to fulfill on earth, and I hope this book empowers you to take a hold of it. Are you ready to live by the truth? Will you pursue the Teacher Himself? If you reach out your hand, God will take it, and lead you to your promised land of divine health. Your destiny is waiting.

"The lions may grow weak and hungry, but those who seek the Lord lack no good thing. Come, my children, listen to me; I will teach you the fear of the Lord" Psalm 34:10-11 NIV.

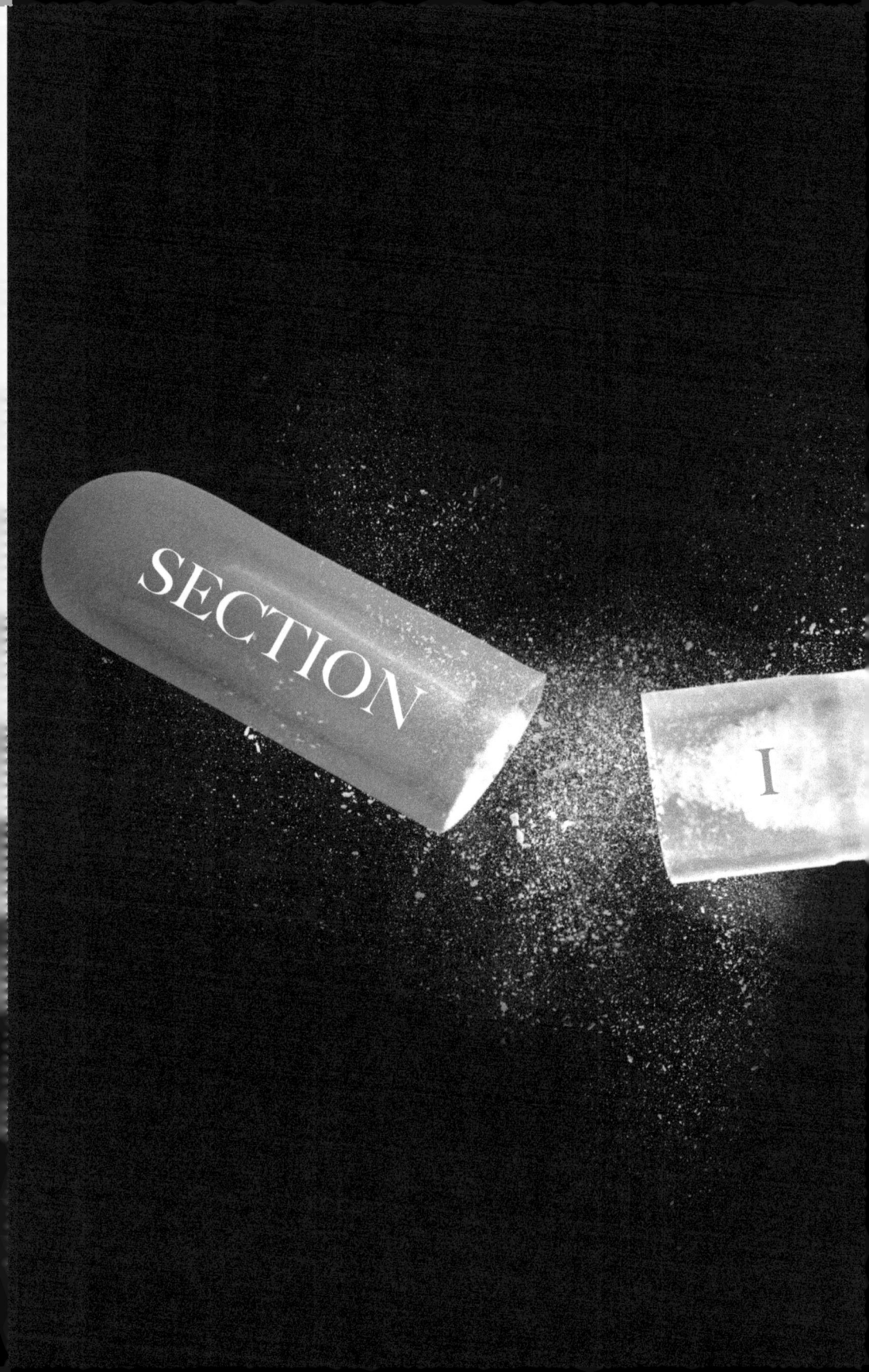

SECTION I

JOURNEYING TOWARDS HEALTH WITH GOD

Resolving complex health struggles is no easy task. On a personal level, or on a national level, there are so many factors to consider, and so many valid opinions about which solution or strategy is best. Where do you even start? Let my life be used as a testimony: I've found that a conversation with God is the only place to start. Man's wisdom will always contain some truth and some falsehood. But God's wisdom is pure, reliable, and right. He is the Good Shepherd! He knows how to lead us, so let's learn how to follow.

CHAPTER 1
SURVIVING OR THRIVING?

REALITY CHECK...

Did you know, according to the CDC (Centers for Disease Control & Prevention)[1]:

- Over half the population of adults in the US have a chronic disease - such as heart disease, stroke, type 2 diabetes, cancer, chronic lung disease, etc.

- And 40% of these adults actually have two or more of these diseases.

- Chronic diseases are the cause of 70% of the deaths in the US, killing more than 1.7 million Americans every year.

- Chronic disease accounts for 86% of our nation's health care costs, accounting for 81% of hospital admissions, 91% of all prescriptions filled, and 76% of all physician visits.[2]

- The average total health spending for a family of four with workplace coverage, rose to $7,726 in 2018, a 67% increase from 10 years ago.[3]

- According to CDC predictions, by 2025, 164 million Americans will be affected by chronic disease.

The statistics don't lie... the numbers are increasing - chronic disease is out of control!

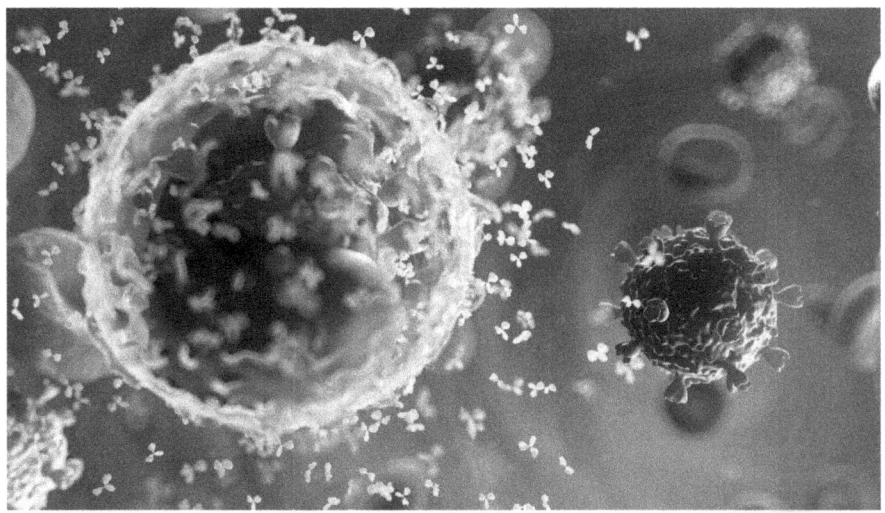

Can you imagine if chronic disease were eliminated completely? What would America look like? The truth is, the majority of chronic disease can be prevented, delayed, and even alleviated through simple lifestyle changes.[4] We all already know what we should do: eat nutritious meals, exercise, limit alcohol, and not smoke (and avoid second-hand smoke).[5] The CDC says these changes alone could reverse the trend. So what's the real problem? Some might suggest that we're uneducated as to what healthy meals consist of, or that we battle stress, and then indulge in emotional eating or other unhealthy comforts. We become lethargic and find it easier to pop a pill than go for a walk. I would agree that all of this is true and very problematic, but I think there's more to it. Behind the scenes, we have a spiritual enemy pulling strings on a large scale, in order to steal, kill and destroy our lives and health.

Let me start by telling you about my story...

MY JOURNEY

Many years ago, I was in a bad place. I worked six days a week without breaks, and constantly felt tired, irritable and anxious. I didn't sleep well and that increased my stress and added memory issues. I had no energy. I was eating all the wrong foods. I was an emotional wreck! But I just kept going, because, you know, that's what everybody does! Working too much, being tired, eating poorly - that's just life right? But is that the life God wants for us? Sooner or later, bad habits build up and our inner illness starts manifesting symptoms we can't control or hide. That's what happened to me. My eyes were bloodshot and weepy — and not just a little bit — people thought I was crying constantly, but I wasn't. My eyes looked swollen and red, as if I had broken blood vessels. As a dentist, face to face with clients all day, I was afraid of what my patients would think. Maybe they would think I was high and wouldn't want me to treat them. How was I going to get referrals if people thought I was out drinking all night? I learned how to joke about it. I'd say, "I just broke a blood vessel in my eye so don't worry I can still see," as I laughed it off. But the truth was, I was afraid. I had no idea why my eyes were reacting this way. I started to get really depressed and frustrated with my whole life. I wanted my energy levels back. I wanted clear eyes again. I wanted to feel and look better. I wanted to hear God. I was motivated to make a change. So, I made a list of all the possible underlying problems in my life which looked something like this:

Underlying Problems:

- My diet and lifestyle
- Bad habits
- Negative thoughts
- Toxic people
- Fear
- Lack of exercise
- Polluted environment
- A spiritual disconnect
- Destructive emotions

I was a mess, and this was going to be hard work. But I figured I had to start digging through each issue and try to rebuild my life.

I marched into Whole Foods Market on my lunch hour to buy anything that seemed healthy. "How about tofu? That's supposed to be healthy right?" I kept eating it, but my eyes started to get really itchy. I didn't make the connection until I was complaining to my receptionist who suggested, "Maybe it's what you ate?" A lightbulb went on that would light a significant portion of my path to health. Isn't it amazing how *sometimes God speaks through someone else, without them even knowing it!* This is how God first began to guide me. So, I went online and found out that tofu is made of soy, and soy can cause many risks to health. As soon as I read that, I made a decision to never eat tofu again! But more than that lone decision, my mind was being awakened to the fact that *what I eat affects how my body functions. And certain things that seem healthy, may not actually be healthy!* Breakthrough number one and two!

I realized I needed to learn more about what was healthy for my body, so, the second part of my journey began. I went to a naturopathic doctor to learn about food. What could go wrong? Except, everything. I had endless allergy tests. I tried so many elimination diets and all they produced was a long list of things I was allergic to. Even 'normal' foods were debilitating. Healthy foods like avocados still triggered my symptoms. I felt like I couldn't eat anything! I remember trying ostrich burgers just to try and find something I could eat without a reaction. It was ridiculous! Nothing was working. I began to spend a lot of money on supplements and tests. I lost an unhealthy amount of weight. I was convinced I needed to get rid of the allergens, but the process was taking so long. I became desperate. So I went to a medical doctor to get "magic pills." I hoped it would be an easy fix. I really understand people's desire to just take whatever the doctor gives you so that your sickness will go away. "If it will fix me, I'll take it!" The doctor looked at my red eyes and said it was probably Conjunctivitis, a bacterial infection, possibly brought on by allergies. They recommended a whole month of CIPRO antibiotics, which has very strong warning labels, so I decided to read about the side-effects online: "an increase in ruptures or tears in the aorta, which is the main artery in the body, significant drops in blood sugar levels, ruptured tendons, pain, "pins and needles" sensations, and depression, anxiety, thoughts of suicide and other mental health issues."[6] The FDA (Food & Drug Administration) reports that, "CIPRO can cause side effects that may be serious or even cause death."[7] Whoa! CIPRO (or fluoroquinolones) is not a weak allergy medication. Serious side effects can even begin after the first or second dose, and the after effects can last longer than a year!

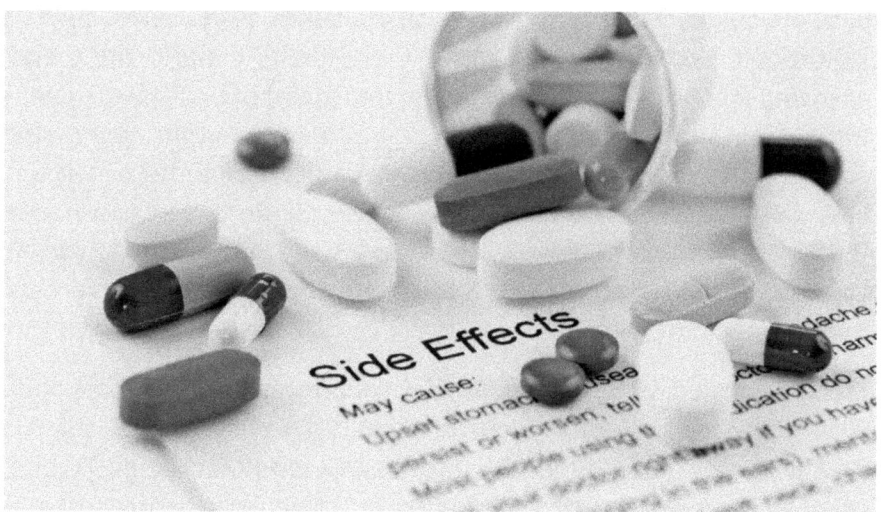

I thought, "I can't risk that!" I really just wanted to take a pill and make the whole thing go away, but I didn't feel comfortable taking this kind of drug for a whole month. It could have been very destructive to my body and I didn't want to create more problems. So I took the prescription, walked out, and never filled it. Here's an important thing to remember: **Sometimes our intuition or gut feeling is actually God's Spirit encouraging us in another direction.** Even though it seemed like I had no other option, I had to listen to that inner voice that these drugs were not the right choice. But what would I do instead? Well, I went back to the naturopath who did many different, but specific, lab tests that were not standard tests in a medical office. One of the tests revealed that I had an underactive thyroid, due to stress. The mystery of my health became more complicated. After many treatments, some parts of my body finally began to feel a bit better, but my eyes remained itchy, watery and now, painful! Pressure had begun to build up behind my eyes, so it felt as if my optic nerve was going to burst. I thought I was doing everything right. What was I missing? I had so much fear. I was irritable, and fatigued. It was so frustrating to spend so much money on all these naturopathic appointments, and so much money on supplements and treatments, with no firm solutions! Although I learned a lot on my naturopathic journey I was exhausting my funds and not yet fully healed.

I went back to the eye doctor. I conveniently avoided mentioning the fact that I didn't fill the prescription for CIPRO. This time, he referred me to a neuro ophthalmologist for a brain scan. The doctors saw a knot of intertwined vessels in the front of my brain that might be causing the pressure. I was relieved that they may have found the cause, until they said, "You'll need brain surgery." WHAT! No one is getting ready to operate on my brain!

This is when I first began to really cry out to the Lord. I remember the long drive from DC to Maryland praying in my car: "Lord... brain surgery? No Lord. This is not my portion. Lord show me what to do! Anything, I'll do it!" Tears were running down my face. I was desperate. I had to chase God! I had to run to after Him, pursue Him for answers. I wasn't giving in to deadly drugs or someone cutting open my brain! Only Jesus could help me!

Then, through a simple comment from my cousin, I realized how kind and compassionate God is. She came to town for a visit, and we were chatting. I mentioned that I had a slight headache. She began sharing a story about her own headaches. She said she had felt pressure in her head so she had a brain scan, and the doctors noticed a clump of vessels in the front of her brain. Her doctor told her this was a natural occurrence, probably hereditary, and not likely the cause of her headaches. At that moment, a light bulb went on! My blood vessels were not broken! It was just something that ran in my family line. This was a major spiritual turning point for me in my life. I had cried out to God for wisdom, and without any other prompting, my cousin comes to visit and brings up the exact situation I was experiencing.

God is so real! And He hears us! And He is able to open our eyes to the answers. It is such a comfort to know we aren't alone and God really is helping us. He cares about us and sympathizes with how we feel.

"Trust in the Lord with all your heart;
do not depend on your own understanding.
Seek His will in all you do,
and He will show you which path to take.
Don't be impressed with your own wisdom.
Instead, fear the Lord and turn away from evil.
Then you will have healing for your body
and strength for your bones" Proverbs 3:5-8 NLT.

OUR EVER-PRESENT HELP

Having God reveal His character to me was a big deal. He was listening. He knew the answers. And He loved me enough to share them with me. So I kept asking God for answers and, over time, He kept showing me more of who He is, and more of how I am made in His image. Our relationship took on a whole new depth of communication and trust, which was not something I was familiar with.

Growing up, I only knew God on the surface. I thought the Bible was just a story book, not something that actually happened, and is still happening! I accepted Jesus into my heart when I was a little kid, but I didn't understand what that really meant. I didn't know God was a real person. As I grew up, I became engrossed in the world, doing worldly stuff I shouldn't have been doing. There were times I searched for God, but I didn't really know where to find him. I had grown up in an episcopal church, then during my University post grad program, I discovered more entertaining churches where the community was fun to be part of, but it still seemed quite shallow. I remember feeling the Lord tell me, "you really need to look deeper."

> **God has a way of changing your circumstances to cause you to search for Him on a deeper level than you've ever known before.**

Then, I became ill. Very visibly ill. I mean, when your eyes are bleeding, and you're losing weight when you're already thin, you can't hide how you're really doing! When your skin starts turning colors, long sleeved blouses only help for so long. People start looking at you differently. My illness was a big blow to my self-esteem. In my university days, I really cared about my image and I was always trying to look my best. I thought I was all that and a bag of chips! But I couldn't hide my symptoms or the reality that there was something seriously wrong with me.

God brought me to the end of myself. To the end of medical advice. To the end of naturopathic solutions. It was just me and Him. I began to turn to Him and cry out for answers, "Lord, you can do anything! I know you can heal me. You designed the perfect body that heals itself. Tell me God, how come the whites of peoples' eyes are white, and mine are red. Why? Give me wisdom! Show me what I need to do to be completely healed, and I'll tell the world." *This was a major breakthrough. I learned how to converse with God for wisdom about my health.*

The Bible says:

"If any of you lack wisdom, you should ask God, who gives generously to all without finding fault, and it will be given to you. But when you ask, you must believe and not doubt, because the one who doubts is like a wave of the sea, blown and tossed by the wind. That person should not expect to receive anything from the Lord. Such a person is double-minded and unstable in all they do" James 1:5-8 NIV.

God speaks to people in many different ways: in dreams, in visions, through others, in prophecy. On my journey towards health, I really worked on my relationship with the Lord. *God and I talked as naturally as an ongoing phone conversation.*

I loved to ask the Lord questions and watch how He would answer them in different ways. He taught me in my quiet time through prayer, in worship, or we would talk together when I went for a walk. As I would pray and ask for guidance, I would see God move as I trusted Him to guide my steps. God is so real and relational. He became closer to me than most other people in that horrible time. He was truly my friend that stuck closer than a brother (Prov. 18:24). He was always there for me, and He will be there for you too.

God loves to hear you speak to Him in your own way. You don't need 'special words,' but if you're stuck or uncertain, here is a prayer you can pray:

> "Lord, you created me to walk in divine health.
> Good health is my God-given birthright.
> I ask You for Your wisdom for my healing,
> God, which is far greater than man's limited opinion.
> Lord, I ask You to lead me into the truth. Please guide me.
> How do I obtain the healing You've created for me?
> What is the next step that I should take?"

Then listen. ***Become expectant that as you seek you will find.*** Keep asking. Keep persisting in prayer. God will meet you and He will guide you. He is your Savior.

"Then they cried to the Lord in their trouble, and He saved them from

their distress. He sent out His word and healed them; He rescued them from the grave. Let them give thanks to the Lord for His unfailing love and His wonderful deeds for mankind" Psalm 107:19-21 NIV.

In my journey, when I felt I couldn't figure out what my body needed to get better, I felt God tell me, "Go back to the very beginning." It turns out, He has hidden much revelation in Creation. Let's go back and take a look at day one...

ENDNOTES

1   "About Chronic Diseases." Centers for Disease Control and Prevention. Centers for Disease Control and Prevention, October 23, 2019. https://www.cdc.gov/chronicdisease/about/index.htm.

2   "The Growing Crisis of Chronic Disease in the United States." Partnership to Fight Chronic Disease. Accessed September 18, 2019. https://www.fightchronicdisease.org/sites/default/files/docs/GrowingCrisisofChronicDiseaseintheUSfactsheet_81009.pdf.

3   Mercado, Darla. "Here's Why Your Workplace Health Insurance Is so Expensive." CNBC. CNBC, August 19, 2019. https://www.cnbc.com/2019/08/19/heres-why-your-workplace-health-insurance-is-so-expensive.html.

4   Willett, Walter C. "Prevention of Chronic Disease by Means of Diet and Lifestyle Changes." Disease Control Priorities in Developing Countries. 2nd edition. U.S. National Library of Medicine, January 1, 1970. https://www.ncbi.nlm.nih.gov/books/NBK11795/

5   "About Chronic Diseases." Centers for Disease Control and Prevention. Centers for Disease Control and Prevention, October 23, 2019. https://www.cdc.gov/chronicdisease/about/index.htm.

6   Ambardekar, Nayana. "Ciprofloxacin Risks and Side Effects." WebMD. WebMD, March 31, 2019. https://www.webmd.com/cold-and-flu/fluoroquinolones-safety-risks.

7   "Medication Guide." fda.gov, September 2008. https://www.fda.gov/media/73412/download.

CHAPTER 2
GOD SPEAKS THROUGH CREATION

"In the beginning God created the heavens and the earth. The earth was formless and empty, and darkness covered the deep waters. And the Spirit of God was hovering over the surface of the waters. Then God said, "Let there be light," and there was light" Genesis 1:1-3 NLT.

When you can have conversations with the Creator of the Universe, you can learn some pretty amazing things. God wants to reveal Himself to us. That's why He gave us the Word. But He doesn't reveal everything upfront all at once. He gives us a little, and then waits for us to ask for more. When I began seeking God for insight into my health, I began to wonder, "Why did He create things the way He did?" "What can creation teach me about how He made me?" The more I talked with God about my health, and read the Word, the more I became curious. I'd ask God, "why" all the time. "Why did you create the stars?" "Why did you make my body out of the dust of the earth?" Let me share with you some of what He showed me.

THE LIGHT OF LIFE

Light was the very first thing that was created. Think about this for a moment. God, in His infinite wisdom and perfect design, first created light, and then created things that would be dependent upon it. God designed creation so that life begins with light and is sustained by light. This holds a key to our design. Jesus Christ is called "The True Light." John says of Jesus:

"He was with God in the beginning. Through Him all things were made; without Him nothing was made that has been made. In Him was life, and that life was the light of all mankind... The True Light that gives light to everyone was coming into the world" John 1:2-4,9 NIV.

Just as we need sunlight to give our bodies a healthy dose of Vitamin D, so we need to depend on Jesus to sustain our life. When I first began my healing journey, I didn't know the depth of how much Jesus had to be a part of it. One day it clicked: healing is not attainable without Jesus. If you want to walk in complete wholeness, you have to know what Jesus did on the cross for you. I knew the facts, I knew He saved me, but I didn't know that His death and resurrection gave me power and victory to live life differently. For the first time, I began to walk out my salvation. It's sort of like getting a suntan, the more time you spend in the sun (and with the Son), the more your appearance begins to change, from the inside out. The Bible says as we draw near to the Son, we begin to brightly reflect His glory, and are transformed.

"We can all draw close to Him with the veil removed from our faces. And with no veil we all become like mirrors who brightly reflect the glory of the Lord Jesus. We are being transfigured into His very image as we move from one brighter level of glory to another. And this glorious transfiguration comes from the Lord, who is the Spirit" 2 Corinthians 3:18 TPT.

This also points to an element of our destiny. Just as He is The Light, so we, as His creations, are called to reflect His light. In Matthew 5:14, Jesus calls us *"the light of the world"* created to shine for His glory!

Creation holds countless parallels for us. The sun 'rises from the dead' after the darkness of night to provide life-giving energy to the earth, just as The Son of God rose from the dead to give life to our sinful bodies. The sun rises in the east and sets in the west, and in the book of Matthew it says, *"For as the lightning flashes in the east and shines to the west, so it will be when the Son of Man comes" Matt. 24:27 NLT.* The sun is at its peak at twelve noon, and it was at age twelve that Jesus 'peaked' and began preparing for His ministry by sitting in the temple questioning the teachers of the law.

God has created a universe filled with messages for us, if we are hungry to learn more about Him. Jesus tells us that creation is where wisdom hides: *"There will be signs in the sun, moon, and stars" Luke 21:25.* As if the twinkling of the stars is just to catch our attention; as if He's whispering, "Let me show you what the stars mean. Do you want to know?" The Scriptures are full of revelation that we may not see at first. It takes digging and a hunger! How hungry are you to search out His wisdom for your life?

FROM DUST TO DUST

When I began to ask God how I could restore my health, I realized that the Bible says that we are made from the dust of the earth. As I did my research, I learned that the earth is full of minerals that my body needs to function well: calcium, chloride, magnesium, phosphorus, potassium, sodium, and sulfur, chromium, copper, fluoride, iodine, iron, manganese, molybdenum, selenium, and zinc. These minerals are found in soil, and rocks, and water that are then absorbed by plants as they grow, or animals as they eat; these are then passed onto us. Of minerals, clinical nutritionist, Dr. Bruce Bistrian, says, "Each one plays a role in hundreds of body functions. It may take just a very small quantity of a particular mineral, but having too much or too little can upset a delicate balance in the body."[8] Once again, God's creation gives us clues as to how to restore our body's health! Science has continued to validate the significance of the creation story. Have you ever wondered why people feel refreshed when they are close to nature? Perhaps it is because we were created from it! We were raised in the Garden of Eden. Nature is our truest home! Our modern urban lifestyle hinders us from having regular, direct physical contact with the earth. We walk and drive on concrete, not soil. But God created the earth's surface with a vast supply of electrons and minerals that we need for proper health. Emerging scientific research confirms that our disconnection from the earth may in fact be a major contributor to physiological dysfunction[9]. In the Journal of Environmental and Public Health, researchers discuss the significance of "Earthing." Earthing (or grounding) refers to walking barefoot outside in order to transfer the Earth's electrons from the ground into the body. Reconnection with the Earth's electrons has been found to promote better sleep, reduce pain and alleviate other physiological impacts related to general well-being.[10] Isn't God's creation amazing? We are made up of what the earth is made of! This is why I know the body can heal itself as it receives these elements from the earth.

THE SECRETS OF SOUND AND WATER

Before the earth was formed the Bible says:

"The earth was formless and empty, and darkness covered the deep waters. And the Spirit of God was hovering over the surface of the waters... Then God said, 'Let there be a space between the waters, to separate the waters of the heavens from the waters of the earth.' And that is what happened. God made this space to separate the waters of the earth from the waters of the heavens. God called the space 'sky'" Genesis 1:2,6-8 NLT.

We are surrounded by water, both above and below. Believe it or not, at any moment, the atmosphere contains an astounding 37.5 million billion gallons of water, in the invisible vapor phase. If it were all to switch from vapor to liquid, the entire surface of the earth (ocean included) would be covered with one inch of rain.[11] Water is not only around us, it is also within us! Science confirms, our bodies are actually made of 60 percent water.[12]

So let's back up a bit and consider the implications of all of this. From the very beginning, God was hovering over the waters. Then, He spoke, and the water shifted. The powerful sound of God's voice initiated creation. The Bible reveals that sound actually shapes matter, and science confirms it. Scientists have played music around water, and observed how the crystalline shape of water molecules change with different tones and vibrations. Even yelling, or encouraging, will physically change the structure of the water. So, if water is within our bodies, guess what? The music, words, and sounds that we surround ourselves with will physically shift the water inside of us! This brings on a whole new concept as to why God instructs us to guard our tongues and speak with love to one another: *"Don't use foul or abusive language. Let everything you say be good and helpful, so that your words will be an encouragement to those who hear them" Ephes. 4:29 NLT.* God knew it would actually shift our internal design. He's hidden keys to our emotional wellness in creation! When the Holy Spirit showed this to me, I became a lot less negative with my words. Just as God spoke and created, when I spoke, I also created, and changed the shape and nature of the water within me. To enjoy the physical health God created me to have, I needed to speak, and surround myself with joy and truth.

THE FREQUENCY OF WELLNESS

When God spoke, the sound not only caused everything on earth to take shape, it infused everything with energy! We know that when God spoke from Mount Sinai His voice shook the earth (Heb. 12:26). The powerful vibrations in His voice made the earth respond. Science has studied creation's intricacies and discovered that everything in creation is made up of tiny atoms held together by energetic vibrations. Water, for example, is made up of two hydrogen molecules and one oxygen molecule. The speed of vibration of these components determine if the water remains liquid, turns to ice, or vaporizes. Everything we see, from plants, to rocks, to furniture, to food is infused with energy and has a vibrational frequency; including human beings! Nowadays, they can even measure the frequency of things we can't see, like thoughts and emotions. Negative thoughts vibrate slower, on a low frequency, and positive thoughts vibrate faster, on a high frequency. These discoveries give more clues to our health and wellness. But what does all of this mean for us?

In 1992, Bruce Tainio, of Tainio Technology & Technique, built the first calibrated frequency monitor which identified that a healthy body resonates at a frequency of 62-70 MHz, and when the frequency drops to 58 MHz, that is when disease starts.[13] Bacteria, viruses, and disease each have their own frequency, which can be eliminated by exposure to higher frequencies. Most foods have their own frequencies too! Much of the food we eat (canned and processed food) literally has zero MHz frequency, so we are eating dead food. No wonder we're such a sick nation! Fresh food, however, has an energy signature of 15 MHz, fresh herbs up to 27 MHz and essential oils even up to 320 MHz! We can literally infuse our body with health by understanding and applying how God created the universe.

Ultimately, God is the power source behind all of creation. So, it makes sense that when we are connected to Him, we operate at the highest frequency. The Bible tells us to fill our thoughts with what is good, and science tells us that when we focus on good things, our frequency increases.

"And now, dear brothers and sisters, one final thing. Fix your thoughts on what is true, and honorable, and right, and pure, and lovely, and admirable. Think about things that are excellent and worthy of praise" *Philippians 4:8 NLT.*

"Always be joyful. Never stop praying. Be thankful in all circumstances, for this is God's will for you who belong to Christ Jesus" *1 Thessalonians 5:16-18 NLT.*

God is teaching us how to keep our vibrational frequency high! God says always be joyful. Not just when things are going well. No matter how difficult things look, we have to know that God is going to turn it around for His glory. He's going to work it for our good. Our part is to have joy, even in the midst of chaos. Joy comes from trust. The Word says, *"Sing a new song unto the Lord. Let the whole earth sing to the Lord!"* *Psalm 96:1 NLT.* This song is literally sound therapy to your internal organs. It will raise your internal frequency promoting health, vitality, and spiritual well being. God also says to never stop praying. It's like He's saying, "Never be disconnected from me. Keep that channel of communication open. Be in my presence." Just like Jesus did! He was always going off to quiet places to commune with the Father. When we do these things we are operating with the frequency of heaven. Love, joy, peace, kindness, gratitude, engaging in prayer, and praise and worship, all of these things increase our vibrational frequency, leading to health and wellness in our body, soul and spirit.[14]

ALTERNATIVE MEDICINE

Some people may be concerned that beliefs about energy are tied to Eastern spiritualism or New Age, but actually, it's more deeply rooted in God's majestic creation! The Bible says that we can learn about God through what we can observe in Creation: Romans 1:20 says, *"For since the creation of the world God's invisible qualities—His eternal power and divine nature—have been clearly seen, being understood from what has been made, so that people are without excuse"* (NIV). For centuries, mankind has been observing the energy in creation, each tradition giving it a different name - frequency, vitality, Qi, etc. Albert Einstein said, "Everything in life is vibration." As Christians, we know the true Source of that energy: God spoke the sound that put the universe into motion. Science just backs up what the Bible has already revealed. Scientific study reveals more of who God is, and who we are, so that we can align ourselves with God's original design and live intentionally with health and vibrancy.

Over the years, many have felt conflicted about the contrasting approaches of eastern and western medicine, but both perspectives provide insight into how God has created our bodies, and how we can liberate ourselves from illness to function in full health. More holistic approaches to wellness, like using essential oils and mindfulness practices, have been increasing in popularity as people can partake without fear of negative side-effects found in western pharmaceuticals. On the flip side, though Western medicine has been under attack for being "dangerous," "unnecessary," and "unnatural," it does provide some benefits. Western medicine offers allopathic medication that can quickly alleviate negative symptoms, to allow people to resume their daily lives with minimal interruption or discomfort. For example, a dose of ibuprofen could quickly clear up a headache, but it is important to note that such pharmaceuticals are often toxic and do not address the root cause of illness. Western medicine is also very helpful in emergency situations, like car accidents, where surgery or physical therapy is required. The injured patient can go to an emergency room and find the cause of their medical issue within a few hours due to laboratories, X-Rays and other procedures.

Eastern medicine, such as ayurvedic medicine, or traditional chinese medicine, takes an entirely different approach, focusing on the energy balance in the body, and the bond between mind, body and spirit. Eastern medicine is also known as "alternative medicine" or "holistic medicine." Many criticize Eastern medicine due to the lack of medical research in support of it, however, people do seem to benefit. Diagnosing illness from an Eastern approach, requires evaluating the entire person (and sometimes even external influences like the calendar year, or the local geography)[15] and seeking to heal all imbalances. It emphasizes the body's own ability to heal itself while promoting lifestyle changes. Rather than relying on pharmaceutical drugs, tests, and operations, Eastern medicine relies on natural resources, like teas, herbs and essential oils drawn from the extract of fruits, vegetables and spices. The effects are often slower, but they do bring healing to the root of the problem.

The spiritual, or energetic, aspect of Eastern medicine is often where the controversy lies. Because the approach to healing involves body, soul, and spirit, the healing practices may include activities such as meditation, acupuncture, and tai chi. At first glance, these may seem not biblical, or more in line with New Age practices. It's good to be evaluative and discerning, but not immediately dismissive. A closer look into some of these theories reflect what God has shown us in creation. We have to remember that we are energetic beings created from the earth so movement of energy is healing to the body. Remember, everything God created is good, but Satan likes to take those good things and create false imitations of them, perverting and twisting what was once pure. Our goal in pursuing health is to return to a pure understanding of what is true and intended for us. We must use wisdom and discernment from the Holy Spirit when we make choices within both Eastern and Western medicinal practices.

I recently tried out a healing machine, based on quantum physics, that balances the body's frequency and uses acupuncture to unblock energy flow. It was very beneficial. Some people limit their opportunity for healing because they are uncertain of alternative medicine. But don't get tied up in fear from pursuing health. We need to untangle the truth from Satan's distortion. The truth is that all energy comes from God, and He alone is worthy of our devotion and worship. God's desire is to heal us and He inspires the development of healing modalities. The struggle comes when Satan twists mankind's understanding of the source of that energy, so that people give credit to other religions and begin to trade the Word of God for false philosophies. But, if I am grounded in the Word and committed to my faith, I can use alternative healing methods and continue to worship my God, the Creator and Sustainer of everything. I am not aligning myself with any false god or participating with dark spirits, or compromising my faith. I am pursuing wellness through the methods available to me. I am appreciating the diversity of God's creation and learning from many who have devoted themselves to understanding how to best achieve health. Of course, I use discernment in choosing which practitioners to learn from, and I reject any spiritual activity or ideology that doesn't align with God's word, but I can still benefit from various perspectives on wellbeing. In your journey, if you're unsure, ask God. You can trust the Holy Spirit within you to guide you into truth. **If you are committed to pursue healing *with* God (not on a path you perceive to be apart from Him), then your motives are in the right place.** Don't let a spirit of fear trap you in a cage that keeps you away from pursuing healing that may be helpful for you. Remember, God created everything! And He still holds everything. *"You are from God and have overcome them, for greater is He that is in you, than he who is in the world" 1 John 4:4 ESV.*

THE PURSUIT OF UNDERSTANDING

The reality is, not everybody wants to know the truth. Not everybody is willing to search for it. It takes discernment, and a close relationship with the Spirit of truth. But if we seek, we will find (Matthew 7:7). In order to embody the identity that God designed for us, we need to become comfortable seeking, and dialoguing with, God. **To strengthen our relationship with Him, God hides His treasures of wisdom and then invites us to search them out and chase Him down for answers.** The hungry will be filled with revelatory knowledge and insight into His mysteries. God is always speaking, but too often we're not listening because we're too busy and preoccupied. But His invitation remains:

> *"Indeed, if you call out for insight*
> *and cry aloud for understanding,*
> *and if you look for it as for silver*
> *and search for it as for hidden treasure,*
> *then you will understand the fear of the Lord*
> *and find the knowledge of God.*
> *For the Lord gives wisdom;*
> *from His mouth come knowledge and understanding"*
> *Proverbs 2:3-6 NIV.*

Isn't God amazing? He hides wisdom for us to discover. Everything He made has a purpose, and a message, from the sun, to the water, to our blood! I don't know about you, but this makes me more curious. Every piece of creation is an invitation into a deeper understanding of our God. This can shape your relationship with Him. He wants to show you. If you seek you will find.

Nowadays, I come to Him like a little child and talk to Him about everything. Whatever I read in Scripture, I ask Him, "Daddy, what does this mean?" His responses come in different ways. Sometimes He gives me a sense in my spirit right away of where to go look for the answer. I'll feel compelled to turn to a certain book of the Bible, or He may remind me of a previous message that I heard. Sometimes He doesn't answer right away. But if I'm patient, the answer will come. Sometimes it comes through other people or circumstances, and I say, "Oh, I remember I asked You about that!" He loves when His children are relational and have a hunger to seek Him. Can you hear Him speaking? Are you willing to become a God-chaser? His invitation stands.

"Call to me and I will answer you and tell you great and unsearchable things you do not know" Jeremiah 33:3 (NIV).

I remember one evening I was at a church service where I was really pleading with God to open my spiritual sight. I wanted to see things in the supernatural realm and I asked God to give me clear vision. When the service was over it was quite late, but I decided to take the winding back roads despite the darkness. Although it was a clear night, all of a sudden, out of nowhere, my windshield got sprayed with mud — I could not see anything! I was driving blind. I was so scared I literally thought I was gonna die from oncoming traffic. I heard the Holy Spirit say, "Turn on your windshield wipers," so I did. To my relief, there was no traffic in sight. Where had that mud come from? But what was even more amazing is that my windshield wipers cleared the mud without any irrigation - there were no smudges obscuring my vision. I could see perfectly clearly. I believe this was God's sense of humor answering my prayer for spiritual sight. As if to say, "I can remove any obstacle impacting your vision — just follow My voice." After that experience, my spiritual vision started to become clearer and clearer.

You never know how the Lord is going to speak to you, but He loves to do so. He loves when His children are relational and have a hunger to seek Him. Can you hear Him speaking? Are you willing to become a God-chaser? His invitation stands...

ENDNOTES

8   "Precious Metals and Other Important Minerals for Health." Harvard Health, July 2018. https://www.health.harvard.edu/staying-healthy/precious-metals-and-other-important-minerals-for-health.

9   Chevalier, Gaétan, Stephen T Sinatra, James L Oschman, Karol Sokal, and Pawel Sokal. "Earthing: Health Implications of Reconnecting the Human Body to the Earth's Surface Electrons." Journal of environmental and public health. Hindawi Publishing Corporation, January 12, 2012. https://www.ncbi.nlm.nih.gov/pmc/articles/PMC3265077/.

10   Ibid.

11   Ackerman, Steven A, and Jonathan Martin. "How Much Water Is in the Atmosphere?" The Why Files, August 28, 2013. https://whyfiles.org/2010/how-much-water-is-in-the-atmosphere/index.html.

12   The Water in You: Water and the Human Body. USGS. Accessed June 16, 2020. https://www.usgs.gov/special-topic/water-science-school/science/water-you-water-and-human-body?qt-science_center_objects=0.

13   Young, D. Gary. "Aromatherapy Essential Oil Frequency." The Kollinger Telegram, 1999. https://www.ralf-kollinger.de/wp/wp-content/uploads/2013/05/Frequency-Charts-Aromatherapy-essential-oil-frequency.pdf.

14   Dalio, Joe. "Is Vibration Biblical?" Power of PIES, April 22, 2020. https://powerofpies.wordpress.com/2014/04/29/is-vibration-biblical/.

15   Charlton, Emma. "Traditional Chinese Medicine (TCM) - A Different Approach to Essential Oils." Materia Aromatica, January 2020. https://materiaaromatica.com/blog/tcm-a-different-aproach-to-essential-oils.

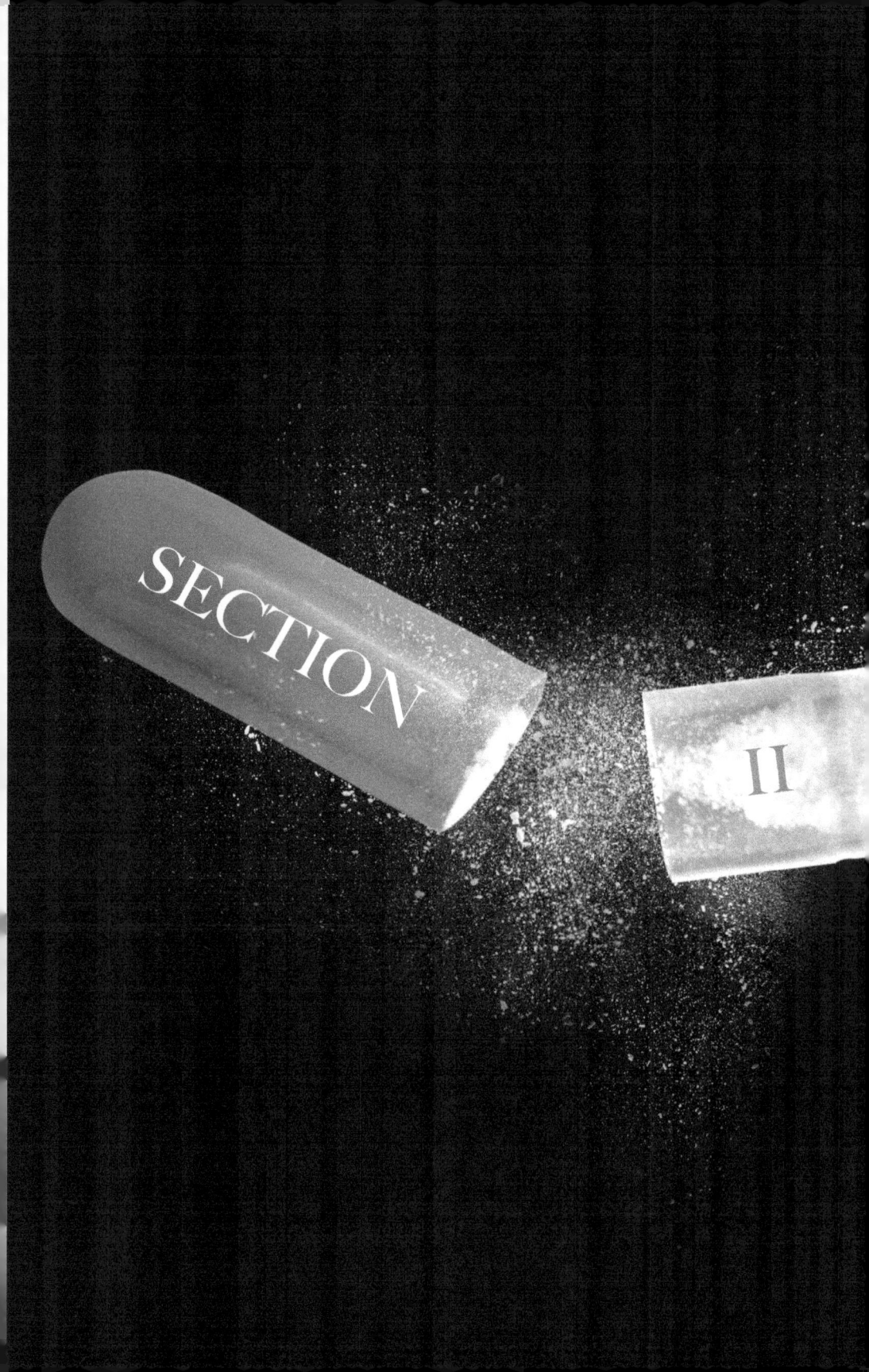

SECTION II

A HEALTHY SOUL

When you begin pursuing health, it's wise to consider all parts of your being — your body, soul, and spirit. Your soul is made up of your mind, your will, and your emotions. They each play a very important role in your life! Your happiness, your perspective, and even the things you believe. When I got sick, before I could even think about changing my diet or exercising to get my body working right, I knew I had to get my mind working right. This section focuses on your mental and emotional health.

CHAPTER 3
RENEWING YOUR MIND

Your thoughts have power. When your thoughts are aligned with the truth of God's word, you will benefit. When they are misaligned, by doubting, fearing, blaming, complaining, you will suffer both emotionally, and physically.

As I sought for solutions to my eye problem, I became more and more aware of how negative my thinking had become. The enemy's lie that I would never be well was a burden on my soul. So I complained to people, I complained to myself, I complained to God. "Why is this happening to me?" This pattern repeated enough times that I knew I needed a change. I knew this negativity was not my portion. After all, I had read about what happened to the Israelites when they murmured and complained in the desert. I did not want that outcome! I also began to realize, as humbling as it was, that the example I was showing to others would be my testimony! My words and my attitude needed an upgrade. I began to pray along with Proverbs 139:23-24:

"Search me, O God, and know my heart! Try me and know my thoughts! And see if there be any grievous way in me, and lead me in the way everlasting!" (ESV).

WHAT IS THE MIND?

What is the mind, anyway? The mind is the manifestation of thought, perception, emotion, determination, memory, and imagination that takes place in the brain. We can see and touch the brain, whereas, we cannot see or touch the mind. The brain is like hardware composed of nerve cells and blood vessels, and the mind is software. It is commonly thought that the brain and mind are one and cannot be separated. As science has advanced, we now know that thoughts in the mind can affect the physical brain. Have you seen those images of a brain scan with what looks like electrical wiring firing in different colors as thoughts connect across the synapses? Your brain is filled with many, many connections — like branches on a tree.

Imagine each thought as its own tree with many branches. The more branches, the more intelligent and accessible the thought will be. Each thought tree is made up of cells called neurons (nerve cells) and the branches are called dendrites. You have one trillion of these trees in your brain and one tree can grow up to 70,000 branches, which means we have three million years' worth of information storage space in our brain! Isn't that amazing!

CAN THINKING MAKE YOU SICK?

Researchers say that 87 percent of illnesses that plague us today are a direct result of our thought life.[16] The mind-body link is an ongoing symphony of chemicals playing through your body 24 hours a day. The way we think will affect the functioning of that whole electrical-chemical cycle. Our physical bodies function optimally when they have stable internal chemical conditions. If we allow negative thoughts that come from worry, fear, anger, or irritation throw off our internal balance, studies show that we can actually disrupt our brain function.[17] In other words, negative thinking can literally cause brain damage! Toxic thinking damages your ability to reason and communicate well. Even if you are feeling stressed about something silly or unlikely, the amygdala and the thalamus (which help communicate sensory and motor signals) will release the same stress-producing hormones through your system, as if the threat you're imagining was real. Dr. Caroline Leaf, author of *Who Switched off my Brain*, says, *"The average person has over 30,000 thoughts a day. Through an uncontrolled thought life, we create the conditions for illness making ourselves sick... Medical research increasingly points to the fact that thinking and consciously controlling our thought life is one of the best ways, if not the best way of detoxing our brain. Detoxing allows us to get rid of toxic thoughts and emotions that can consume and control your mind."*[18]

Rick Hanson, a neuropsychologist, suggests that your thoughts can actually change the *physical* structure of your brain. His studies have found that your thoughts and experiences can produce new synapses and even alter your genes, changing the very structure of your brain. He explains that the neuroplasticity of the brain causes it to be shaped by the synapses that are frequently firing — "the brain takes its shape from what the mind rests upon."[19]

What does your mind rest upon? The Bible says, *"Have this mind among yourselves, which is yours in Christ Jesus, who, though He was in the form of God, did not count equality with God a thing to be grasped, but emptied Himself, by taking the form of a servant, being born in the likeness of men. And being found in human form, He humbled Himself by becoming obedient to the point of death, even death on a cross"* Phil. 2:5-8 ESV.

As we think like Jesus thought, we begin to actually receive the mind of Christ (1 Cor. 2:16). The Bible also says that we can actually be transformed through the renewing of our thought life.

"Don't copy the behavior and customs of this world, but let God transform you into a new person by changing the way you think. Then you will learn to know God's will for you, which is good and pleasing and perfect" Romans 12:2 NLT.

DETOXING YOUR BRAIN

But how does someone actually change their thoughts? How does someone renew their mind?

First we have to know who we are, and where our mind was formed. We were created by God. I like to think that we are spiritual beings having an earthly experience. This means that although our lives are here on earth, our true home and identity exists in heaven. Even now, Christ has given our spirits seats in the heavenly realms. Ephesians 2:6 says, *"And God raised us up with Christ and seated us with Him in the heavenly realms in Christ Jesus" (NIV).* What would your thought life be like if you looked at your life from heaven's perspective? Would you complain as much? Would you have a broader perspective? Would you worry less, knowing that you have a seat secured in heaven for you? Aligning your thoughts with the truth of heaven's perspective is a foundational part of renewing your mind.

The Bible says, "We destroy people's defenses, that is their arguments, and all their intellectual arrogance that oppose the knowledge of God. We take every thought captive so that it is obedient to Christ" 2 Cor. 10:5 GWT.

In other words, identify the negative thought, the wrong belief, and take it captive! March it over to Jesus until it becomes obedient to the truth of His word. **You can literally detox your brain, and purify your emotions by intentionally changing your thinking.** Consciously controlling your thought life means not letting any old thoughts rampage through your mind whenever they feel like it. It means being alert to the devil's schemes to fill our minds with negativity and self-criticism. We have a tendency to believe these words and dwell on them, because the human mind is easily misled, our heart is easily consumed, and we forget to ground ourselves on the truths of God. Taking your thoughts captive means learning to engage interactively with your thoughts, analyzing them before you decide to either accept or reject them. When you notice a negative or untrue thought entering your mind, stop it in its tracks. Reject it forcefully! And then, declare the truth instead. **You have the God-given authority to take each negative thought captive, and tell it to submit to the truth of Christ Jesus.**

"So letting your sinful nature control your mind leads to death. But letting the Spirit control your mind leads to life and peace. For the sinful nature is always hostile to God. It never did obey God's laws, and it never will" Romans 8:6-7 NLT.

Because the mind of the flesh is at enmity with God, our best chance at victory is to return to the mind of God that was intended for us from the beginning, before the flesh became corrupted.

BEING TRANSFORMED

The Garden of Eden is where our identity began. Just imagine it! God declares, *"Now let Us conceive a new creation—humanity—made in Our image, fashioned according to Our likeness. And let Us grant them authority over all the earth"* Genesis 1:26 THE VOICE.

You are made in God's own image, and given authority over all creation! That is your identity! Let's reflect on this for a moment, so we can better understand how to align our thoughts with who God created us to be. Our beginnings are glorious, yet humble. Adam was made to reflect the very image of God — He was also formed from the dust of the ground (Gen. 2:7). And what filled him? God's own breath.

Although God made us to be like Him, our thoughts toward ourselves should not be boastful, as if we are supreme beings, in the same way that God Himself is supreme. We are not little-gods. We are humans, created from the earth, by an all-powerful Creator who gives us His very breath to sustain our lives. We can maintain a reverent awe for God, and a healthy humility towards ourselves, because we are fully dependent upon Him. Like Adam and Eve, we are simply reflections of who God is.

This is where a positive-self-perception comes in. He made us with care and intention which means we are valuable to God. We have worth because He invested His very nature into us! We were created "in His image" — according to His likeness. This signifies that we can feel good about ourselves because we have His goodness within us. God designed us to reflect His character. He also placed us in a beautiful garden, to enjoy His creation and His presence because He wants to bless us, and enjoy a relationship with us. Let your thoughts toward yourself reflect how much God delights in you, and values you. Afterall, He looked at all He had made, and said, "it is very good" (Gen. 1:31).

Lastly the Garden of Eden shows us that we have been given a purpose. We have been granted authority over the earth by God Himself. This means you are not helpless, incapable, directionless, or useless! Take those thoughts captive! You are a steward of God's creation and of His character within you. *"For we are his workmanship, created in Christ Jesus for good works, which God prepared beforehand, that we should walk in them" Ephes. 2:10 ESV.* We have a role to play on earth. Look at how God revealed this to Adam. He brought him all these animals to receive names. You could say that Adam was the first zoologist! Now my thinking is: how do you go from being dust made alive by God's breath to naming all the animals we know of today? How does dust become trustworthy of governance? Only by receiving the mind of God! Adam was the first person to share an intimate and personal relationship with the living God. He spent time with God. He knew

God's heart. He thought like Him. This enabled Him to accomplish his assignment.

I am taking us back to the garden so we can see who we really are, and how God really ordained us to think! **The degree that you are able to get back the mind God intended will be the degree you are able to manifest the life and nature of God.**

THORNS OR FRUIT?

When you think of the Garden of Eden, what do you imagine? I think of lush green trees, beautifully textured foliage, with colourful flowers and hanging fruits — a true paradise. What if you could create a similar flourishing garden within your own mind, through your thought life?

Do you remember the parable of the Farmer scattering seed? Jesus shares an analogy of a farmer who scatters seed (God's word) on different types of soil (different people). The type of soil determined what could grow. In Matthew 13:20-23 He explains, *"The seed on the rocky soil represents those who hear the message and immediately receive it with joy. But since they don't have deep roots, they don't last long. They fall away as soon as they have problems or are persecuted for believing God's word. The seed that fell among the thorns represents those who hear God's word but all too quickly the message is crowded out by the worries of this life and the lure of wealth, so no fruit is produced. The seed that fell on good soil represents those who truly hear and understand God's word and produce a harvest of thirty, sixty, or even a hundred times as much as had been planted"* (NLT).

Another way to think about it is this: when God's word comes to us, it comes in seed form. If we allow it to take root and grow, our thoughts will thrive until they become mighty trees. But if our minds are filled with negativity, then these pure seeds may be crowded out, and other weed-seeds of fear or worry will sprout and fill our minds with their crooked branches.

When we develop a lifestyle of thinking in alignment with God's word, our minds begin to resemble the Garden of Eden, filled with positive thoughts like beautiful lush green trees. Negative thinking keeps our mind barren, fruitless, with a mind filled with ugly, mangled, thorny trees that hurt us and those around us.

What type of soil describes your heart? The good news is that no matter what condition the garden of your mind is in, you can make a choice to restore it. You can till the soil, clear out the rocks, repent, and turn back to God. This willingness to renew your thoughts prepares the soil to receive God's word so it can take root. As you tend your mind's garden like a faithful farmer, guarding against invasive and negative thoughts, you will soon have beautiful green trees breathing life and hope and joy into your thoughts and emotions.

Even Albert Einstein said, *"I want to know God's thoughts... The rest are details."* So, now the question is: how badly do you want this transformation? You can change your life by meditating on the truth of the word of God. When you fill your mind with His truth, instead of entertaining the accusations of the enemy, and remaining stuck in the cycle of complaining and worrying, your brain will be transformed. The Bible instructs:

> *And now, dear brothers and sisters, one final thing. Fix your thoughts on what is true, and honorable, and right, and pure, and lovely, and admirable. Think about things that are excellent and worthy of praise. Philippians 4:8 NLT*

Are you ready to experience the freedom of a transformed mind? I **encourage you to read more of the Word of God than you do now.** Whenever you have free time — read it! Ponder what you read. Ask God to give you His revelation. He wants to reveal Himself to you. God tells Joshua in the Old Testament: *"Keep this Book of the Law always on your lips; meditate on it day and night, so that you may be careful to do everything written in it. Then you will be prosperous and successful" Joshua 1:8 NIV.*

If you don't know how to read the Bible, there are endless resources on the internet. You can simply use Google and type in the search bar, "Scriptures about peace," or "What the Bible says about who I am in Christ." Sites like Bible.org allow you to study by topic, or book, with different translations and ministry resources. Some translations, like the New Living Translation, or The Passion Translation, use everyday language to make it easy to understand. The Amplified Version is very inspirational! I encourage you to do what I did: **get hungry for understanding and just keep asking God for wisdom.** Keep reading the Word until it becomes a natural part of your thought-life.

CHOOSING YOUR FAVORITE SCRIPTURES

Do you have favorite Scriptures that you've memorized so they are on-hand when you need them? This is a powerful practice! I've chosen some of my favorite scriptures to declare when the enemy wants to pull me into negativity. Here are some of my go-tos:

- If you're stressed and tired, declare Matthew 11:28-30 over yourself and memorize it, to remind yourself who to lean upon:

  "Come to me all you who labor and are heavy laden, and I will give you rest. Take My yoke upon you and learn from me, for I am gentle and lowly in heart, and you will find rest for your souls. For My yoke is easy and My burden is light" (NKJV).

- If you're sick, declare Isaiah 53:5 in faith:

  "He was wounded for our transgressions, He was bruised for our iniquities; the chastisement for our peace was upon Him, and by His stripes we are healed" (NKJV).

- If you are anxious, remember Isaiah 26:3:

  "You keep him in perfect peace whose mind is stayed on You, because he trusts in You" (ESV).

- If you feel unloved, remember Ephesians 1:4-5:

  "Even before he made the world, God loved us and chose us in Christ to be holy and without fault in his eyes. 5 God decided in advance to adopt us into his own family by bringing us to Himself through Jesus Christ. This is what he wanted to do, and it gave Him great pleasure" (NLT).

- Do you feel like giving up? Declare Phiippians 4:13:

  "I can do all this through Him who gives me strength" (NIV).

With every negative thought that you replace with a God-given one, you are causing more positive synapses to fire and shape your brain! This is how you take back control from the devil, and get your thought-life back. This is how you start getting healthier emotionally, mentally and physically. **It's never too late to do something about what is going on inside your body and mind.** No matter how negative a person you think you are — there is hope! If you are ready to make a change, ask for forgiveness for agreeing with the negativity and lies of the enemy.

I encourage you to write out a daily affirmation; something that is personal to you. Say it aloud every day and begin to walk in the truth God has for you.

My daily affirmation:

> "Heavenly Father, I want to glorify You in my body, mind, and spirit. I want to live with the mind of Christ. I belong to You. Lord help me develop self-control and patience to persevere. I commit my ways to You. Transform my mind with Your Word. Help me to make the lifestyle changes that will give me a healthier body, mind, and spirit. I trust You Lord, and I know You will bring this to pass."

ENDNOTES

16   "Dr. Caroline Leaf Says That Research Shows That '87%-95% of All Illnesses Are a Result of Thought Life.'" PRWeb, April 13, 2012. https://www.prweb.com/releases/2012/4/prweb9398089.htm.

17   Newberg, Andrew. "Why This Word Is So Dangerous to Say or Hear." Psychology Today. Sussex Publishers, August 1, 2012. https://www.psychologytoday.com/us/blog/words-can-change-your-brain/201208/the-most-dangerous-word-in-the-world.

18   Christa Gifford, "Who Switched Off My Brain? The Danger of Toxic Thinking," September 16, 2012, https://christablackgifford.com/who-switched-off-my-brain/.

19   Toohill, Kathleen. "Here's How Negative Thinking Is Changing Your Brain." ATTN, July 31, 2015. https://archive.attn.com/stories/2587/what-negative-thinking-does-your-brain.

CHAPTER 4
CLEANSING YOUR HEART

Where there is negative thinking, you'll most likely find negative emotion. Be on guard — the enemy loves to weave a tangled web between thoughts and emotions. Once his lies begin to take root in your mind and your emotions start to distort, discerning truth becomes very muddy. This is exactly what the enemy wants. You have to be so careful not to let this toxic confusion drag you into a downward spiral of depression and despair. **If you want to become healthier, mentally, emotionally, and physically, you have to interrupt the negative pattern.**

FEAR VS. FAITH

There are two groups of emotions that are polar opposites: negative, fear-based emotions, and positive faith-based emotions. Fear does not come from God — it comes from the enemy.

"For God has not given us a spirit of fear and timidity, but of power, love, and self-discipline" 2 Timothy 1:7 NLT.

Satan prowls around looking to consume us with fearful thoughts. Have you ever been lured into his trap of worry? Staying awake at night thinking about all the possible things that could go wrong, and playing through different scenarios in your mind. The worst part is, the more you worry, the more you are feeding the fear, and then, the fear becomes a reality! When you open the door to the enemy through worry and fear, he loves to come in and make it all come true. *"**Be alert** and of sober mind. Your enemy the devil prowls around like a roaring lion looking for someone to devour. Resist him standing firm in* *the faith" 1 Peter 5:8-9 NIV.*

The enemy wants to keep you in a constant state of fear. **Fear is the root of all stress.** Dr. Caroline Leaf explains how research shows that fear triggers more than 1,400 physical and chemical responses.[20] When fear enters your mind as a thought, you experience physiological changes that occur at a cellular level. This stress causes negative and damaging alterations internally with negative implications to your health.

Most people live in a constant state of stress which causes chronic inflammation in the body. The body reacts to stress as a type of infection and tries to overcome it by producing inflammation. This is the starting place of many diseases. Prolonged stress can have serious consequences on your health by keeping your internal environment in a constant state of disarray. God has warned us about this:

Philippians 4:6-7 "Do not be anxious about anything, but in every situation, by prayer and petition, with thanksgiving, present your requests to God. And the peace of God, which transcends all understanding, will guard your hearts and your minds in Christ Jesus" (NIV).

OVERCOMING TOXIC EMOTIONS

When I began working through the fear in my life, I realized that much of it developed during my childhood. I'm sure all of us have some form of negative childhood experiences — whether from a teacher, parent, schoolmate or friend. These childhood wounds don't disappear with age, so we become wounded adults. Then, when our own kids come along, we become wounded parents. What I didn't realize is how elaborate the devil's schemes are to infect us and our family line for generations.

It isn't only my own wounds that affect me, but the wounds of those who have gone before me! Toxic residue can be passed through the bloodline.

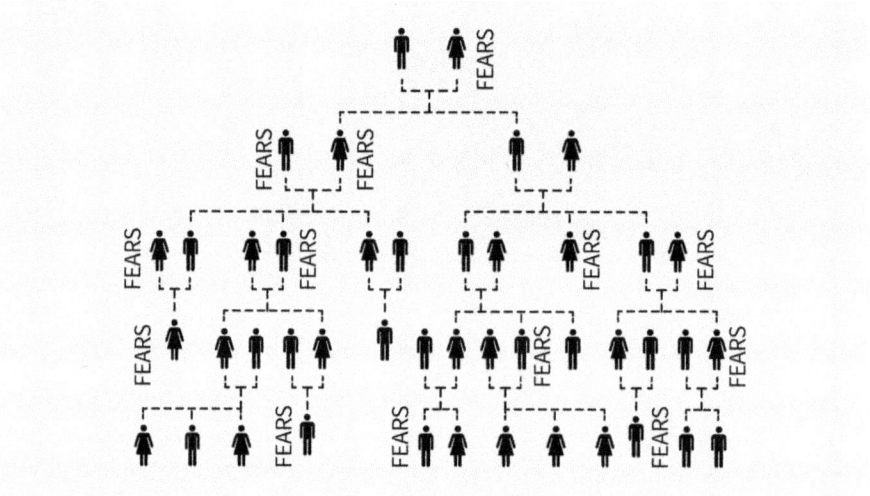

Scientists have discovered that phobias, fears, and memories can be passed down generationally.[21] It's called "transgenerational epigenetic inheritance." A neuroscientific study trained mice to dislike a certain smell, and the aversion was passed down two generations. They found physical changes in the descendant's sperm and in the brain related to the aversion. This was a huge revelation for me! I thought my fears were my own, but they had multiplied in the toxicity of my generational line.

We cannot avoid the fact that we live in a body of flesh. All flesh has been corrupted by sin in the Fall, so we are subject to the consequences of that sin, even if it was our ancestors who committed it. I had to learn prayer strategies to break off these generational curses, and renew my mind according to the word of God. I began to pray this prayer over myself:

"My mind is bound to the mind of Christ because He lives in me. Therefore, I command all toxic thoughts to dry up and disintegrate in Jesus name. I invite the breath of God to enter those dry places in my mind to realign with the purpose of Father God's destiny for my life."

As I worked through my wounds, I realized that fear doesn't only relate to anxiety. One of the most powerful fear-based emotions is hate. It grows out of a fearful desire for self-protection, hurt and unforgiveness, and spreads like weeds in a garden until everything else is crowded out. The enemy loves to hide roots of unforgiveness in our hearts, and then watch them take root, until thorns begin to poke through in our behavior.

Feelings of hatred, anger, rage and helplessness are powerful and dangerous emotions that affect the hormonal balance of your physical body. Each emotion triggers a neural impulse with chemical and electrical representation in the body. Negative emotions can cause chronic stress and drain your brain of the chemicals needed for happier emotions. According to Dr. Gayle Rogers, when we hold on to painful memories, the negative energy within them can either get stuck in, or course through the brain, heart, subconscious and the entire body, releasing toxic contaminants as they travel.[22] If hatred is destroying your internal balance, no wonder God says, *"Don't let the sun go down on your anger" Ephes. 4:26b CSB. Don't keep this toxicity in your body for more than a day! The Bible says: "But when you are praying, first forgive anyone you are holding a grudge against, so that your Father in heaven will forgive your sins too" Mark 11:25 NLT.*

REACHING OUT

If you don't feel able to deal with what you are facing, remember that God is able, and He makes you able because He is right there with you. I have found in my darkest times, that reaching out to Jesus as my companion is sometimes the best friendship I could ask for. Whatever you're facing, don't suffer alone. When you're struggling to overcome toxic emotions, it's best to find a mentor or an accountability partner to help you through; to keep you on track. Find somebody you can bounce things off of, so you don't stay stuck in your own perspective; somebody who can help you rise up and become who God has called you to be. Ideally this will be someone who can also provide wise counsel, not just a sympathetic friend who may enable you to stay stuck. If you don't have supportive mentors around you, consider seeking out a Christian counsellor, or an intercessor. Intercessors will pray for you and check in on you, and are generally very encouraging relationships to have. Do whatever it takes to get clear of the toxic emotions inside of your heart. Once you're free, you can finally start living without the heavy weight of pain dragging you down.

THE NEED TO FORGIVE

When I was seeking God for my healing, He spoke to me about the necessity of healing my emotions. God told me my total healing would come when I forgave my mother for trauma I had experienced as a child. My dad worked all the time, so he wasn't often around, and even if he was home he was not present emotionally. I felt very disconnected from him. I realized later that I needed to forgive him for not protecting me. Living in a house where my mom was regularly harsh in words and actions was a very traumatizing environment to grow up in. I knew I was carrying unforgiveness, anger and bitterness toward my mother, and I wasn't prepared to let it go. I didn't want to forgive her. I just kept thinking, "How can you claim to love me when you say those things? You birthed me!" Part of me wanted to punish her for it all. I wrestled with God on this. In my stubborn pride, I would try and manipulate her so that she would apologize for her actions instead of letting God handle things His way. I held onto unforgiveness for a long time. The enemy could not get me to reject God but he lured me into defiantly rejecting my mother by infecting my mind with repetitive reasons why I needed to harbor unforgiveness toward my mother. As I meditated on those reasons, the root of bitterness deepened. I didn't realize the damage I was doing to myself.

Psalm 66:18 says: *"If I had cherished sin in my heart, the Lord would not have listened" (NIV).* My unforgiveness was hindering my prayers. It was affecting my relationship with God. And it was affecting my health. We see this consequence in the Scriptures, when God allowed the Israelites to face diseases and sickness when they disobeyed Him:

"If you refuse to obey all the words of instruction that are written in this book, and if you do not fear the glorious and awesome name of the Lord your God, then the Lord will overwhelm you and your children with indescribable plagues. These plagues will be intense and without relief, making you miserable and unbearably sick. He will afflict you with all the diseases of Egypt that you feared so much, and you will have no relief. The Lord will afflict you with every sickness and plague there is, even those not mentioned in this Book of Instruction, until you are destroyed" Deuteronomy 28:58-61 NLT.

When the Israelites would turn back to Him, He would heal their land and take sickness from their midst:

"You must serve only the Lord your God. If you do, I will bless you with food and water, and I will protect you from illness" Exodus 23:25 NLT.

"If you listen to these regulations and faithfully obey them, the Lord

your God will keep His covenant of unfailing love with you, as He promised with an oath to your ancestors... And the Lord will protect you from all sickness. He will not let you suffer from the terrible diseases you knew in Egypt, but He will inflict them on all your enemies" Deut. 7:12,15 NLT.

I was bringing the curse of unforgiveness upon myself by my refusal to be obedient to God's word:

"Then Peter came to Him and asked, "Lord, how often should I forgive someone who sins against me? Seven times?" "No, not seven times," Jesus replied, "but seventy times seven" Matthew 18:21-22, NLT.

In John 13:34, Jesus said, *"A new commandment I give unto you, that you love one another as I have loved you, that you also love one another"* (KJV).

God commands that we walk in love. It's not optional. No matter how hard it was for me to forgive, the Lord said to me, "you've got to deal with that if you really want to be well." My choice to not forgive my mom allowed the devil legal right to hold me in bondage to sickness. It wasn't until I stopped rehearsing all the offenses in my mind towards her that my heart could begin to heal. I had to start looking at my mom through Jesus' eyes. I could never have done that without the Lord. When Jesus hung on the cross wounded unjustly by sinners, He said, *"forgive them Father for they know not what they do"* (Lk. 23:34). I had to do the same, gather all of my suffering, and finally release it to Him in His words, "*It is finished*"(Lk. 23:46). I want my mom and dad to be blessed, because deep down, I love them. Now that I have finally released my offense, when I look at them, I don't see any of the abuse anymore. I see two people who did the best they could, and that is good enough for me. The act of forgiving was my seed of obedience to God's word. My decision to forgive realigned me and opened me again to allow God to do His work in me. If I hadn't forgiven, I would have cut myself off from being forgiven by Father God.

"For if you forgive other people when they sin against you, your heavenly Father will also forgive you. But if you do not forgive others their sins, your Father will not forgive your sins" Matthew 6:14-15 NIV.

Our ability to receive forgiveness is connected to our ability to forgive others. When we forgive others, we free Father God to forgive us. We can lose this right if we refuse to forgive others for their offenses against us. As I released my mother to the Lord, my joy was restored and I felt better physically. I was reconnected to the Lord, and I began to experience true inner freedom.

THE PROCESS OF FORGIVENESS

The Process of forgiveness is simple. It takes humility and consistent obedience:

1. Decide
   You will never forgive if you wait until you feel like it. Just decide to do it. Once you decide you are planting your seed of obedience so it can start to grow.

2. Depend
   You cannot forgive without the power of the Holy Spirit. Ask Him to help you.

3. Obey
   Do what the Word tells you to do.
   - Pray for your enemies and those who abuse and misuse you

(Lk. 6:26-27).

- Bless them and do not curse them (Rom. 12:14).

4. Continue
    This may not bring immediate breakthrough because the heart
    has many layers. Continue to decide. Continue to depend.
    Continue to obey, and pray for them. Over time, you will find your
    heart begins to change, and breakthrough will come.

SPIRITUAL ROOTS OF DIS-EASE

*"A joyful heart is good medicine, but a crushed spirit dries up the
bones" Proverbs 17:22 ESV.*

Unforgiveness is the singular, most popular poison that the enemy uses
against God's people; it is deadly. It causes everything from mental
health problems like depression, to high blood pressure, stomach
problems, back pain,[23] and even cancer. In fact 61 percent of cancer
patients have issues with unforgiveness.[24] Unforgiveness is a disease
of relational separation. It puts a barrier between your relationship
with God, with yourself, and with others.

SEPARATION FROM GOD

In my own journey, I began to see how the enemy wanted to
subtly weave the isolation of separation into all areas of my life.
My family attended an episcopal church which wasn't strong
in promoting biblical values or teaching practical application. It
was a religious setting and none of the doctrines really made
any sense to me. In my young life, I began to feel separated from
God. I wondered how my family could go to church when such
negativity and hypocrisy was going on at home. I felt separated
from my earthly father and from my heavenly father. I see now,
that my parents lack a real relationship with the Lord and didn't
know how to act any differently. Many earthly fathers do not
represent God the Father well. Mankind is diseased for this

reason. They were treated poorly by their own fathers or there was no dad at all in the home, so, the cycle continues with generations who don't understand that God is love. That there is a loving father who would do anything to regain connection to those He loves — after all, God sent His only begotten Son, who willingly gave His life for us.

"For this is how God loved the world: He gave His one and only Son, so that everyone who believes in Him will not perish but have eternal life" John 3:16 NLT.

SEPARATION FROM YOURSELF

If it's possible to be separated from oneself, I was. I constantly struggled with lack of self-esteem and guilt. I had believed the things my mother said about me. I didn't have positive voices to encourage me. I could never be good enough. Jesus said, *"Every kingdom divided against itself will be ruined, and every city or household divided against itself will not stand" Matt. 12:25 NIV.* The enemy wanted me to be divided against myself, in my own body. The word of God convicted me; it told me that I was created *"in the image of God" (Gen. 1:27),* that I was loved: *"See what great love the Father has lavished on us, that we should be called children of God! And that is what we are" 1 Jn. 3:1 NIV.* I realized if I didn't love myself, I stood in opposition with God. How could I not love myself, if I am his masterpiece (Ephes. 2:10)?

SEPARATION FROM OTHERS

Because I always remembered what my mom said to me as a child, bitterness and unforgiveness festered within me as I grew up. I did not like being around her and felt unworthy in all my relationships. I didn't trust people. I felt isolated. I felt like I was the only one with these issues. So, I withdrew from people. Can you see the enemy's hand? If we are not careful, the roots of unforgiveness will spread like weeds growing deep in the soil of our heart, creating separation — the exact opposite of God's greatest desire: reconciliation with His people and unity amongst the family of God.

CAN EMOTIONS MAKE YOU SICK?

It's the enemy's vicious cycle to lure you into negative emotions and then have your body slowly break down from the poison they release. If he can pull you into hatred, or fear, or negativity, your physical body begins to break down. In fact, when toxic emotions are released, the cardiovascular system (your heart) is the first target of these nasty chemicals. Studies show that emotional states like depression and anxiety increase the physical risk of heart disease over time, that anger may cause irregular heart rhythms, and high stress is related to high blood pressure.[25] We've got to protect our heart, by guarding which emotions we allow it to dwell on!

"Above all, guard your heart, for everything you do flows from it" Proverbs 4:23 NIV.

The heart is not just a pump for your blood, it is a mini-brain. Research shows that the heart considers and *thinks* about information it receives from the brain. It acts as a still small voice that checks our thoughts for integrity and wisdom. The heart submits to the brain, at times, and other times, vice versa. Your heart is very sensitive to what you think and feel. Your heart's brain acts like a checking station for all the chemicals produced by emotion and thought.

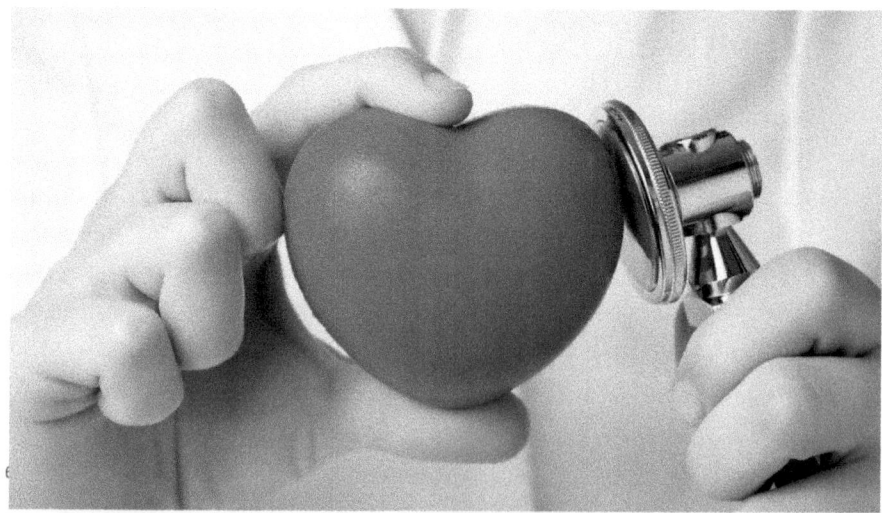

Do you need a heart check up? Proverbs 23:7 says, *"For as he thinketh in his heart, so is he" (KJV).*

Traditional Chinese Medicine also upholds the belief that organ health is directly related to emotional health. Practitioners believe negative emotions restrict the energy flow around specific organs. Here is a list of which organ is affected by which emotion:[26]

> **Spleen** - worry, dwelling or focusing too much on a particular topic, excessive mental work. Symptoms of a spleen imbalance include poor digestion, lack of appetite, pale lips, excessive menstrual flow, loose stool.
>
> **Lung** - grief, sadness, or detachment. Symptoms of a lung imbalance include, shortness of breath, fatigue, cough, pale complexion, dry skin.
>
> **Liver** - anger, resentment, frustration, irritability, bitterness, flying off the handle. Symptoms of a liver imbalance include red face, bitter taste in your mouth, jaundice, nausea, sighing, blurred vision.
>
> **Heart** - lack of enthusiasm and vitality, mental restlessness, depression, insomnia, despair. Symptoms of a heart imbalance include heart palpitations, excessive dreaming, spontaneous sweating, poor memory and concentration.
>
> **Kidney** - fearful, weak willpower, insecure, aloof, isolated. Symptoms of a kidney imbalance include dry mouth, vertigo, night sweats, poor short term memory, weak knees, hair loss, lower libido.

If you know you are heart-sick about something or someone, I want to encourage you to do what it takes to pursue healing. God wants to make you whole. He designed you to be joyful and healthy. He wants to restore you and use you as His vessel, as His hands and feet, to bring heaven to earth.

I know it can be intimidating to deal with what's inside, but He knows how to work on your heart, even if you don't know how to sort it out yourself. Start with the Lord's prayer, *"Our Father..."* Remember, He is a loving Father who is there for you. *"Your kingdom come, your will be done, on earth as it is in heaven" Matt. 6:10 NIV.* His will is to help you become healthy again — from the inside out. Satan wants to keep us fragmented and broken, not knowing who we are, heart-sick, feeling unloved. We can heal and repair by allowing God to touch those areas of trauma, so darkness will dissipate and light will shine forth. Less of us, more of Him. Then, people will be drawn by the light within us, because of the time we've spent drawing close to the Spirit of the Lord. We will then have the wisdom and the insight to help others around us. We may have to stay hidden under the shadow of His wings for a season as He does His work in us. Healing is a process. So, be patient, but be intentional. It will take time, but God's mercies are new every morning!

ENDNOTES

20   Leaf, Caroline. SWITCH ON YOUR BRAIN: The Key to Peak Happiness, Thinking, and Health. Ada, MI: BAKER Book House, 2018.

21   Gallagher, James. "'Memories' Pass between Generations." BBC News. BBC, December 1, 2013. https://www.bbc.com/news/health-25156510.

22   Gayle Rogers, The Whole Soul: Rescripting Your Life For Personal Transformation (Lakebay, WA: Kingdom House Publishing , 2014), 79.

23   Valeo, Tom. "Forgive and Forget." WebMD, August 25, 2008. https://www.webmd.com/mental-health/features/forgive-and-forget.

24   Johnson, Lorie. "The Deadly Consequences of Unforgiveness." CBN News, June 22, 2015. https://www1.cbn.com/cbnnews/healthscience/2015/june/the-deadly-consequences-of-unforgiveness.

25   Davis, Ann. "How Our Emotions Affect Our Heart Health." How our emotions affect our heart health | Edward-Elmhurst Health, March 19, 2019. https://www.eehealth.org/blog/2019/03/emotions-heart-health/.

26   "The Emotions." Chinese Medicine Living, November 16, 2016. https://www.chinesemedicineliving.com/philosophy/the-emotions/.

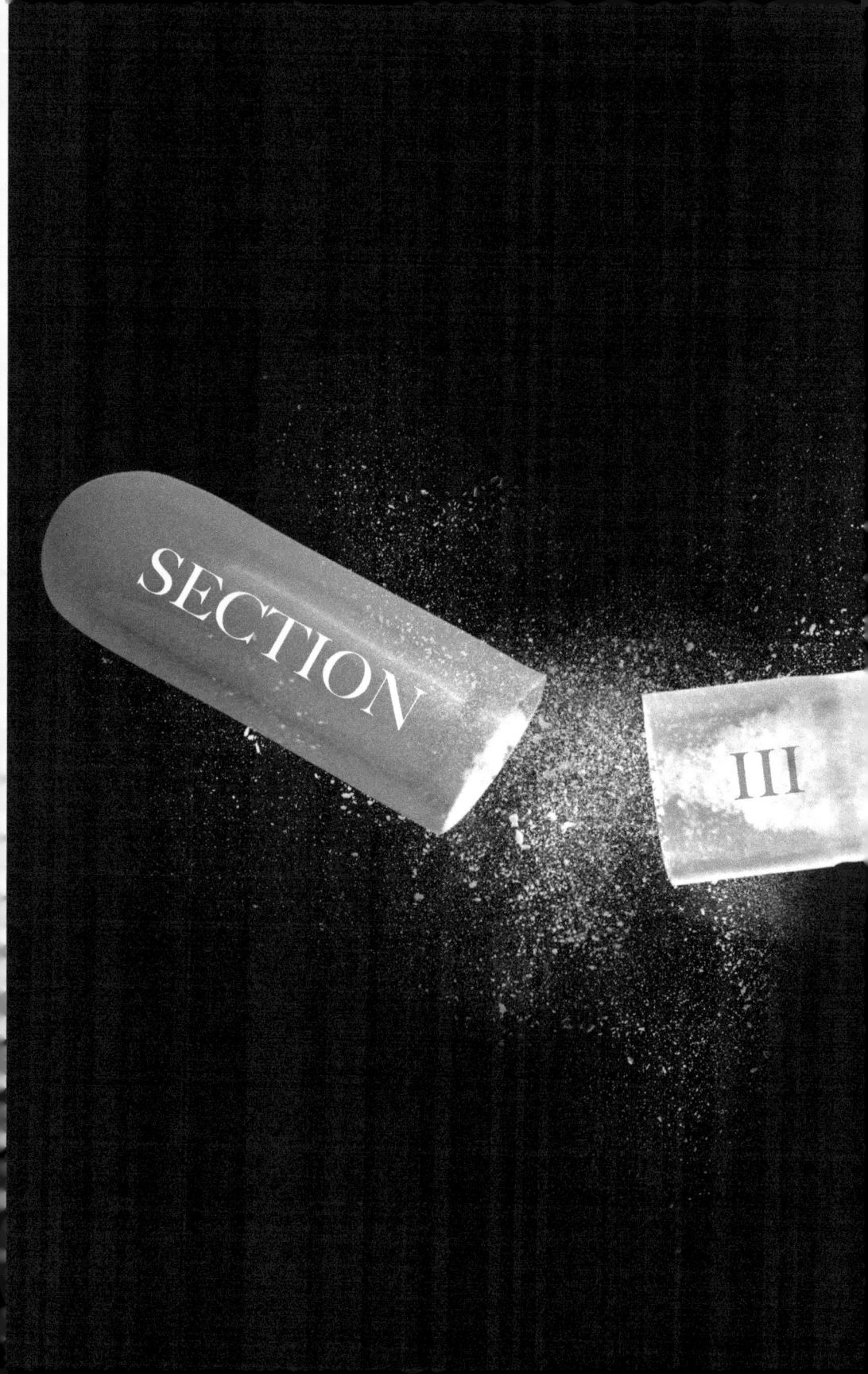

SECTION III

A HEALTHY SPIRIT

You may think that if you can get your mind and heart healthy, eat a balanced diet, and exercise you can live a holistically happy life. This is far from the truth. Without addressing the other major part of your God-given identity — your spirit — you ignore the True Source of health, and leave yourself unguarded and exposed to an enemy much more significant than your calorie-count. To pursue a healthy spirit, you must know what strengthens it and what weakens it. In other words, you must know who will attack it and how, and what methods you can use to strengthen yourself to remain standing. Who is this invisible force of darkness we battle against daily, in our mind, emotions, and even physically? What are our spiritual tools to guard against the enemy, and claim our victory? Let's find out.

THE WAR ON HEALTH

CHAPTER 5
SPIRITUAL
FOUNDATIONS

The Art of War, written by Sun Tzu in 500 B.C. has become a bestselling guide to winning a battle. Focusing on ancient Chinese military tactics, his philosophies form strategies for victory in many different contexts. He writes, "It is said that if you know your enemies and know yourself, you will not be put at risk even in a hundred battles. If you only know yourself, but not your opponent, you may win or may lose. If you know neither yourself nor your enemy, you will always endanger yourself."[27] You may think, "Of course I know myself and know about the enemy!" But there is knowing, and then there is *knowing*. The more deeply you understand, the stronger your foundation will be, and this will directly affect the skill and strength of your spiritual conviction in battle.

KNOW YOUR ENEMY

Satan is not a little horned devil in a red suit; he actually had a high ranking position in the heavenlies. He wasn't just a low-level angel — he was a guardian cherub. Cherubim are supernatural creatures associated with the throne of God, involved in worship and praise. Angels and cherubim serve God in worship or act as His messengers. The book of Ezekiel describes how Satan was once adorned with precious stones and was anointed with purpose, but his heart became proud and he was cast out of heaven to earth.

This is what the Sovereign Lord says:

"You were the seal of perfection,
full of wisdom and perfect in beauty.

You were in Eden,
the garden of God;
every precious stone adorned you:
carnelian, chrysolite and emerald,
topaz, onyx and jasper,
lapis lazuli, turquoise and beryl.
Your settings and mountings were made of gold;
on the day you were created they were prepared.
You were anointed as a guardian cherub,
for so I ordained you.
You were on the holy mount of God;
you walked among the fiery stones.
You were blameless in your ways
from the day you were created
till wickedness was found in you
Through your widespread trade
you were filled with violence,
and you sinned.
So I drove you in disgrace from the mount of God,
and I expelled you, guardian cherub,
from among the fiery stones.
Your heart became proud
on account of your beauty,
and you corrupted your wisdom
because of your splendor.
So I threw you to the earth;
I made a spectacle of you before kings" Ezekiel 28:12-17 NIV.

Satan was given honor and an esteemed role in God's presence. You could say that he was heaven's worship leader! He experienced the powerful presence of glorious worship that was lifted to God, and decided he wanted it for himself. He wanted to be like God. Now, Satan is taking what he experienced in heaven and he's trying to duplicate it on earth — with himself at the center. He is striving to build a kingdom unto himself. Remember in the wilderness when he tried to tempt Jesus by offering the glory and authority over the kingdoms of earth in exchange for worship? (Luke 4:5-6). He was looking to receive the same worship that God was getting in heaven, for himself on earth.

Isaiah 14:12-15 says:

> *"How you have fallen from heaven,*
> *morning star, son of the dawn!*
> *You have been cast down to the earth,*
> *you who once laid low the nations!*
> *You said in your heart,*
> *'I will ascend to the heavens;*
> *I will raise my throne*
> *above the stars of God;*
> *I will sit enthroned on the mount of assembly,*
> *on the utmost heights of Mount Zaphon.*
> *I will ascend above the tops of the clouds;*
> *I will make myself like the Most High.'*
> *But you are brought down to the realm of the dead,*
> *to the depths of the pit"* (NIV).

Satan is a heavenly being who has been kicked out of heaven and cast down to earth. He was once a beautiful archangel who became corrupted.

His punishment from God brought him such shame that he has positioned himself as the archenemy of God and all humanity. He uses demons, evil spiritual beings, to accomplish his specific agenda: He opposes God by destroying mankind. His primary weapons are deception and temptation. Satan is limited — he cannot create, he can only corrupt. So, if he wants to build something, he has to convince man to do it. His work table is the mind of man. Satan will mess with thoughts, twist logic, and cloud the truth. He counterfeits all that God does, taking what God intended for good, and luring people into traps like addiction to sugar, gluttony, lust of the flesh, pride, and greed. Satan wants to separate you from God any way he can. He loves making the things of this world so consuming, so captivating, and so distracting that we don't spend quality time with God anymore. Our own lives become our priority, not the kingdom of God. And then he stirs disillusionment and doubt. He creates chaos in circumstances and then whispers, "where was God?" *Jesus refers to Satan as a thief that has come to steal sheep from the flock. He says, "The thief comes only to steal and kill and destroy..." Jn. 10:10a NIV.* Think about that for a minute. There is a spiritual being who has only one agenda: to take you out!

You may not have realized it, but you were placed on a battlefield when you were born. God created you with a destiny, and Jesus died so that you could fulfill it. Satan will do anything he can to stop you from fulfilling it, and he will strike without warning.

One time, he literally stopped my legs from moving! I was planning to attend a class at church about clearing bloodlines of generational sin. The morning of the class, I could not move my legs to get up out of bed. It was as if a demonic force was holding me down and didn't want me to go. A fire rose up in me and I said, "Get off of me now you foul spirit, the blood of Jesus consumes you!" It left, and I got up and went to the class. If you're ever in a situation where you're not sure what to do, just call on the name of Jesus!

"So that, at the name of Jesus every knee shall bow [in submission], of those who are in heaven and on earth and under the earth" Phil. 2:10 AMP.

The enemy is such a deceiver, and works through intimidation. Don't let this testimony trick you into being afraid of him! Instead, let it raise in you a shout of victory that authority has been given to the children of God! Don't you want to uncover his agenda in your life? Don't you want to see what he's lying to you about? Don't you want to defend yourself? Prepare yourself for battle! The victory is yours! Know your enemy!

1 Peter 5:8-9 says, *"Be sober [well balanced and self-disciplined], be alert and cautious at all times. That enemy of yours, the devil, prowls around like a roaring lion [fiercely hungry], seeking someone to devour. But resist him, be firm in your faith [against his attack— rooted, established, immovable], knowing that the same experiences of suffering are being experienced by your brothers and sisters throughout the world. [You do not suffer alone]" (AMP).*

STRENGTHEN YOUR SPIRITUAL DEFENSES

Gaining spiritual health involves learning to defend your spirit man. Just like the immune system guards your physical body against illness, so your spirit-man must rise up as the defender of your soul. Your mind, will, and emotions are the doorways to greater mental and emotional and even physical illness. You need to learn how to guard those doors, and keep your soul from being contaminated by the evil one.

There is a wide range of perspectives on how Christians should go about guarding their doors. Some Christians feel you shouldn't talk about the devil at all; they don't want to give him any glory or attention. While the motive is honorable (because the devil doesn't deserve any of the glory he so desperately seeks), we can make great strides forward when we open our spiritual eyes to see the traps laid out before us. It's not a matter of giving him credit by talking about him, it's about being wise to his schemes. This way we can be ready for the battle so we don't get wounded.

How can we become aware of his schemes? First, learn from the Word of God about his methods.

1. **Be on guard when you notice self-condemning thoughts -**

   We know that Satan is referred to as the Accuser of the brethren so our antennas should go up when we notice critical thoughts. When he puts these thoughts in your head in what seems like your own voice, it is really the powers of darkness manipulating your mind. Once you become aware, you can expose his lies and tell him to shut up! That's what Jesus did! Jesus took authority to tell the devil to *"Be quiet" and follow His orders (Lk. 4:32).*

2. **Stop any double-mindedness, second-guessing, or paranoia in its tracks -**

   The Bible also shows us that Satan loves to create fear and doubt, so in response, we must squelch any double-mindedness, second-guessing, or paranoia before it begins to spiral.

   I remember when my practice required a marketing specialist in order to recruit new patients. I was treating a gentleman one day, and he was telling me about how his wife worked for a Periodontist (gum specialist), and she had really increased his practice. He suggested I talk with her and I thought it was a good idea so I met with the two of them. In our conversation, they mentioned that they were Jehovah's Witnesses. The Lord had been speaking to me about John 3:16, and my desire was growing to reach the lost on a deeper level. Was this my opportunity? I was so caught up in my desire to show God's love to all people, that I almost missed the voice of discernment in my spirit that the enemy was laying traps for me, and that really, hiring her was not a good idea. I kept second-guessing myself. Afterall, this was an opportunity to improve my practice and share the gospel, so I thought. But I had so much doubt and confusion — my mind began to spiral. I decided not to hire her, but I was still really concerned about whether or not I had made the right decision. So, I sat beside my open window with a heavy heart and I looked into the sky saying, "Lord, give me a sign that I did the right thing today by not hiring this lady." All of a sudden, on a clear night, there was a quick flash of lightning in the sky. No storm clouds, no rain. Just a response to my question. I was in awe at this wondrous sign! My heart jumped for joy that I made the right decision.

If we don't develop strong discernment skills, then we will be easily swayed by the enemy's tactics. We may think our doubt is our own, but just like Satan did in the Garden of Eden, the enemy is the one that whispers seeds of doubt that rattle our confidence. He loves to get us twisted up in confusion. The Bible reminds us to ask God when we need wisdom. But when you ask Him...

"Just make sure you ask empowered by confident faith without doubting that you will receive. For the ambivalent person believes one minute and doubts the next. Being undecided makes you become like the rough seas driven and tossed by the wind. You're up one minute and tossed down the next. When you are half-hearted and wavering it leaves you unstable. Can you really expect to receive anything from the Lord when you're in that condition?" James 1:6-8 TPT.

Steady yourself in the Lord. Be on guard against the enemy's strategy to cause you to doubt, and stand against it. In Christ, you can gain the confidence to be unshakeable. Don't fear. Don't be double-minded. Remember who is the solid Rock under your feet!

3. **Don't dwell in guilt or shame -**

The enemy also capitalizes on guilt and shame. Don't play his game of dwelling on past hurts, and beating yourself up. The more we ruminate, the more we believe his lies and compromise our self-image. He'll tempt you to feel like a victim — but in fact, you are the victor! You've been redeemed! You are the head and not the tail! (Deut. 28:13). Confess your sins and receive the joy of your salvation! God has forgiven you, so follow his lead and forgive yourself also.

4. **Not dealing with past trauma -**

    Many people don't realize they have trauma. We try to "let the past be the past." But painful emotions that we don't address linger inside until they are healed. The enemy loves to work through our past hurts and keep using them to hinder us. Be aware of the enemy's strategy to stagnate your growth, and in response, be intentional to heal and rise into the fullness of life that God has designed for you! God has bigger plans for you, so don't waste any more energy avoiding the things of the past. Pursue healing, and start living!

    My father tragically lost his father when he was very young, leaving his widowed mother to raise four children. Earning only a maid's wages, life became a challenge for all of them. The oldest was only 10 years old, but he had to help raise his brothers and a sister. They were very poor and they lived in a lot of fear. The whole family was traumatized by loss. Some of these siblings still have nightmares to this day. They didn't even realize they had trauma — it was just how life was for them, and they were focused on surviving. But Satan uses those undealt-with memories to haunt them, and to remind them of why they should be afraid. He twists and compounds those emotions so they begin to damage all sorts of relationships and situations, but it all stems back to his access point: unhealed wounds. Imagine if those disturbing memories and emotions were healed. Imagine the new level of freedom, hope, and joy my family would be able to experience. Christ is our healer. He is able to minister to our deepest wounds.The spirit of fear may be intimidating and oppressive, but it is just a spirit. God is God. He is fully able to overcome and enable you to live with power, love, and a sound mind (2 Tim. 1:7).

    Be intentional to seek healing for your traumas. Find an experienced Christian therapist, or minister, who specializes in bringing healing to past wounds. Also, consider a deliverance ministry to break any stronghold the enemy has on your family bloodline. Don't let your past determine your future. Once you remove the burdens of your past, you will be liberated to experience the victorious future that God has designed for you.

CREATED FOR DOMINION

People in the church often get scared when you mention demonic activity, but really, we have nothing to be afraid of. Jesus holds the keys to death and hell, so we have the victory in Jesus. Demons tremble at Jesus' name, and that same Jesus lives within you and me. Understanding the limits of the devil's authority is important. When Jesus died, He went down to Hades and then rose to give the keys of authority to us (Rev. 1:18). Now we, as His followers, have His authority to regain dominion over the earth. We are the ones with all the power! If you're not currently walking confidently, knowing the authority Christ has given you, I want to encourage you to learn more about your identity in Christ. See yourself as He sees you: a righteous warrior armed with the sword of the Spirit which is the word of God, upholding the shield of faith, with a helmet of salvation that declares you belong to the Kingdom of light. You must grow in confidence that Jesus has given you dominion, learning how to operate within the power Christ has given you, or else the enemy is going to presumptuously walk all over you. It's up to you! If you don't learn how to exercise the power of the Mighty One who lives in you because you are too consumed by the things of this world, then you are living spiritually weakly, with no authority. You are a part of the army of God, by the blood of Jesus you've made the cut, so don't live as an untrained soldier. Your true identity is mighty in God, but only those who decide to be like David — a man after God's own heart — who knew who he was, and knew who God was, can have the courage to stand up to their Goliaths and say, *"I come against you in the name of the Lord Almighty, the God of the armies of Israel, whom you have defied. This day the Lord will deliver you into my hands, and I'll strike you down and cut off your head" (1 Sam. 17:45-46).*

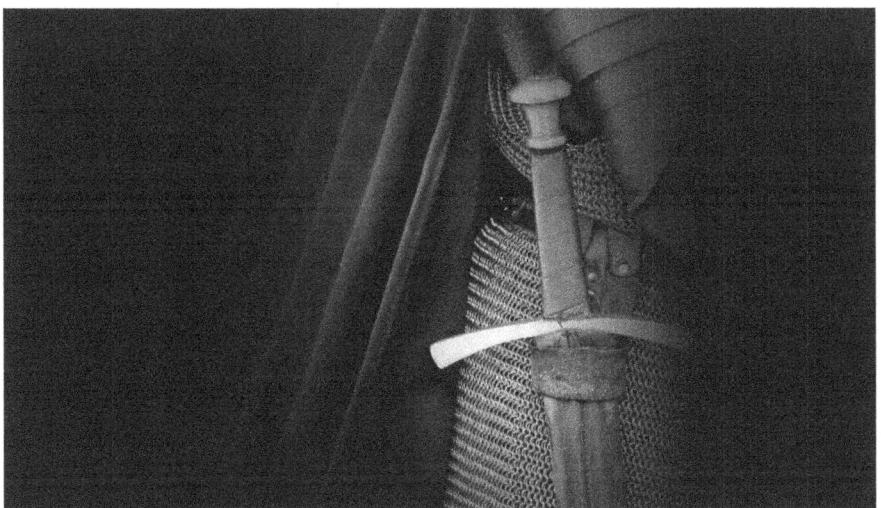

The sad reality is that Satan is not threatened by most Christians — they don't really do much to oppose him. In fact, religion is his playground! He loves stirring dissent, disunity, gossip, greed, and even promoting someone to a high position only to expose their sin publicly and cause many others to doubt the truth of God. He delights in getting people addicted to following laws until they're rule-bound followers like the Pharisees — filled with self-righteousness, but little love, and no power.

True faith is not about stellar church attendance. It's about a true and deep, authentic connection between you and your God that gives you confidence, faith and power to live as Jesus lived. God's "ecclesia" (true church) is filled with people who want to bring about God's government on earth and are willing to sacrifice the pleasures of their own life to achieve it. They refuse to be deceived by the world, so they've renewed their minds with truth. They don't live by fear, but by the truth of the Word, and by faith. They are lovers of the Lord, they reflect Christ's humility, and their devotion and worship of the One true King is a mighty force to be reckoned with. This is what scares Satan. This is who we as Christians are called to be. This is what true spiritual health looks like!

We don't need to be afraid of the devil — he's the defeated one. God sits on His throne, and laughs at His enemies (Ps. 2), and promises to make them our footstool (Heb. 1:13). He gives His disciples authority over scorpions (Luke 10:19). God promises that He will crush the devil under our feet (Rom. 16:20). God has made it clear: our spiritual foundation is strong, the enemy is weak, and we can live victoriously!

ENDNOTES

27   Parmar, Amardeep. "10 Quotes From 'The Art Of War' That Will Transform Your Life." Live Your Life On Purpose. Medium, August 31, 2020. https://medium.com/live-your-life-on-purpose/10-quotes-from-the-art-of-war-that-will-transform-your-life-a571381f57c8.

CHAPTER 6
SPIRITUAL ROOTS OF ILLNESS

Have you ever wondered where sickness comes from? Is it just from our poor health choices? Or does God have something to do with it? Can the devil create sickness? Does God allow that? Can sickness be fully spiritual in nature? These are worthy questions to ask God about as you read this chapter, and as you study the Scriptures. More than obtaining "yes" or "no" answers, our goal should be to seek understanding of how the spiritual realm operates alongside the natural realm. God reveals this to us in His Word.

Jesus says: *"Simon, Simon, Satan has asked to sift each of you like wheat. But I have pleaded in prayer for you, Simon, that your faith should not fail" (Lk. 22:31 NLT).* We can see from this statement that actions in the spiritual realm can affect what happens on earth; and actions on earth (like prayer) can affect the spiritual realm. Both realms are intertwined and affect one another. The more we understand these dynamics, the more we can manage ourselves with wisdom. We can also observe that the spiritual realm operates by levels of authority. God is the highest authority, and He has angels who serve Him, and humans who follow Him. The devil is a fallen angel, so he carries no authority unless it is given to him by humans, or by God Himself. The spiritual realm also operates according to spiritual laws, similar to how earth functions within laws of physics, such as gravity. One of those spiritual laws is that obedience to God brings blessing, and disobedience, or rebellion against Him, brings a curse.

THE SIGNIFICANCE OF OBEDIENCE

Although the devil has been stripped of his authority, he understands how the spiritual realm works and uses it to his advantage. He knows that when we are disobedient, we break the spiritual law of blessing. We are stepping outside of God's protective covering and opening a part of ourselves to the rule of the kingdom of darkness. When we disobey, it's as if we are handing the devil the keys to a part of our soul to come in and create chaos and harm.

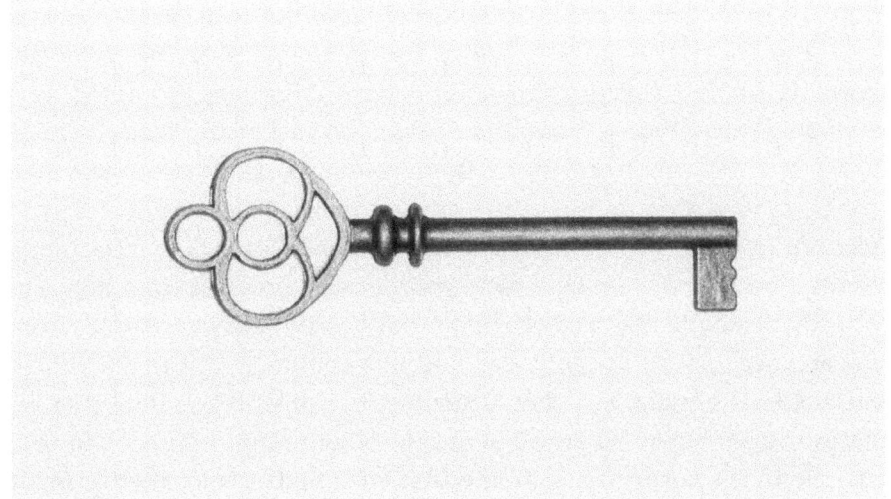

Although Jesus' blood gives us access to His victory over Satan, our rebellious choices can give the enemy a legal right to traffic in our lives, and bring destruction. I came to realize the true meaning of the phrase "when the Lord truly becomes Lord over your life." As my trust has developed in Him, I am willing to say, "Okay Lord!" even though I may be kicking and screaming. I no longer have to understand *why*, because I realize that it is part of my growth path which will eventually get me to my ultimate destiny.

I remember when the Lord asked me to join a church that I didn't want to attend. I had been attending a mega-church, which was pretty much run like a business: efficient, effective, but with very little room for the Holy Spirit to move. I was comfortable, but I kept sensing it was time to grow more spiritually. I felt the Lord's nudge to find somewhere else to attend that allowed more of the flow of the Holy Spirit. One day, I was going for a detox treatment and the practitioner began to emphatically invite me to her Spirit-filled church where she had seen so many miraculous things. I agreed to check it out, but I was resistant. This church was from a different culture than mine. I wasn't used to socializing with people from different backgrounds. So, I went one week but then pulled back. The congregation certainly moved in the power of the Holy Spirit, but I didn't feel like I fit there. It just wasn't as comfortable as what I was used to. So, I told the Lord, "No, Lord. I don't want to go there." But then, I began to notice a negative shift in my business. Just prior to this, I had been experiencing financial blessing in my dental practice. But after I told the Lord "No," I noticed that the insurance checks weren't coming in anymore, and the patients weren't calling as much anymore. What was blooming, was suddenly stagnating. It was quite obvious, so I asked the Lord, "What's going on?" He reminded me of Deuteronomy 8:18, *"Remember then the Lord, your God, for He is the one who gives you the power to get wealth" (NABRE)*. It was like a spiritual NEWSFLASH — God is in charge of my income, not me! I couldn't afford not to do what He told me to do! My disobedience had opened a door to the enemy to steal from me and dry up God's supply, and God was pointing it out to encourage me towards obedience. I felt a healthy fear of God knowing that He holds everything in His hands. I decided that I had to go back to that church for His purposes, not mine, and I just had to trust Him. To insist on what I wanted was to rebel against Him.

And guess what? As I obeyed God, I received so much more at that little church than I could ever have imagined. I stayed there for two years, and I grew tremendously! I was able to engage with God's Spirit in a close-knit group which made it more personal. I had never seen the Holy Spirit move like that! The community was amazing. We'd go to each other's houses and have all night prayer and praise to the Lord. Our spiritual warfare together was incredibly powerful. I learned so much about how to overcome fear and be who God called me to be. Truly, I am who I am today because of what I learned in that church. I can't bear to think what I would have missed out on in my spiritual development if I had remained disobedient.

Obedience to God shuts the door on the enemy. It keeps us walking on the right path, and it legally denies Satan's access. God's call to obey isn't meant to be a heavy yoke of burden, or rules and laws. **God's call to obedience is an invitation into His goodness and mercy.** He only has good things for us. When we love Him and obey Him, goodness and mercy will follow us all the days of our lives. Through obedience, we become naturally aligned to receive His blessings. Moses described the abundant life of blessing for those who obey:

"If you fully obey the Lord your God and carefully follow all His commands I give you today, the Lord your God will set you high above all the nations on earth. **All these blessings will come on you and accompany you if you obey the Lord your God:**

You will be blessed in the city and blessed in the country.

The fruit of your womb will be blessed, and the crops of your land and the young of your livestock—the calves of your herds and the lambs of your flocks.

Your basket and your kneading trough will be blessed.

You will be blessed when you come in and blessed when you go out.

The Lord will grant that the enemies who rise up against you will be defeated before you. They will come at you from one direction but flee from you in seven.

The Lord will send a blessing on your barns and on everything you put your hand to. The Lord your God will bless you in the land He is giving you.

The Lord will establish you as His holy people, as He promised you on oath, if you keep the commands of the Lord your God and walk in obedience to Him. Then all the peoples on earth will see that you are called by the name of the Lord, and they will fear you. The Lord will grant you abundant prosperity—in the fruit of your womb, the young of your livestock and the crops of your ground—in the land He swore to your ancestors to give you.

The Lord will open the heavens, the storehouse of his bounty, to send rain on your land in season and to bless all the work of your

*hands. You will lend to many nations but will borrow from none. The
Lord will make you the head, not the tail. If you pay attention to the
commands of the Lord your God that I give you this day and carefully
follow them, you will always be at the top, never at the bottom.
Do not turn aside from any of the commands I give you today, to
the right or to the left, following other gods and serving them"*
Deuteronomy 28:1-14 NIV.

When you accepted Jesus as your Lord and Savior, you made a covenant
with God. That contract is an agreement to serve Him as the Lord over
your life. In other words, **God is in the driver's seat! You follow His
lead.**

THE COST OF DISOBEDIENCE

Disobedience, on the other hand, forms an unwritten agreement with
the devil. God protectively instructed Adam and Eve not to eat from
the tree of knowledge of good and evil or they would surely die. But
the serpent whispered, "you won't die — give it a try!" They decided
to agree with the devil. They abandoned God's leadership and gave
the devil the authority to lead them. As a result, they were banished
from the Garden of Eden (Gen. 3:24), and God set a cherubim and
a flaming sword to guard the way back to the tree of life. This act of
discipline was a sign of the Lord's love. If sinful humanity was allowed
to eat from the tree of eternal life while under the dominion of Satan,
they would be trapped in sin forever! God guarded the tree, until His
Son, Jesus, came to break the curse, and He could once again open the
path to give us eternal life, so we could live forever in His favor and
blessings.

*Hebrews 12:6 says, "For the Lord disciplines those He loves and
punishes each one He accepts as His child" (NLT)*

If you know there are areas of your life that you are not walking in
obedience to God, and you are trying to obtain blessing and health,
you've first got to get back into right spiritual alignment. The reality is,
your spirit will naturally connect itself either to the Spirit of God, or to

the spirit of the world.

The spirit of the world roams around, trying to ensnare us in it. But you are called to be a child of the Kingdom of Light. God wants to give you health and power to have dominion and power to push back the kingdom of darkness. But, the reality is, you won't have any power to do that until you walk in obedience. You've got to get rid of that rebellion in your life, and remember who is Lord. You can't get healthy without Christ at the center.

God has taught me obedience in many ways throughout my life— sometimes through very small things. I once purchased a second-hand Louis Vuitton purse on eBay that I just loved. It was the real thing, and it was big and beautiful. I felt the Holy Spirit tell me to give it to someone at the church. My heart wanted to rebel. I loved that purse! I used it all the time, but I had a choice to make. I knew the consequences of disobedience were always worse than whatever gain I hoped to hold onto. So, I gave the purse away. And by the goodness of God, I found a brand-new Louis Vuitton purse on eBay, and despite the fact that I missed the payment deadline, the seller contacted me personally to ask, "Would you still like to purchase this?" That never happens on eBay! It was as if God Himself was offering me something better than I had given away. He is such a good Father. He is always preparing more blessings for us around the corner.

Adam and Eve most likely didn't realize the significance of their choice to disobey. Their simple choice to eat the forbidden fruit set all the generations after them on a crooked path. Disobedience always comes with a lot of unforseen ramifications, including diseases. You can read a full account of the warnings Moses gave regarding curses for disobedience in Deuteronomy 28:15-68, but here's a sample:

"However, if you do not obey the Lord your God and do not carefully follow all his commands and decrees I am giving you today, all these curses will come on you and overtake you:

You will be cursed in the city and cursed in the country.

Your basket and your kneading trough will be cursed.

The fruit of your womb will be cursed, *and the crops of your land, and the calves of your herds and the lambs of your flocks.*

You will be cursed when you come in and cursed when you go out.

The Lord will send on you curses, confusion and rebuke in everything you put your hand to, until you are destroyed and come to sudden ruin because of the evil you have done in forsaking Him. ***The Lord will plague you with diseases until He has destroyed you from the land you are entering to possess. The Lord will strike you with wasting disease, with fever and inflammation,*** *with scorching heat and drought, with blight and mildew, which will plague you until you perish. The sky over your head will be bronze, the ground beneath you iron. The Lord will turn the rain of your country into dust and powder; it will come down from the skies until you are destroyed.*

The Lord will cause you to be defeated before your enemies. You will come at them from one direction but flee from them in seven, and you will become a thing of horror to all the kingdoms on earth. Your carcasses will be food for all the birds and the wild animals, and there will be no one to frighten them away. ***The Lord will afflict you with the boils of Egypt and with tumors, festering sores and the itch, from which you cannot be cured. The Lord will afflict you with madness, blindness and confusion of mind.*** *At midday you will grope about like a blind person in the dark. You will be unsuccessful in everything you* *do; day after day you will be oppressed and robbed, with no one to rescue you" Deuteronomy 28:15-29 NIV.*

If you want to walk in full health you need to walk with God; there's no way to do this without Him. You can't just say "I'm saved" and just do what you want to do. There's a price to pay to walk with God. **God loves people and wants them healed and set free, but this is only accomplished when we are walking closely with Him.** When you take care of God's business and do whatever He is telling you to do, He will take care of you!

I remember I had an elderly patient come into the office who was blind in his right eye. His right eye had no pupil! He was such a nice man. I felt the nudge from the Holy Spirit to pray for him right there in the dental chair... but I didn't do it. I let fear creep in. How would he react if I brought spirituality into this professional appointment? What if he complained to the referral office, and I lost future business? Later on that evening, in my prayer time, I had to repent because I knew that I did not do what the Lord asked. I said to the Lord, "If you bring him back to the office, I will pray for him." Meanwhile, I felt an urgency, and began to pray and intercede for him right then and there. I really did not expect him back because I had only done a consultation and he decided he wasn't going to get treatment. Well, don't you know it, a couple of weeks later his name showed up on my schedule! I started root canal treatment on him and when I was finished, I felt a boldness rise up in me. I told him that I was a disciple of Christ and that I had been praying for him and I would like to pray for him now. He said, "I would love that! I know Jesus too, but what you don't know is that I had an appointment yesterday at Johns Hopkins Hospital. Previously, the doctor saw an infection in the back of my right eye and they were going to have to remove the whole eyeball. But at yesterday's appointment they discovered the infection was gone and they cancelled the surgery." The patient started tearing up as he was sharing his story and thanking me for praying for him! Of course, the tears came streaming down my face as I prayed for him again. The Lord had prompted me to pray for this man during his first appointment because God loved him and wanted to release healing over him, but I had disobeyed! What if I hadn't repented and just went on about my business? I remembered the urgency the Lord gave me at home while I was praying for him. My repentance put me back on track to intercede for this patient's miracle! I believe those prayers saved that man's eye.

REVERENTIAL FEAR

As I've wrestled with sickness and suffering, I've had to come to terms with the fact that my life is for God's purpose, not my own. If I live my life my way— eating what I want, doing what I want, and getting careless spiritually, I end up suffering for it, and others do too. I'm not perfect, but my mistakes remind me that God's way is really the only way!

The realization that I have to deny what I want, in order to follow God's wisdom for my health, has helped me to develop a lifestyle built on the fear of the Lord. The fear of the Lord is a deep reverence for his holiness, and an ongoing choice to trust His wisdom over my own. It keeps me obedient. It gives weight and significance to the little choices I make for Him throughout my day. Gaining a healthy "fear of the Lord" has been a significant safe-guard for me as I learn to maintain a healthy lifestyle in the blessing of the Lord.

As I began to grow spiritually and get deeper into the Word, I came across many passages that made me tremble at the righteousness and the holiness of our God. These are some of the scriptures that have motivated me to maintain humility and choose obedience as a lifestyle.

"Aaron's sons Nadab and Abihu put coals of fire in their incense burners and sprinkled incense over them. In this way, they disobeyed the Lord by burning before Him the wrong kind of fire, different than He had commanded. So fire blazed forth from the Lord's presence and burned them up, and they died there before the Lord.

> *Then Moses said to Aaron,*
> *"This is what the Lord meant when He said,*
> *'I will display my holiness*
> *through those who come near me.*
> *I will display my glory*
> *before all the people.'"*
> *And Aaron was silent" Leviticus 10:1-3 NIV.*

Aaron was a priest, who had committed his life to serve alongside Moses, yet God did not spare his two sons who took the Word of the Lord casually. God shows no favoritism. He hates sin. He commands holiness. And He will do whatever it takes to teach His people how to honor what He says.

In another story, God rebukes Miriam and she gets struck with leprosy because she spoke against the leader God had chosen:

"Then the Lord came down in a pillar of cloud; He stood at the entrance to the tent and summoned Aaron and Miriam. When the two of them stepped forward, He said, "Listen to my words:

> *"When there is a prophet among you,*
> *I, the Lord, reveal myself to them in visions,*
> *I speak to them in dreams.*
> *But this is not true of my servant Moses;*
> *he is faithful in all my house.*
> *With him I speak face to face,*
> *clearly and not in riddles;*
> *he sees the form of the Lord.*

Why then were you not afraid to speak against my servant Moses?" The anger of the Lord burned against them, and He left them. When the cloud lifted from above the tent, Miriam's skin was leprous it became as white as snow. Aaron turned toward her and saw that she had a defiling skin disease, and he said to Moses, *"Please, my lord, I ask you not to hold against us the sin we have so foolishly committed" Numbers 12:5-12 NIV.*

We must take God seriously, and understand that our physical well-being is directly related to our spiritual well-being. Miriam's story shows us that sin can be the root of our physical illness— though this isn't always the case— we cannot ignore that sometimes it is. We see this in the New Testament as well:

"Some men came carrying a paralyzed man on a mat and tried to take him into the house to lay him before Jesus. When they could not find a way to do this because of the crowd, they went up on the roof and lowered him on his mat through the tiles into the middle of the crowd, right in front of Jesus. When Jesus saw their faith, He said, 'Friend, your sins are forgiven'" Luke 5:18-20 NIV.

The man was made well through the forgiveness of his sin, and through the power of faith in Jesus Christ. Coming in through the roof to see Jesus exhibited great faith. The paralyzed man's friends knew that if they could just get him into the presence of Jesus he would be healed. They were expectant of a miracle and they got one! He was forgiven of his sins, and he picked up his mat and walked home praising God. This tells me that at the same time he was healed, he was forgiven.

"If we confess our sin He is faithful and just, to forgive us our sin and purify us from all unrighteousness" 1 John 1:9 NIV.

God's word is clear that sin can result in physical illness. And His character shows us that He is passionate about removing it from our lives. But sometimes, we unwittingly and unknowingly allow the ways of the world into our lives, and we give the devil a legal right to hold us.

SIN IN THE BLOODLINES

Now, maybe you have repented of all your known sin and believe you are living an obedient lifestyle, but you are still battling persistent illness; there may be one other spiritual aspect to consider. One area of sin removal that Christians do not often consider is sin that is passed down through our bloodlines.

Our generational line can be traced all the way back to creation: Adam and Eve are our ancestors! Our bloodline contains behavioral and spiritual patterns that have been recorded in the flesh throughout the generations before us. These patterns identify strongholds the enemy has established; these may include iniquity, or repeated sin in a particular area, or covenants made to other gods. For example, do you know of families where every member in the family suffers from sickness, or repeated financial disaster, premature death, divorce, or addiction? Research confirms these generational patterns exist. Children who grew up around domestic violence often find themselves in similar situations as adults. Drug addiction or alcoholism in the family is also repeated among children raised by alcoholic parents.[28] What's happening here? Some could be learned behavior, but often there is a spiritual root. If people in our bloodline (our ancestors) lived in idolatry, they, knowingly or unknowingly, made an agreement with the devil by allowing these behaviors to take root in their lives. This curse can be passed down to us and from us to future generations. This contract has to be broken. The devil will strive to influence each generation to keep that contract open. This is how both physical disease and mental health issues are passed down from generation to generation. If Satan can continue to traffic sin through your life, he then has a legal argument that he presents in the heavenly courtroom: that he has a right to *"steal, kill, and destroy" (Jn. 10:10),* because you keep letting him in.

"The Lord, the Lord, a God merciful and gracious, slow to anger, and abounding in steadfast love and faithfulness, keeping steadfast love for thousands, forgiving iniquity and transgression and sin, but who will by no means clear the guilty, visiting the iniquity of the fathers on the children and the children's children, to the third and the fourth

generation" Exodus 34:6-7.

Some people call these "familial spirits" or generational iniquities, which are passed down from generation to generation. Sin opens the door to demonic forces within families, luring them into the same related sin. These familial spirits are assigned to a family to keep generations bound to these sinful behaviors. We seem to accept it as a part of our lives because "that's just the way it's always been in our family" all the way back to great uncle Joe and his mother! Satan wants to use this generational structure for evil, but God wants to redeem each generation for good, to fulfill His purpose.[29] He set apart Abraham, Isaac, and Jacob for generational blessing to extend through the twelve tribes of Israel, all the way down the line to us today!

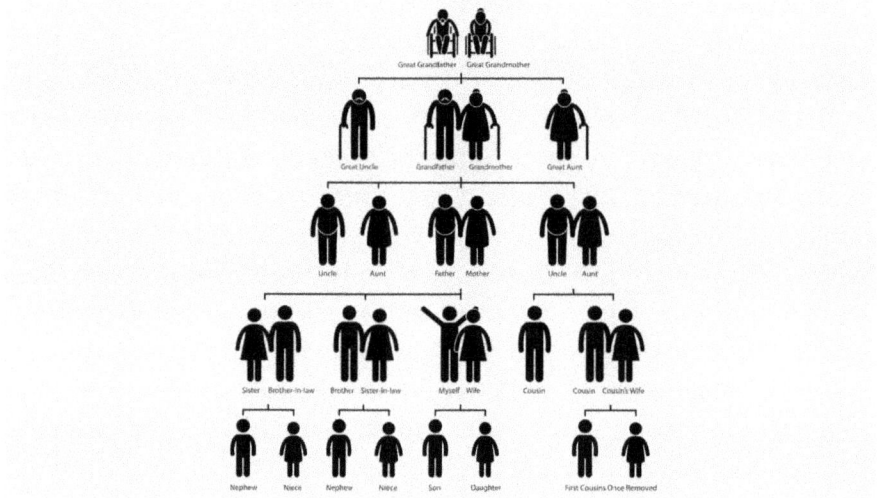

If you're wondering if anything has been passed down through your bloodline, consider any patterns in what your ancestors have struggled against mentally/emotionally, spiritually or physically. Kathy DeGraw, author and prophetic deliverance minister, suggests creating a family tree and marking down all physical and emotional sickness that each member of your family has experienced: alcoholism, anger issues, divorce, diabetes, depression, fear, greed, suicide attempts, etc.[30] Look for commonalities to discover any generational curses. Then, do whatever you can to heal your ailments naturally first. For example, don't pray to break off a curse of diabetes, and then start eating sugar and bread and all the things that trigger diabetes. Take all the actions you can to heal your body, (exercise, eat a healthier diet, decrease the stress in your life). Do all you can do, and at the same time pray that Satan's spiritual foothold would be removed and the curse of diabetes be broken.[31] **Your body, mind, and emotions must be in agreement with your spiritual declaration.**

Through observation and prayer, you can discern the specific case (generational curse) that the enemy has used to hold your family in bondage. Remember, we have been given the Holy Spirit of Truth to give us revelation about our current situation. Ask Him to guide you. He is your greatest counsellor!

"God conceals the revelation of His word in the hiding place of His glory. But the honor of kings is revealed by how they thoroughly search out the deeper meaning of all that God says" Proverbs 25:2 (TPT).

BREAKING THE CURSE

If you suspect you are under the influence of a familial spirit, you can break its hold on you. Josiah is an example of this. Both Josiah's father and his grandfather Manasseh lived in disobedience to the Lord, but Josiah decided to break the cycle and follow the example of King David, his ancestor, who lived more than ten generations before![32] His testimony is recorded in 2 Kings 22:2, *"He (Josiah) did what was right in the sight of the Lord and walked in all the ways of his father (ancestor) David and did not turn aside to the right or to the left" (AMP).*

If you can see how you are following the example of your parents or grandparents, and you want to break the pattern, Dr. Venner J. Alston, author of Next Level Spiritual Warfare, offers a simple prayer to help move you towards freedom:

> *"Father, I thank you for the power of redemption paid for me through the life, death, burial, and resurrection of Jesus. Lord, thank you for revealing iniquitous patterns that are affecting me and hindering my prayers. These patterns are things that became a part of my life as I grew up watching behaviors in my family. I acknowledge these patterns are unrighteous and do not*

agree with your word. These patterns hinder my prayers. Lord, I repent today and refuse to walk in ungodly patterns. Beginning today, let me walk in the redemptive gifts You have placed in my family. Like Josiah, I choose to walk in righteousness. Today I choose freedom, in Jesus name."[33]

In my life, I could see that the spirit of fear was present in both my parents' bloodlines; I could see it affecting so many of my relatives. And guess what? I inherited it too! The devil counted on me leaving that door to fear open in my life the way my ancestors had. But the Word of God tells me that in God's kingdom there is no reason to live in fear. Fear is actually a sin. I had to learn that it takes power, love, and a sound mind from the Holy Spirit to overthrow the spirit of fear. 2 Timothy 1:7 says: *"For God did not give us a spirit of timidity or cowardice or fear, but [He has given us a spirit] of power and of love and of sound judgment and personal discipline [abilities that result in a calm, well-balanced mind and self-control]" (AMP).*

A powerful lesson in my battle against fear was to learn to fear the Lord more than anything or anyone else. Proverbs 9:10 says, *"The fear of the Lord is the beginning of wisdom and the knowledge of the Holy One is insight" (ESV).* From the Word, I observed how the heroes of the faith faced their own fears. Abraham was called to take Isaac, the child of promise that he and Sarah waited so long for, and offer him as a sacrifice to the Lord. He clearly feared God more than his own fears when he acted in obedience, and so God saved Isaac. I am not so sure I would have been that brave! Moses teaches us that **the fear of God is meant to be an attitude that protects us from sin.** He said to the children of Israel in Exodus 20:20: *"Do not be afraid. God has come to test you, so that the fear of God will be with you to keep you from sinning" (NIV).*

Trials and testing are just going to be a part of life! So, I had better respond the way God intended: **not to fear the trial, but to fear the God who controls the trial.** As I've learned to replace my fears with the fear of the Lord, I have been set free from many anxieties. Now, this is still a process; the enemy knows the history of fear in my family bloodline, but I am determined to break the cycle. As I continually choose to stop receiving the spirit of fear in my life, I begin to enjoy the Spirit of Life that God offers me through Christ Jesus. After all, Christ came so that I could enjoy life in abundance as I walk in fellowship with Him.

If you can trace a physical, emotional or mental ailment that has plagued your generational line, you can invoke the power of the blood of Jesus to cleanse your blood line. Below is an example of a prayer once you have done your preparatory work: readying your physical health (making healthy choices in your area of weakness), readying your emotional health (offering forgiveness to all parties), and your mental health (aligning thoughts with truth). These steps of readiness show that you are truly ready for the obedience it takes to make the changes necessary, so that your spirit can line up with the wisdom of God functioning in the rest of your body. (Note: It is always wise to join in faith with other Christians and pray this together as you do warfare against the devil's hold on your life.)

"I repent of and renounce any participation or agreement with the evil one in my life, specifically in the area of _____. God forgive me and/or my ancestors for_____. In the name and authority of Jesus Christ I now break every related curse that has plagued my family line back to the 4th generation and beyond. I cast you out in the name of Jesus Christ. I command you not to affect me anymore, and to flee from me once and for all, in the name of Jesus. I command you— soul, body, mind, and emotions— to line up with the word of God and submit to His authority and healing. I receive the full forgiveness of the Lord Jesus Christ, and I bow my knee to Him alone. Thank you, Lord, that your power has set me free to walk in health and wholeness and to live a life of victory in the mighty name of Jesus."[34]

With sin removed and bloodlines cleansed, you are preparing yourself to receive everything Jesus died for you to have. Remember, walking out our salvation is a continuous journey. So take what you've learned so far, put those tools in your toolbelt and keep moving forward! There's more and more grace, and more and more revelation still to come.

ENDNOTES

28   Dr. Venner J. Alston, Next-Level Spiritual Warfare, First (Victoria, BC: Friesen Press, 2018), 56.

29   Ibid, 57.

30   DeGraw, Kathy. "Prayers, Decrees to Break Your Family's Generational Curses." Charisma News, April 6, 2019. https://www.charismanews.com/opinion/75824-prayers-decrees-to-break-your-family-s-generational-curses.

31   Ibid.

32   Dr. Venner J. Alston, Next-Level Spiritual Warfare, First (Victoria, BC: Friesen Press, 2018), 57.

33   Ibid., 57-58.

34   Robert T. Henderson, Receiving Healing from the Courts of Heaven: Removing Hindrances That Delay or Deny Your Healing (Shippensburg, PA, PA: Destiny Image Publishers, 2018), 28.

CHAPTER 7
WINNING YOUR BATTLE

When you are battling for your health, it can be so frustrating searching for the root of the problem. I know, I've been there! It can feel like you are fighting an uphill battle, and, at times, you may think you are inherently flawed. But this is not true. When God created you, He knew exactly what He was doing. When He breathed life into you at conception, every cell in your body began to be uniquely and intentionally placed for health and wellness and purpose. Let's take a closer look at how He made us, what went wrong, and how we can be restored.

DAMAGED DNA

Within your cells, you have a unique DNA blueprint that determines all of the qualities of who you are. It's what makes you, you. No one on earth has been given the same DNA as you have. DNA is not passed down from generation to generation in a single block because not every child gets the exact same 50 percent from mom's DNA and the same 50 percent from dad's DNA. Each egg and each sperm has a unique genetic makeup, creating different combinations for each set of siblings. Studies show that you may only share half of the same genetic code as a brother or sister.[35] You are uniquely you!

You're probably familiar with the DNA image of the double stranded helix joined by ladder-like prongs. Though the textbook image is stiff and static, in its natural state, your DNA is dynamically charged with energy, moving and bending with the waves of change occurring within your cells.[36] DNA is your unique, energy-infused identification card. But you are not just physical matter held together energetically, you are also an eternal spirit. Humanity received its life from the breath of God Himself. Even when your temporary, fleshly body dies, your spirit will live on in eternal life with Christ, or in eternal suffering separated from His presence. Just as your physical body can become ill, so your spirit can be corrupted. This spiritual reality directly affects your physical reality. When God created Adam, his physical DNA was whole and his spirit was pure. The first man, made in the image of God, formed by God's own hand. The Bible says, *"the life of the flesh is in the blood" Lev. 17:11a ESV,* and Adam's blood was perfectly clean, carrying God's pure DNA. Can you imagine if we had blood like that today? Our bodies would never experience sickness or decomposition!

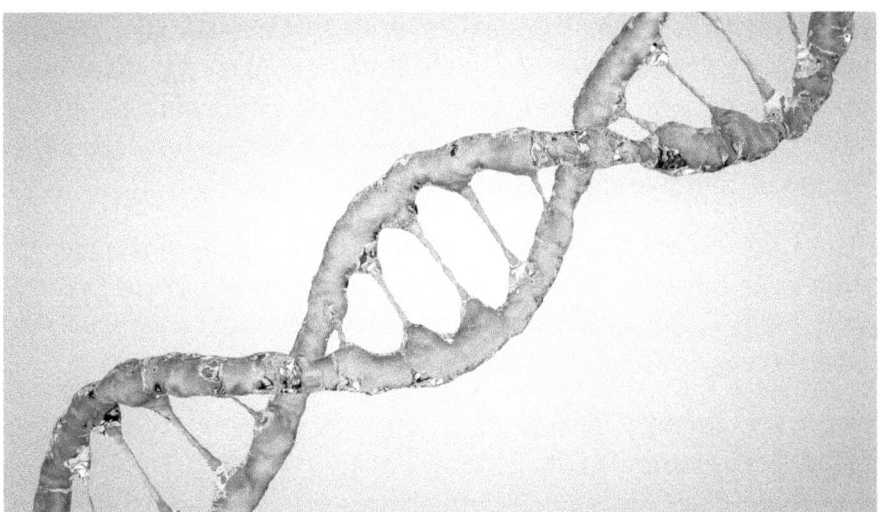

But when Adam sinned in Genesis 3, his life-blood changed; the process of death and decay began in his body, and he passed it on to all of us. Our blood carries stored information going all the way back to Adam (imagine that!), and this information influences who we are. Because Adam and Eve's blood had become contaminated with sin, all of their descendants (including us) would be conceived in iniquity, would struggle against sin, and would ultimately, both physically and spiritually, die. As the Bible says, *"The wages of sin is death" Rom. 6:23.*

JESUS HAS MADE THE WAY

Ever since this encounter with the serpent at the Tree of Knowledge of Good and Evil, humanity has been aging, experiencing poverty, sickness, and death. To save us, God needed to do a miracle. It was necessary for Jesus, as the Son of God, to come with perfect blood, divine DNA, and reverse the curse of Adam. He came as the second Adam, that would restore health, and the dominion of the earth back to the sons and daughters of God.

Jesus was not conceived by man but by the Spirit of God. In the womb of the Virgin Mary, He took on the chromosomes necessary for flesh, and with the heavenly DNA template in His blood, He became the perfect being to restore humanity to its original state. Untainted divine blood flowed through His veins, which He offered for the redemption of the world *"...whoever believes in Him will not perish but have eternal life" Jn. 3:16 NLT*. **To follow Jesus as our Savior, is to receive the gift of His blood, and thereby, a redeemed genetic code.**

"For you know that you were ransomed from the futile ways inherited from your forefathers, not with perishable things such as silver or gold, but with the precious blood of Christ, like that of a lamb without blemish or spot" 1 Peter 1:18-19 ESV.

"Jesus also suffered...in order to sanctify the people through His own blood" Hebrews 13:12 ESV.

We have now become a part of Jesus' bloodline. We belong to the royal family of God. Chosen. Adopted. Transformed.

"God decided in advance to adopt us into His own family by bringing us to Himself through Jesus Christ. This is what He wanted to do, and it gave Him great pleasure" Ephesians 1:5 NLT.

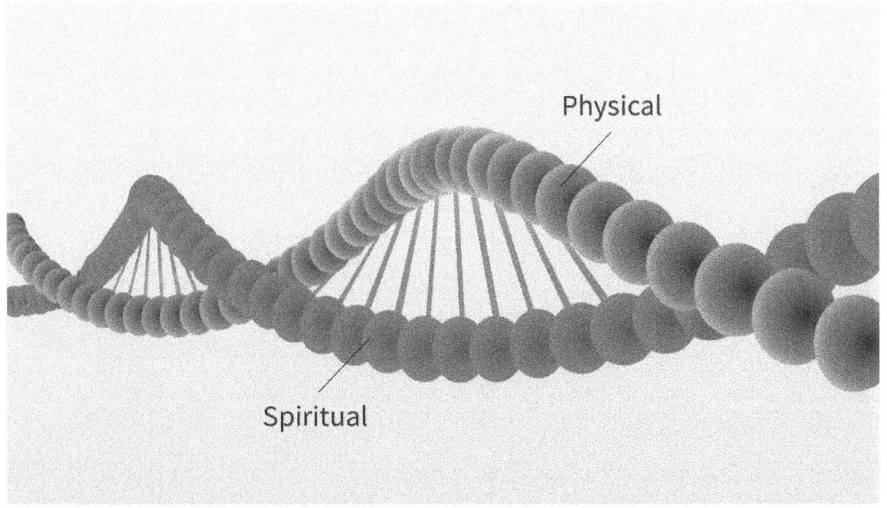

The physical blood of Christ brings us spiritual healing and physical healing. Imagine it like this. Your DNA strand has 2 strands that form the double helix. Let's say one of them represents your spiritual well-being and the other represents your physical well-being. When sin entered the human bloodline, the devil hijacked the DNA by corrupting the spiritual strand of the double helix, which allowed decay and death to affect the physical strand as well. However, when we come to Christ, Jesus' righteousness restores this hijacked spiritual strand, releases divine power to break every curse, and brings physical healing as well. His righteous blood overrides the previous mutated DNA. From the point of salvation, the Spirit of God continues to work within us, transforming us to become more and more like Christ. This is the process of sanctification.

Now, even though Jesus has restored us, we can still allow spiritual corruption into our lives when we choose to sin, giving Satan the same influence to corrupt our whole selves. But God, in His mercy, gives us opportunity to repent, and when He sees the righteous strand of Christ in our blood, we are freed from all condemnation. Hallelujah!

"In Him we have redemption through His blood, the forgiveness of sins, in accordance with the riches of God's grace" Ephesians. 1:7 NIV.

"Now in Christ Jesus you who once were far off have been made near by the blood of Christ" Ephesians 2:13 ESV.

HEAVEN'S COURTROOM

The decision declaring us guilty, or acquitted by Jesus' blood happens in the courtroom of heaven. Did you know that heaven has its own courtroom? It's a real place! The book of Daniel describes it like this:

"I watched as thrones were put in place
and the Ancient One sat down to judge.
His clothing was as white as snow,
His hair like purest wool.
He sat on a fiery throne
with wheels of blazing fire,
and a river of fire was pouring out,
flowing from His presence.
Millions of angels ministered to Him;
many millions stood to attend Him.
Then the court began its session,
and the books were opened" Daniel 7:9-10 NLT.

Isaiah confirms:

"The Lord takes His place in court; He rises to
judge the people" Isaiah 3:13 NIV.

Isn't it amazing how our earthly experiences are often just a reflection of what is going on in heaven? Just as in a human courtroom there is both a prosecutor and a defender, so there is in heaven also.

God stands beside us as our defender:

> *"For He stands at the right hand of the needy one,*
> *to deliver him from his accusers" Psalm 109:31 ISV.*

Satan is the prosecutor:

> *"... For the accuser of our brothers and sisters*
> *has been thrown down to earth—*
> *the one who accuses them*
> *before our God day and night" Rev. 12:10b NLT.*

Satan is an incessant accuser, and he is constantly slandering us and accusing us of sin, because he knows that if we are found guilty, he then has a legal right to bring chaos and destruction into our lives. Because God is righteous, Satan knows He will not turn a blind eye to sin. His holiness does not allow Him to compromise standards of right and wrong. He is a God of justice. Our enemy, also known as 'The Accuser' likes to take advantage of this fact and use it against us.

Satan might say something like, "God, have you considered Janet? She is holding unforgiveness toward her brother in her heart. She refuses to humble herself. You can't dismiss that can You?" The devil loves to accuse the body of Christ in the Courts of Heaven.[37]

Satan knows that if there is sin, God, in His perfect character, must judge it. **Though our sin does not remove our salvation which is given freely by faith in Christ (Ephes. 2:8-9),** undealt with sin in our life can break our fellowship with God.[38] In the Lord's prayer, Jesus teaches His disciples to commune with the Father regularly by asking God for the forgiveness of their sins (Lk. 11:4).

I have learned that the reason many people are not healed is because there is an open case in the heavenlies against them due to undealt-with sin. I'd like to recommend the books: Accessing the Courts of Heaven and Receiving Healing from the Courts of Heaven by Robert Henderson. When I was seeking my own healing, they changed my life and I'm sure they will change yours too! They discuss how sometimes the suffering we face in life is due to choices we have made that have legal implications in the courts of heaven. Once you understand the legal process, you'll have more knowledge in how to win the battles you face on earth.

TURNING FROM SIN

Sometimes, without asking God, we don't realize what sin we need to turn from. The enemy spiritually blinds us to truth about ourselves. Other times, we just don't want to take an honest look at what is really going on. A helpful spiritual practice is to ask God to show you what you need to repent of. Humble yourself, listen, and see what He brings to your heart and mind.

In 1 Samuel 15:19-23, King Saul denies that he has any sin to repent of. The prophet Samuel rebukes him and reminds Saul that God told him specifically not to take any of the plunder after the battle with the Amalekites. It takes Saul a while to admit it to himself.

"Why did you not obey the Lord? Why did you pounce on the plunder and do evil in the eyes of the Lord?"

"But I did obey the Lord," Saul said. "I went on the mission the Lord assigned me. I completely destroyed the Amalekites and brought back Agag their king. The soldiers took sheep and cattle from the plunder,

the best of what was devoted to God, in order to sacrifice them to the Lord your God at Gilgal."

But Samuel replied:

> *"Does the Lord delight in burnt offerings and sacrifices*
> *as much as in obeying the Lord?*
> *To obey is better than sacrifice,*
> *and to heed is better than the fat of rams.*
> *For rebellion is like the sin of divination,*
> *and arrogance like the evil of idolatry.*
> *Because you have rejected the word of the Lord,*
> *He has rejected you as king."*

Then Saul said to Samuel, *"I have sinned. I violated the Lord's command and your instructions. I was afraid of the men and so I gave in to them" (NIV).*

Sin is serious business. God takes it seriously and so should we. Sin, whether a one-time offense, or a lifestyle of rebellion, causes a separation between us and God.

> *"Surely the arm of the Lord is not too short to save,*
> *nor His ear too dull to hear.*
> *But your iniquities have separated*
> *you from your God;*
> *your sins have hidden His face from you,*
> *so that He will not hear" Isaiah. 59:1-2 NIV.*

We have to acknowledge our sin and turn to Jesus with it in order to restore fellowship with the Father. Otherwise, we face the attacks of the enemy against our mind, emotions, spirit, and body. Sin has natural consequences. We must be hasty to confess and keep ourselves in right standing before the Lord. Taking the medicine of self-honesty, and regularly practicing repentance is great discipline for your spiritual health!

THE DANGER OF PRIDE

God invites us into repentance in order to remove the enemy's grip. Don't let the devil tell you it is someone else's fault so you don't need to repent. This builds up pride in your heart, hindering your freedom.

"God resists the proud but gives grace to the humble" James 4:6 CSB.

We must be particularly careful to guard against unforgiveness. Our ability to receive God's forgiveness is connected to our ability to forgive others. **If we refuse to forgive others for their offenses, we forsake our right to be forgiven of our own offenses.** The Bible is clear: *"For if you forgive other people when they sin against you, your heavenly Father will also forgive you. But if you do not forgive others their sins, your Father will not forgive your sins" Matt. 6:14-15 NIV.* Withholding forgiveness is a stubborn refusal of the gift that Jesus paid a high price for us to have, and it gives the enemy an open doorway to harm us. This stubbornness of heart can often be traced generationally.

Forgiveness is not optional in God's kingdom. Make sure you are walking in forgiveness towards everyone; this includes forgiving yourself, forgiving God of any offense you've taken against Him, and forgiving all of your relatives and ancestors. Take a moment now and ask God if there is anyone in your life that you need to forgive.

THE POWER OF REPENTANCE

The good news is, no matter what sin we have in our lives, we have a weapon that even Satan cannot overpower: repentance! If we look throughout scripture, God shares many examples showing us how important repentance is:

"If my people, who are called by my name, will humble themselves and pray and seek my face and turn from their wicked ways, then I will hear from heaven, and I will forgive their sin and will heal their land" 2 Chronicles 7:14 NIV.

"Repent, then, and turn to God, so that your sins may be wiped out,

that times of refreshing may come from the Lord" Acts 3:19 NIV.

Satan may bring arguments and accusations against us before the Lord, but when we come to God with a repentant heart, no amount of sin, rebellion, or generational curses can withstand the flood of forgiveness that God pours out in response to genuine repentance. Jesus died on the cross so we could be forgiven. He enables us to win our court cases in heaven!

"If we confess our sins, He is faithful and just and will forgive us our sins and purify us from all unrighteousness" 1 John 1:9 NIV.

I used to think repentance just meant saying, "I'm sorry." **But repentance really means having genuine remorse in your heart, and also changing from that sin by way of your actions.** Let us be quick to repent when we mess up! Repentance opens the way for us to receive and anticipate the blessings of our Heavenly Father.

Are you ready for God's blessings? Do you believe they will come? Though Satan would have us doubt, the price Jesus paid on the cross grants us resounding confidence in God's irrevocable will for us to be healthy and walk in wholeness.

Sickness and disease are the devil's handiwork intended to destroy us. Through Jesus Christ, God has given us a legal right to overcome.

"My dear children, I am writing this to you so that you will not sin. But if anyone does sin, we have an advocate who pleads our case before the Father. He is Jesus Christ, the one who is truly righteous. He Himself is the sacrifice that atones for our sins—and not only our sins but the sins of all the world" 1 John 2:1-2 NLT.

I had purchased a piece of property with some colleagues in dental school. They were unbelievers, but decent people, and it seemed like it was going to be a good investment, so we went for it! In retrospect, I did not ask the Lord if I should do this before I leaped at the opportunity, and consequently, we had so many problems with that property. It got to the point where we just couldn't afford it anymore, and we had to sell. But even that wasn't easy! In the span of about 6 months we took it on and off the market three times. My prayers weren't working and I felt blocked. My intercessor had me read a short book about the Courts of Heaven. I didn't know anything about what this court was, but I searched the Scriptures, and found it was real. God is not only Heavenly Father but also Judge and He addresses cases in His heavenly courtroom. So, I adjusted the way I prayed. I imagined myself going into the courts of heaven and I asked God to hear my case as a judge. I got down on my knees before Him and I asked Him to forgive me for jumping into this investment without even discussing it with Him. I asked Him to forgive me for becoming unequally yoked into a covenantal (contractual) relationship with unbelievers. I asked Him to look at the blood of Jesus that covered my sin, and to forgive me so that this property could sell and I could be free of it. I promised to only enter covenantal relationships that He led me into. After months of struggling, only two or three days after my prayer, a buyer came forward, ready to purchase the property. It was truly a miracle.

THE POWER OF FAITH

Do you remember in sunday school, cutting out paper shields and helmets learning about how to "put on the full armor of God?" It's cute to see the little ones running around with paper swords, but as you mature in Christ, you realize the absolute necessity of putting on this armor. It makes a big difference in the spiritual realm! God has given us armor to wear, to stand in self-defense against the enemy's accusations and attacks. One of your primary defensive weapons is your shield of faith.

"Finally, be strong in the Lord and in His mighty power. Put on the full armor of God, so that you can take your stand against the devil's schemes. For our struggle is not against flesh and blood, but against the rulers, against the authorities, against the powers of this dark world and against the spiritual forces of evil in the heavenly realms. Therefore put on the full armor of God, so that when the day of evil comes, you may be able to stand your ground, and after you have done everything, to stand. Stand firm then, with the belt of truth buckled around your waist, with the breastplate of righteousness in place, and with your feet fitted with the readiness that comes from the gospel of peace. In addition to all this, **take up the shield of faith, with which you can extinguish all the flaming arrows of the evil one.** *Take the helmet of salvation and the sword of the Spirit, which is the word of God. And pray in the Spirit on all occasions with all kinds of prayers and requests. With this in mind, be alert and always keep on praying for all the Lord's people" Ephesians 6:10-18 NIV.*

Faith is very, very powerful. Jesus says that even a mustard seed of it can move mountains (Matt. 17:20). Satan knows faith blocks his agenda so he is constantly spewing out lies to cause you to stumble and question what is true. Remember the devil's tactics in the garden? Luring Eve to eat the fruit by creating doubt in God's Word (the opposite of faith). We must hold our shield of faith high as we battle for health. Even when the doctor tells you bad news, the Lord wants you to believe God's report. You just say "Nope! I'm going to believe the Lord. He is all powerful and all knowing. Sickness is not my portion!" We have to re-learn what truth is. We have to remember who we are in Christ. The fellowship in the garden between God and man was spirit-to-spirit. His breath gave us breath. Our unity with God was perfect. We can still have this divine connection, and experience divine health, through faith.

A lady at my friend's church was diagnosed with cancer. She told the doctor: "I'm not receiving that. I don't have that. I don't care what you see!" She believed that by Jesus' stripes she was healed. She didn't tell her family about the diagnosis. She got my friend to stand with her in faith. They met together and regularly declared the scriptures over her situation and they worshipped the Lord. Why? Were they begging God for something? No. They already had reason to celebrate. They already had the victory! The devil was just lying. Jesus says, "It is finished!" He's done it all for us! Don't let the enemy bombard you with the lies of this world. He may have influence on the earth right now, but Jesus has already stripped him of his authority.

After some time, the lady went back to the doctor and asked to be re-tested, and the cancer was gone! She had reminded the devil of the truth. She had exercised her spiritual authority as a spiritual being, seated in heavenly places. God wants us to think like He does, because He loves us.

"And without faith it is impossible to please God, because anyone who comes to Him must believe that He exists and that He rewards those who earnestly seek Him" Hebrews 11:6 NIV.

God, the Father of our Spirit, longs to commune with us so we have to build our spiritual muscles resisting our flesh. Our flesh believes whatever the world says. Our flesh is trying to battle the chemical warfare of medications and GMOs and all the other nasty tactics of the enemy. It must hurt God's heart to see His people suffering unnecessarily. **It's as if God is saying, "Don't you know how much I love you? Let go of the lies so that you can have real freedom in me. You're believing a false report!"** No matter what fiery darts that are thrown at you, if your spirit is stronger than your fleshly body, you win. When you know who you are in Christ, you can say, "Come on, give it your best shot! It can't stick to me." Faith moves mountains— it's the currency of heaven.

"Now faith is the assurance (title deed, confirmation) of things hoped for (divinely guaranteed), and the evidence of things not seen [the conviction of their reality—faith comprehends as fact what cannot be experienced by the physical senses]" Hebrews 11:1 AMP.

Let's look at a story from Scripture:

> *"One Sabbath day as Jesus was teaching in a synagogue, He saw a woman who had been crippled by an evil spirit. She had been bent double for eighteen years and was unable to stand up straight. When Jesus saw her, He called her over and said, 'Dear woman, you are healed of your sickness!" Then He touched her, and instantly she could stand straight. How she praised God!'"*
> *Luke 13:10-13 NLT.*

For eighteen long years, this woman was bound to the enemy's rule over her life. The devil had a legal hold to keep her infirm, but through the prayer from Jesus, she was brought to the courts of heaven[39] to overturn any agreement (known or unknown), that had allowed Satan control over her. Jesus broke that contract, and loosed her from the infirmity. In that moment, the agreement with the enemy was made null and void. She was finally aligned to the rule of God in her life and was able to receive His anointing.

Whatever you are battling, take your need into the courts of heaven and plead your case. If you have knowingly, or unknowingly, given Satan access to your life, the wisdom from Heaven's throne room will set you on the right path again. **When your obedience is complete and the Lordship of Christ is firmly established in your life, you have great authority to wipe out all of the enemy's plans and schemes**

from your personal life. Jesus stands beside the Father interceding on your behalf, so that you may live fully alive and free in Jesus Christ.

"Who will bring any charge against those whom God has chosen? It is God who justifies. Who then is the one who condemns? No one. Christ Jesus who died—more than that, who was raised to life—is at the right hand of God and is also interceding for us" Romans 8:33-34 NIV.

When you believe you are healed, you are acknowledging the all-sufficiency of what Jesus did on the cross. He died so we could live, fully and abundantly, both now, and in eternity. Many times, Jesus spoke to the infirm and said, *"Your faith has made you well" (Mark 5:25-34; Luke 7:50; Luke 17:19; Luke 18:42).* So, I encourage you: keep walking by faith. No matter what your situation looks like. God is watching your response. Are you going to give up? Are you going to be found whining and complaining like someone who doesn't know the royal favor they have in Jesus Christ? Or are you going to say, "I believe, by faith, that I am already healed in the spirit, and I am waiting for it to manifest in the natural."

Let the words of your mouth align with God's word. There's life and death in the power of your tongue (Proverbs 18:21). **His Word is true no matter what the physical looks like.** If you feel you need more support in your faith, I encourage you to find someone who operates in a higher realm of authority in the spiritual realm, to pray with. Someone who has built up their faith muscles, and has confidence as they pray in accordance with the authority of the Word. In this spiritual walk, there are always higher heights to discover; and at each level, God teaches us more about faith. As we grow, we get to know His character more personally, and become more confident about how He will act. We have to know Him intimately to hear His will for situations. It's okay to act on what you know right now, just keep growing. He loves you so much, and He has already prepared blessings in heaven for you— it is just waiting to manifest on earth. Expect it. If God is for you, who can be against you? (Romans 8:31).

WHEN HEALING STILL DOESN'T COME

If you're reading this, feeling like you've tried everything to get well: you've repented of sin, you've prayed in faith, you've forgiven, fasted, worshipped, you've joined with others to break any generational curses... and you are still sick, please, take heart. God has not forsaken you. Sickness is not a sign of God's absence. Jesus has told us that we would experience troubles on earth, and has given us the comfort of the Holy Spirit to assure us of His nearness in the midst of difficulty (Jn. 16:7,33). Some healings do happen instantaneously. But sometimes they don't. Sometimes God leads us on a journey, and teaches us along the way. If you're waiting for your breakthrough, I encourage you to do a few things:

- Dialogue with God

- Be steadfast and patient

- Humbly let God be God

1. Dialogue with God

Learning to hear God's guidance is a journey in itself, but it begins by reaching out with expectation that He will speak to you. If you want answers, don't demand them, but do search them out, practice listening, and God will teach you. I believe God chose to use my journey through illness to become a testimony to the body of Christ, to show how accessible God is to guide you into wisdom for healing. I didn't always have the clarity about divine healing that I have now, and I know there is still more to come. I had to start where I was and search it out! God revealed more and more to me through different stages, so I would not be overwhelmed, because it is a lot. So much has been hidden from the body of Christ; but if we seek we will find.

"Truth's shining light guided me in my choices and decisions; the revelation of His word makes my pathway clear" Psalm 119:105

(TPT).

Sometimes our communication with God can become blocked. When Adam's relationship with God was broken, Adam hid from God. God had to ask, "where are you?" If you're hiding from God in fear, disappointment, anger, sin, or unforgiveness, your communication with Him will be hindered. God wants to restore your relationship and abide together daily, so that He can guide you into all truth. God wants to reason together with you. The Bible shows us that He seeks us out. In other words, He wants to help us figure life out!

"Come now, let us reason together, says the LORD: though your sins are like scarlet, they shall be as white as snow; though they are red like crimson, they shall become like wool" Is.1:18 ESV.

This scripture reminds me of the heavenly courtroom. As a righteous judge, He invites us to converse with Him in His courtroom, to hear our case, and then, He settles all the matters concerning us. He wants to help you to get rid of the hindrances in your life. He wants to cleanse illness. He wants to forgive sin. He wants to discuss it with you. He is seeking togetherness, continually providing opportunities to communicate and co-labor with Him. So, if you need wisdom for your health situation, go and reason with the Lord. He beckons you to come. Talk to Him and let Him remind you of how you have been made whole by the righteous blood of Christ. Listen and watch for His guidance as He leads you into it.

Let me assure you, getting to the root of illness is not an easy process. It took me years to find my path to health! Sometimes God heals instantly, sometimes He doesn't. Sometimes it's related to spiritual issues, sometimes it's just about your diet! Be patient with yourself as you seek God for wisdom for your situation.

I remember when my dad kept passing out. I'd been praying for him and asking God to show me what the problem was. No one had an answer, he just kept fainting. We saw at least four different doctors. They all wanted to put him on epileptic medication, insisting he must have had a seizure, despite the fact that he's never had a history of seizures. We just knew this wasn't right, so we just kept trusting and asking God to lead us. Finally, God led us to a physician who suggested that it might be "postprandial hypotension," which occurs when too much blood flows from the brain to manage digestion after eating. This was exactly what was going on! My dad loves to eat, and after meals (especially after overeating), his blood pressure would decrease, and then he would pass out. Finally, we had the solution— without drugs, or a wrong diagnosis! Be patient and keep trusting; God will lead you!

Sometimes, like with my dad, God will lead through circumstances, or through that gut feeling that something isn't right. Sometimes, it's just an inclination that I've come to recognize as the Spirit's nudge. For myself, it isn't always easy to hear what God is saying, but I notice that when I pray in the Spirit, or enter worship, I can often hear His voice more clearly. Put yourself in the places of His presence and His word. He will speak. He will guide, in many different ways. But you have to be patient. It may not come after asking just one time! Never underestimate the power of your prayers. You are under the new covenant, which means you are seated in heavenly places. You have more power than you think.

"And God raised us up with Christ and seated us with Him in the heavenly realms in Christ Jesus" Ephesians 2:6 NIV.

Because I am seated with the Lord when I pray, I have confidence that He hears me, so I keep standing in the gap of intercession over myself and over others' lives. I regularly ask Jesus what I need to repent for in my own life, or what will give another person their breakthrough. Even if the answer doesn't come immediately, I choose to wait expectantly. **The main thing is continuing to dialogue with Him.** Don't hold Him at a distance when you don't understand what you are seeing. Keep exploring with Him until you get the answers you're looking for.

2. Be Steadfast and Patient

When God gives you some direction, follow it to the end. God responds to persistent faith. I am reminded of Jesus' parable of the persistent widow in Luke 18:1-8:

> *"One day Jesus told His disciples a story to show that they should always pray and never give up. 'There was a judge in a certain city,' he said, 'who neither feared God nor cared about people. A widow of that city came to him repeatedly, saying, 'Give me justice in this dispute with my enemy.' The judge ignored her for a while, but finally he said to himself, 'I don't fear God or care about people, but this woman is driving me crazy. I'm going to see that she gets justice, because she is wearing me out with her constant requests!'" Then the Lord said, "Learn a lesson from this unjust judge. Even he rendered a just decision in the end. So don't you think God will surely give justice to his chosen people who cry out to Him day and night? Will he keep putting them off? I tell you, he will grant justice to them quickly! But when the Son of Man returns, how many will He find on the earth who have faith?" (NLT).*

God hears your prayers. Even if you don't see your desires manifesting yet, continue to approach Him and bring your needs before Him. Trust that He is listening, and as you pray, listen to Him as well.

3. Letting God be God

Sometimes you just have to let God be God. Even if our will is for healing, His purposes are far above our own:

"For my thoughts are not your thoughts,
neither are your ways my ways,"
declares the Lord.
"As the heavens are higher than the earth,
so are my ways higher than your ways
and my thoughts than your thoughts" Isaiah 55:8-9 NIV.

Someone had asked me to pray for a girl who was only in her twenties and in the hospital with stage four cancer. It gripped my heart, and I tell you, I got so mad at the enemy! I began to bind him and rebuke him and declare and shout and push back the darkness and claim Jesus' life over her. I went to the courts of heaven and demanded that chains be broken and her life restored. How could someone so young be taken out by Satan's evil agenda? Not on my watch! I began celebrating the victory by faith, believing for a complete turn around. And then… she died. This was really hard for me. I began wrestling with God. I began to question the value of my prayers (you see how the enemy keeps pushing in with doubt!); then I sought the Lord about it, and the Holy Spirit reminded me of the Scripture where Jesus said: *"The Son can do nothing by Himself. He can only do what He sees His Father doing" Jn. 5:19 NIV.* I realized I had forgotten to ask the Father what He was doing in this situation. Instead, I just went straight for Satan's jugular! I presumed what God's specific will was for this situation, because I knew His general will is to heal and give life, but God uses all circumstances for His glory. Sometimes, God's final will is fulfilled on the other side of eternity. I don't say that lightly, or as a disclaimer. One of my fellow intercessors who was also praying for this young girl, said that in her prayer time, she could feel the compassion and earnest desire of Jesus to take her home and make her well. As if He said, "Don't worry. I hear your prayers for healing, and I am going to heal her. I'm bringing her home." God knows all the days written in our book before one of them comes to pass (Ps. 139:16). He knows our time. And He knows best. The struggle is, I have to be okay with that. I have to let God be God. As it turned out, her death led to many of her family members getting saved because they wanted to be with her in eternity. God knows what He is doing, even if it's not what we had expected.

This situation taught me that I need to first ask God what His will is. I must ask Jesus to show me what the Father is doing, so I can agree with His will and align myself with His answer. I can't insist on my own will. I have to follow Jesus' example, *"not my will Father, but yours be done" (Lk. 22:42).* **God doesn't promise us our hoped-for outcome, nor all the answers as to why, but He does promise to work everything for our good in the end (Rom 8:28).** When we've done all we can do to make ourselves right before God, and we've brought our petitions to His throne room, we must leave the rest in His hands. Afterall, He is God. And He is good.

ENDNOTES

35   Wetsman, Nicole. "Siblings Can Have Surprisingly Different DNA Ancestry. Here's Why." Why Siblings Can Get Different Results From DNA Ancestry Tests, March 23, 2018. https://www.nationalgeographic.com/news/2018/03/dna-ancestry-test-siblings-different-results-genetics-science/.

36   Baylor College of Medicine. "DNA Is Dynamic And Has High Energy; Not Stiff Or Static As First Envisioned." ScienceDaily. www.sciencedaily.com/releases/2009/07/090713160523.htm (Accessed 30 May. 2020).

37   Robert T. Henderson, Receiving Healing from the Courts of Heaven: Removing Hindrances That Delay or Deny Your Healing (Shippensburg, PA, PA: Destiny Image Publishers, 2018), 112.

38   Bing, Charlie. "Do Believers Need to Confess Their Sins for Forgiveness?" GraceLife Ministries - Bringing Grace to life. Accessed October 20, 2020. https://www.gracelife.org/resources/gracenotes/?id=58.

39   This book helped me to take my healing to the next level: Robert Henderson's Receiving Healing from the Courts of Heaven (2018).

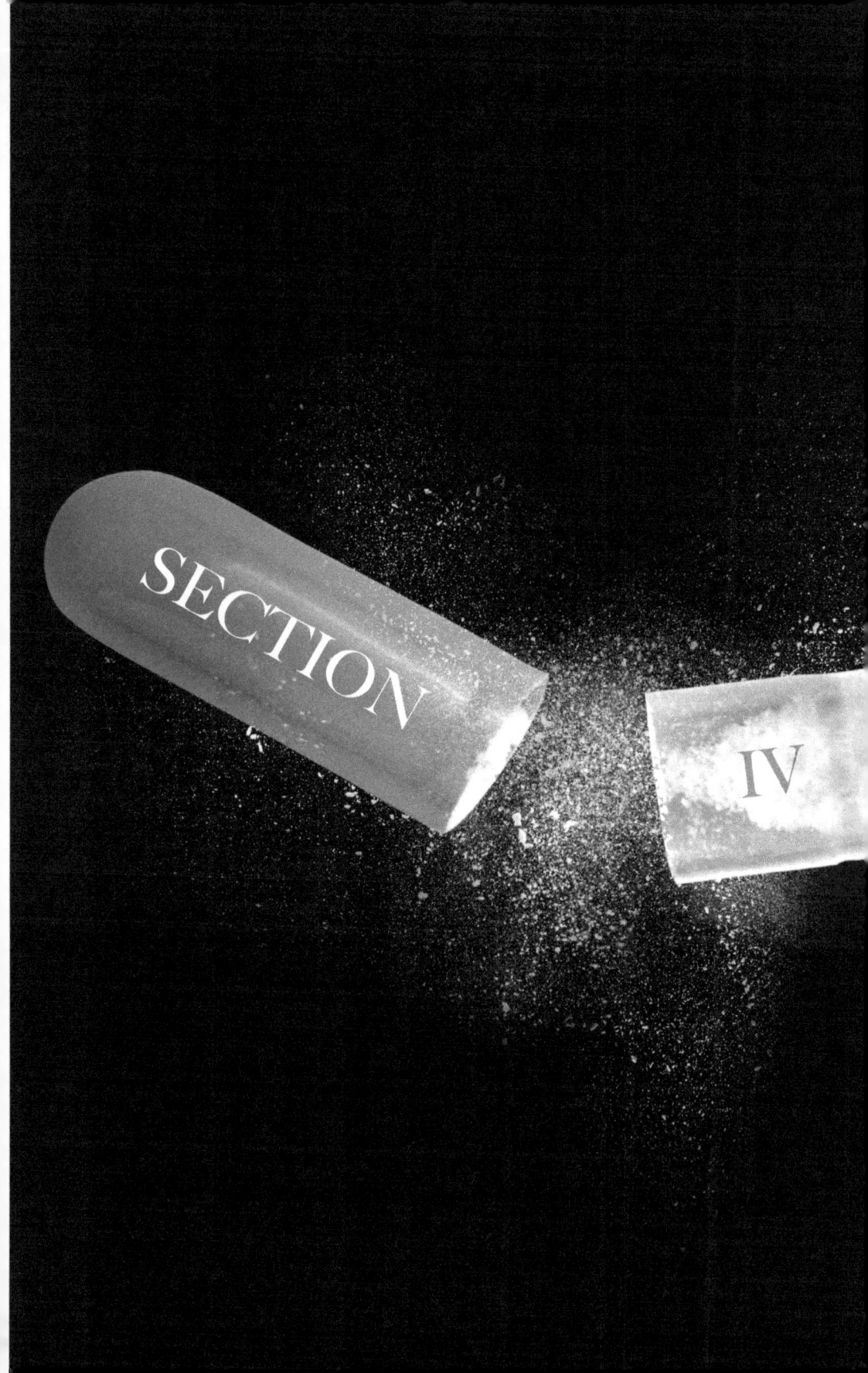

SECTION

IV

A HEALTHY BODY

We can't discuss the war on health without looking at the war going on in our very own bodies. Sometimes we blame spiritual issues, emotional issues or even genetics, and overly complicate the issue, when it's as plain as the nose on our face. What if it simply stems from what you are eating? What if changing a few things in your environment made all the difference? In this section, we will look at physical issues related to health and wellness, which are just as important as the spiritual issues. Remember, you are spirit, soul, and body. Being healthy means taking care of all three.

CHAPTER 8
GETTING DOWN TO THE GUT

Everything in the spiritual realm has a parallel in the natural realm. Just as we engage in a spiritual battle to keep the influences of evil away, so our physical bodies are built to battle for our physical health. Germs, viruses, bacteria, fungi, and parasites are the bad guys that wage war on our bodies from within. But God, in His infinite wisdom, has prepared us for the fight. We have a God-given self-protection system hidden within our physical bodies: our immune system. The immune system is our center for disease control, stocked with the exact artillery necessary to defeat invaders; it acts, not only as defense, but offense too! If the first line of defenders fail to completely eliminate the threat, B cells and T cells are trained to recognize past invaders and offensively seek them out and destroy them before they multiply.[40] Our God knew what He was doing when He designed our bodies! We were built for victorious health!

GETTING TO KNOW YOUR GUT

Did you know that 80 percent of your immune system is found in your gut, otherwise known as your colon? A microscope can show you that tens of trillions of microorganisms line your intestinal tract. These trillions of microorganisms are called your gut microbiota (formerly called gut flora). It contains 1000 different species of bacteria, both good and bad bacteria. In fact, humans typically carry some potentially dangerous fungi, such as Candida, that is kept in balance by the other bacteria. However, when it becomes overloaded, or when antibiotics commonly destroy both good and bad bacteria leaving a void, the bad bacteria (like C. diff) can gain the upper-hand and our bodies become seriously affected. A healthy gut will have rapidly multiplying good bacteria that keeps the bad bacteria in check. The more diverse our bacteria, the better we can digest and enjoy what we eat. The microbiota inside of us also form almost a vitamin distribution plant inside us! These *friends you didn't know you had,* also support you through nutrient assimilation. The microbes digest countless complex carbs and fiber and deploy enzymes to break them down into nutrients.

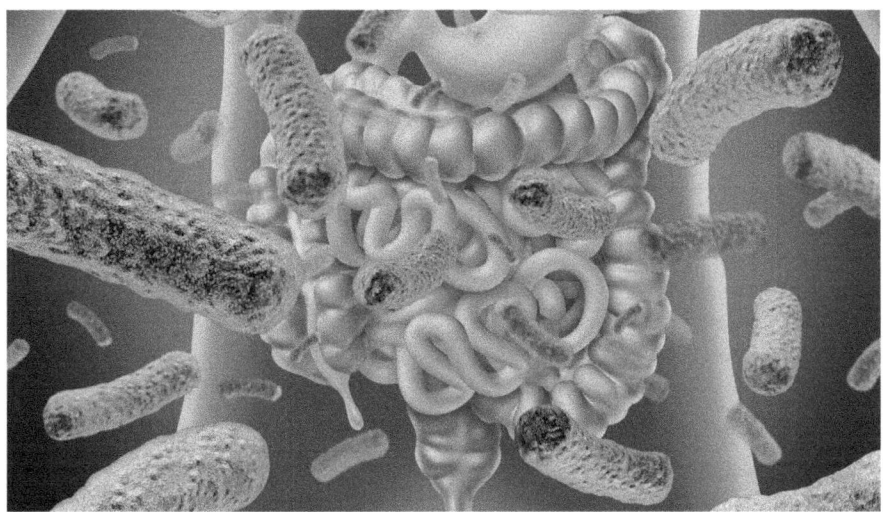

Perhaps you know that over 2000 years ago, Hippocrates (known as the Father of medicine) stated: "All health begins in the gut." It's only now that we're starting to listen! The health of our bodies is largely tied to the health of our gut; one cannot be healthy without the other. Most disease originates in our digestive system. You may have heard the saying, "you are what you eat." But it might be more true to say: "You are what your 'bugs' eat." What we choose to put into our mouths has such a profound impact on our health because each time we eat, we either feed the good bacteria or the bad bacteria. If the bad bacteria get out of balance, diseases are born. For example, sugar (especially in the absence of fiber), strengthens E. Coli and other pathogens that feed on sucrose. The harmful microbes grow, are fought by your immune system, and as a result of the battle, you experience chronic inflammation, which is a common factor underlying many serious illnesses. Alternatively, when we consistently choose whole foods that contain fiber, protein and beneficial fat sources, we are building a microbiota that will promote an anti-inflammatory state of health, and even positive moods.

7 keys to gut health:

1. **Fiber** - the colon works best when it has a lot of bulky material to push through

2. **Water** - along with fiber, water is necessary to keep stool soft so it can move easily

3. **Proper Diet** - consists of fruit, vegetables and whole grains

4. **Exercise** - stimulates the colon and increases peristalsis

5. **Reduce Stress** - under excess stress, the entire digestive system tends to shut down

6. **Probiotics & Prebiotics (friendly bacteria)** - these bacteria break down materials we can't digest, keep harmful bacteria in check and produce some important vitamins. You can purchase probiotics in pill form, or from fermented products like kimchi, miso, yogurt, kombucha, or kefir

7. **Avoid antibiotics** - they kill both good and bad gut bacteria throwing off your internal balance
    Note: if you absolutely need antibiotics to manage your system, just be sure to take a probiotic afterwards to replenish your healthy bacteria

The microorganisms in our gut play a critical role protecting and supporting our overall health. Doctor's are still discovering the intricacies of our microbiome (the genetic make-up of the microbiota). Interestingly, in the gut alone, 3.3 million genes exist; compared to the remaining 22,000 genes in the rest of our body, it forms a very significant part of who we are! In fact, each person's microbiome is 80-90% different from another person's.[41]

When I was seeing the naturopath to get to the bottom of my food allergies, it seemed that my body was rejecting every kind of food I gave it. I spent so much money on supplements and chelation IV's! Looking back with what I know now, of course my body would reject everything because my gut was messed up! I was experiencing toxic overload! The liver normally copes well with the body's everyday toxins, but when the burden exceeds capacity, toxins get dumped elsewhere. For me, these toxins were coming out of my eyes. Other people may experience problems in their skin, their digestion, or even high anxiety etc. Until the gut is cleaned up, and the good bacteria in proper balance, your body won't work the way it's designed to. We must protect and support our community of tiny organisms, and in return, we will thrive. **If you're battling with difficult to diagnose symptoms, start by focusing on restoring your gut health.**

THE DANGERS OF INFLAMMATION

Your immune system starts, before you even swallow, in the tonsils and adenoids as part of the gut protection. There are tonsil-like patches of lymph tissue in the lowest portion of the small intestine called Peyer's patches. These patches contain high concentrations of white blood cells (known as lymphocytes) which help protect the body from infection and disease by detecting antigens, such as bacteria and toxins, and mobilizing the production of antibodies.[42]

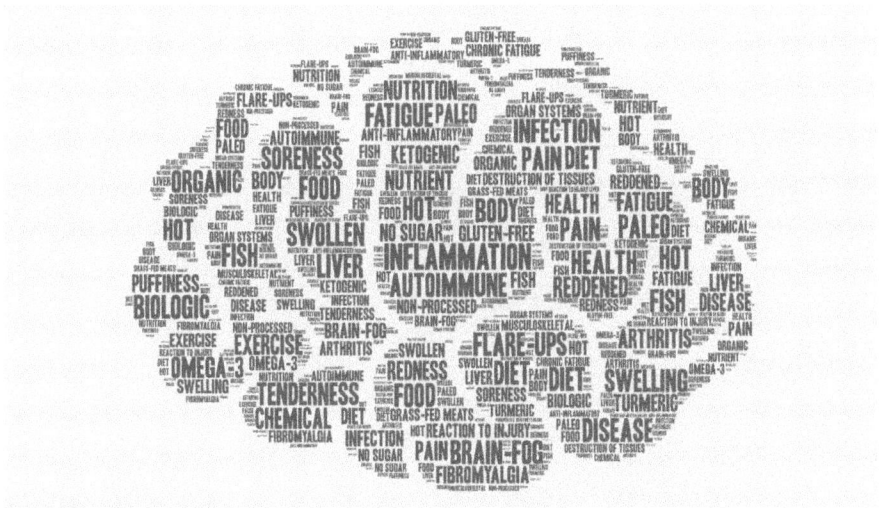

To keep your gut healthy, and to protect your immune system, you've got to keep inflammation to a minimum. The gut is a hotbed of potential inflammation. There are several possible triggers that cause our bodies to be inflamed: food allergies and intolerances, heavy metal poisoning, improperly digested food, and an imbalance of microorganisms within our intestines. All of these triggers act to poison our friendly bacteria, impair the function of our immune cells, and damage our bowel.

The foods we eat can also cause inflammation. Excess omega-6 fatty acids (found in oils such as corn, safflower, sunflower, soy etc.) activate pro-inflammatory chemicals, while omega-3 fatty acids (found in salmon, walnuts, flaxseed etc.) activate anti-inflammatory chemicals. Lori Jo Berg, who writes for the Healthy Gut Company says, "Ideally, these fatty acids would be consumed in a 1:1 ratio. However, modern Western diets commonly contain up to 25 times more omega-6 than omega-3, which further explains why inflamed bodies with chronic pain are so prevalent today."[43] Berg recommends a blood test that will detect chronic inflammation by measuring inflammatory blood markers, such as IL-6 (Interleukin-6). This is a protein in the immune system and if its levels are elevated, it can indicate systemic inflammation.[44]

When I began trying to resolve my health issues, I had no idea about bacteria in my gut, or the dangers of systemic inflammation! I didn't know about the correlation between my immune system and my ongoing gut issues. I hadn't even considered how my actions could support my immune system or severely damage it. There was so much to learn. But as the doctors didn't have clear answers, and there was no magic pill, I was motivated to do my own research. I learned that my body was inflamed and was releasing histamine which was causing symptoms like allergic reactions. I had candida, gas, irritability, anxiety, hives, conjunctivitis, fatigue, and gluten intolerance, just to name a few. I knew I needed to get to the bottom of it all, or else I was on my way to a diagnosis I did not want to hear. No one could lead me to the correct diagnosis but the Holy Spirit. He alone knew the root of my problems.

LEAKY GUT SYNDROME

The Holy Spirit led me to a diagnosis of "Leaky Gut Syndrome" which at that time was still largely unknown. The naturopathic doctors gave me juice and more juice, supplement after supplement, test after test, but no one told me about Leaky Gut. When I read the symptoms in my research, I knew that was my issue.

Symptoms of A Leaky Gut:

1. Chronic diarrhea, constipation, gas or bloating

2. Nutritional deficiencies

3. Poor immune system

4. Headaches, brain fog, memory loss

5. Excessive fatigue

6. Skin rashes, acne, eczema, and rosacea

7. Cravings for sugar or carbs

8. Arthritis or joint pain

9. Depression, anxiety, ADD, ADHD

10. Autoimmune diseases such as Rheumatoid Arthritis, Lupus, Celiac disease or Crohn's.

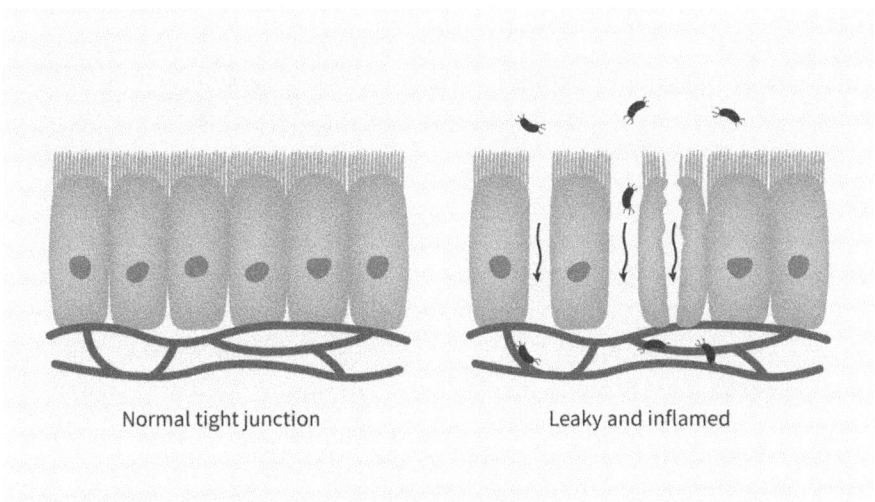

Normal tight junction   Leaky and inflamed

See if you can picture this: the area in the lining of the intestines is called the intestinal barrier. It is only one cell layer thick and acts as a traffic controller; it's a very tight-knit layer controlling what gets in and out of our intestines, and into our bloodstream. This includes nutrients, allergens, toxins, unhealthy bacteria, food particles, GMOs, gluten, and other items. When Leaky Gut occurs, the pores in the lining of the small intestine become wider, so all unwanted guests are allowed to pass through the lining of the intestine into the bloodstream. From there, it's possible to spread throughout the body, causing widespread inflammation, and wreaking havoc on your health.

These unwanted particles irritate your system and cause your body to become inflamed, which can trigger your immune system to go into attack mode. Basically, the immune system says, "Hey, this particle shouldn't be here, so we need to attack it!" This can trigger an autoimmune reaction as the body over-responds to these 'invaders' and our healthy cells are damaged in the attack. Leading functional medicine expert Dr. Will Cole, says this auto-immune response can trigger, contribute to, or worsen a wide range of chronic diseases, "including arthritis, asthma, autism, autoimmune conditions, chronic fatigue syndrome, depression, type I diabetes, type II diabetes, skin disorders, thyroid problems, and weight loss resistance" which have all been linked to gut health issues.[45]

The symptoms of a Leaky Gut can show up anywhere, from the gut to the joints, from the skin to the brain. If you have experienced acne, rashes, eczema, psoriasis, poor skin tone, etc., Leaky Gut may be the problem. For me it was mostly in my eyes. My strong army of gut bacteria had been depleted so I was getting a lot of unwanted items coursing into my bloodstream. Chronic inflammation made my intestinal walls more permeable, allowing these undigested food particles to enter my bloodstream. The seal, or fence, God created between me and them was broken. My intestinal barrier was compromised by diet, and stress. **The inflammatory process going on in my stomach and bowel were enough to disturb the entire physiology of my brain and body and emotions.**

When I began to eat the right foods, I thought I could fix it myself, but my body wasn't digesting any food properly. The food was not the problem: the problem was the food I ate was escaping into the bloodstream triggering an immune response. I was also eating too fast and not chewing my food thoroughly before swallowing. This bad practice, combined with my compromised intestinal lining, resulted in very little assimilation of nutrients and calories into the cells for usage. My excess intestinal gas indicated fermenting of my food from not chewing. I was backed up, and struggled to eliminate waste products through my bowels. Even my skin was trying to purge, through hives!

My holistic doctor got me on the right path. I realized that the foods I needed to stop eating had far more impact on my health than what I needed to start eating! Because I was always rushing from one place to another, I was regularly turning to fast food, microwaved food, processed food, Krispy Kreme donuts with coffee, sodas, sugary caffeine drinks, cakes, cookies, bagels, and croissants... I would feel like crap afterwards, and often, I'd break out in hives. Adding an apple or some celery sticks on top of that regime wasn't going to impact my health much. I had to begin eating real foods. When I started reading food labels, I had to ask, "What am I eating?" All those processed foods have long lists of ingredients, and I didn't even know what those long chemical names meant. It wasn't food! My holistic doctor guided me to cut out the processed foods, and taught me to incorporate live, raw foods into my diet. I thought a raw diet just meant you eat salads all the time, but I learned how to create full and creative meals. Since high heat in regular cooking can kill the enzymes, I learned how to dehydrate my food at a low temperature so that the enzymes stay in the food, and my body could benefit fully. While steaming food is a bit better than frying or grilling, my goal was high nutrition, so a raw food diet made the most sense. I would dehydrate vegetables to make a patty, and I started to make crepes out of dehydrated banana, to top with cashew nut cream and fruit. It was delicious! I learned that ground flaxseed and almond meal when dehydrated could effectively become bread; then top it with some avocado, and you've got yourself a sandwich! I was juicing fruits and vegetables, and drinking fermented drinks like kombucha. Eating 85 percent raw food, plant-based meals, along with regular detoxing, literally transformed me. I can now say that when your gut health and digestion are in sync, you feel pretty darn good! **Your health will restore if you give your body what it**

needs. As Hippocrates said, "Let thy food be thy medicine and thy medicine be thy food."

YOUR SECOND BRAIN

The brain and gut connection is linked to our mental health and plays a major role in our overall well-being; I cannot emphasize this enough. It all starts in the gut! A happy gut is a step in the right direction towards health, balanced moods, and happiness. A happy gut will continue to produce what is needed for the body and brain to function well.

Did you know that your gut has its very own nervous system? Over 100 million nerve cells line your gastrointestinal tract (from esophagus to rectum), send signals from your gut to your brain, and receive signals from your brain to your gut.

This discovery has revolutionized medicine's understanding of the connection between how we think, our digestion, mood, and general health. Scientists call this the **Enteric Nervous System (ENS)**. The ENS acts as a "second brain" and communicates to the "big brain" in your skull through the vagus nerve, which is one of the biggest nerves connecting your gut and *brain.*[46] Though we call it a brain, the ENS can't solve math problems, or ponder retirement plans, the way your big brain can, but it can contribute to how you feel about them!

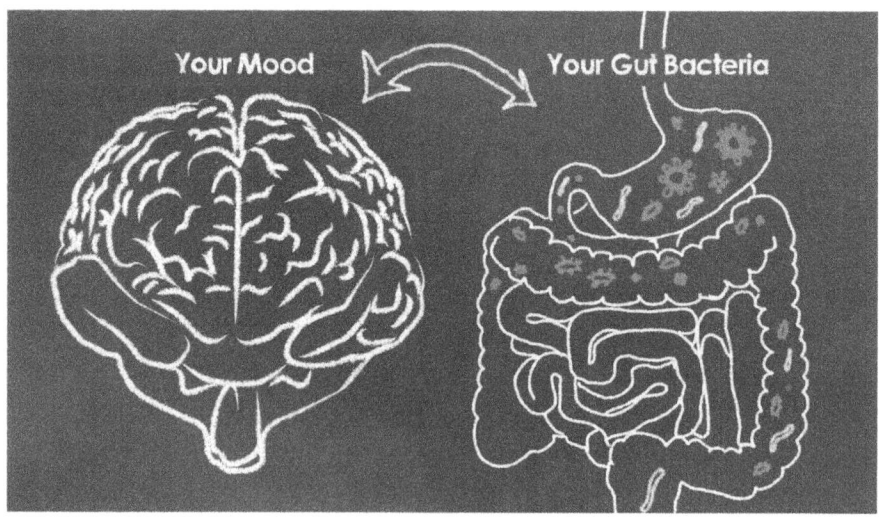

Jay Pasricha, M.D., director of the Johns Hopkins Center for Neurogastroenterology claims that irritation in the gut may send signals to the big brain that can trigger mood changes. In relation to gut issues such as irritable bowel syndrome Pasricha says, "For decades, researchers and doctors thought that anxiety and depression contributed to these problems. But our studies and others show that it may also be the other way around."[47]

Have you ever felt nervous 'butterflies' in your stomach, and wondered whether it is your gut telling you something, or your brain? Maybe it's a conversation between them both! Feelings and emotions are controlled by neurotransmitters. For example, your big brain produces the neurotransmitter serotonin which contributes to feelings of happiness and also helps control your body clock. In your *second brain,* your gut cells, and the trillions of microbes living there, also produce many of the same neurotransmitters, including serotonin. **So, it goes both ways: your brain can send happy feelings to your gut. And your gut can send happy feelings to your brain. It works the same for anxiety or sadness.** The brain and the gastrointestinal (GI) system are intimately connected. Your gut health may even have a role to play in your thinking, skills, and memory.[48]

Here's how it develops:

As we've already established, when the gut is leaky, bacteria is able to cross into the bloodstream. Here, it releases a toxic substance called endotoxin. This endotoxin triggers an immune response. As bacteria continues to leak across the barrier, the immune system is continually activated, producing inflammatory proteins called cytokines, and a substance called lipopolysaccharide (LPS), which also causes inflammation.[49] Inflammation, cytokines, and high LPS in the blood have been associated with a number of brain disorders including severe Depression, Alzheimer's, Dementia and Schizophrenia. In other words, brain disease may originate in the gut!

The same Leaky Gut findings are now being applied to the brain, as researchers have discovered that substances are leaking from the blood into the brain through the blood-brain barrier (BBB). The BBB is a complex regulatory system: it actively transports molecules such as glucose, and oxygen (which the brain needs) and keeps out other molecules from passing over. But the BBB is altered in the presence of inflammation, injury, and degenerative processes.[50] The researchers at Johns Hopkins University School of Medicine have found evidence that Parkinson's disease can be traced from cells in the gut, which travel through the body's neurons to the brain.[51]

DO YOU HAVE LEAKY GUT SYNDROME?

There is one primary test to identify leaky gut Syndrome:

1. **The Intestinal Permeability Assessment** - this test analyzes urine to establish whether or not the gut is releasing larger molecules than are biologically acceptable. It concerns the absorption of two complex sugars, Mannitol and Lactulose. Mannitol is a small molecule and should be absorbed. Lactulose is larger and should not be absorbed significantly. After testing:
   ~~ If the absorption of mannitol is low,
   you can suspect malabsorption
   ~~ If the absorption of lactulose is high,
   you can suspect Leaky Gut
   ~~ If both are normal,
   you likely have healthy gut performance

There are also a range of other tests that can help you discover more information about what is going on inside your gut:[52]

2. **Food intolerance test** - to identify which foods your body has produced antibodies against, which creates low-grade inflammation in your system.

3. **Parasite test** - an imbalanced microbiome can become a breeding ground for parasites, as they take advantage of your compromised immunity. Chronic infections lead to Leaky Gut.

4. **Bacterial dysbiosis test** - this test will help you determine which bacteria might be out of balance so you can target the problem.

5. **Blood test for excess Zonulin** - zonulin is a "gatekeeper" and helps manage what gets through your intestinal lining and what

doesn't. Patients with excess amounts of zonulin have larger pore sizes; they are at risk for a Leaky Gut and other chronic conditions including autoimmunity, metabolic disorders, neurodegenerative diseases and even cancer.[53]

6. **Stool analysis** - to identify bacteria (good and bad), viruses, bacteriophages, fungi, yeast, parasites, and any associated toxins. Some companies provide different quality levels of testing, and support (even including a dietary plan based on your results), so be sure to ask what they provide. You can check out Geneva Diagnostics as a place to start.[54]

SHOULD YOU INVEST IN TESTING?

Despite its growing media attention, many doctors still do not recognize the term "intestinal permeability" or "Leaky Gut." It's better to pursue alternative and integrative medicine practitioners who have worked on gut healing for decades. As I learned, there's a lot you can do from home. Most natural practitioners will recommend removing inflammatory foods from your diet and increasing probiotic intake to support the growth of good bacteria. This is something you can do on your own without spending a lot of money on treatments.

I recommend you aim to follow the steps below for three months and if you still aren't seeing much improvement, then Leaky-Gut testing may help you pinpoint what's holding you back. Listen to your body. Listen to your gut. Listen to the Holy Spirit. Remember, God knows your body better than anyone, so ask the Holy Spirit for insight, and listen and watch for how He leads you. Become an active observer to discover what you need and how to receive the perfect health that God has intended for you.

HOW TO HEAL LEAKY GUT

1. **Eat More Produce (Raw Fruits and Vegetables)** - Plant-based carbohydrates appear to have a beneficial effect on both the lining and the microflora within the gut. Fruits and vegetables contain prebiotics, which appear to help to stabilize the intestinal barrier. Greens, which contain chlorophyll and all its nutrients, are great gut-healing helpers. Eat more greens!

1. **Eat Clean (Minimally Processed) Food** - The typical Western diet contains excessive amounts of unhealthy fats, sugar, and refined carbohydrates, all of which appear to compromise the lining of your gut. Avoid sweetened fruit juices and processed foods containing high fructose corn syrup. Fructose appears to be especially damaging to the gut lining.

2. **Read Those Food Labels** - Read labels carefully. If you don't know what something is, it is likely that your gut doesn't know either. It is not completely known as to what effect preservatives, artificial flavoring, food coloring and other food additives have on gut health, but it is not a stretch to think that such chemicals would be damaging.

3. **Take Prebiotics and Probiotics** - Probiotics are "friendly" strains of bacteria, thought to restore balance and help to optimize

the health of the gut flora. You can purchase a probiotic supplement or eat fermented foods such as yogurt, kimchi, miso, or sauerkraut. Kefir and kombucha are also effective fermented drinks that can aid your gut health. Many research studies have shown that probiotics help strengthen the intestinal lining. Prebiotics are the food that probiotics feed on, encouraging a well functioning gut. Prebiotics are found in high fiber foods like asparagus, leeks, onions, and sugar beets.

4. **Improve Your Diet** - Get off sugar. Get off wheat and dairy. Eat less meat. Get off soy. Avoid GMOs and refined-sugar. Research has shown that each one of these foods contribute to inflammation within the body. Eliminating all of these Leaky Gut triggers from your diet will enable the helpful bacteria in your gut to thrive. I recommend starting with a 90 day trial to see how your body feels after making these changes. It typically takes approximately 3 months for your red blood cells to regenerate, so by this time you'll be able to notice a real difference. Then, if you desire, you can begin slowly reintroducing foods to see how your body responds. Also, drink lots of water — good water. Drink green juice. Eat fermented foods. And completely eliminate the really bad stuff: prepackaged microwave meals, deli meats, heavily processed foods, dairy, soy, sugary drinks. No more!

5. **Increase the Amount of Omega-3 in Your Diet** - One of the main causes of Leaky Gut is inflammation. Since omega-3 is known for its ability to combat inflammation, eating more fatty fish like salmon, or taking a fish oil supplement is very helpful. Flaxseed oil and chia seeds are also high in omega-3s.

6. **Minimize Chronic Stress** - Easier said than done for many of us, but even a few minutes of meditation, or simply sitting quietly a couple of times a week, can slow your breathing and allow better flow of oxygen to your brain. A few deep, slow breaths before meals can aid digestion and is an easy way to remember to intentionally quiet, calm, and ultimately help heal your gut.

7. **Break Away From Pharmaceutical Drugs** - Aim to eliminate your use of OTCs (over the counter drugs), NSAIDs (Nonsteroidal anti-

inflammatory drugs like Ibuprofen and Advil) and antibiotics. Choose to use as few drugs as possible, as they undermine your gut health, promoting imbalances in gut bacteria and weakening the gut wall, which in turn sets the stage for Leaky Gut and chronic inflammation.

As you take these steps to heal your gut, your immune system will be strengthened, your body will be able to absorb more nutrients to give you more energy and clarity, and maybe even improve your mental and emotional wellbeing! When you heal your gut, you prepare your whole body for healthy, happy living.

ENDNOTES

40   "What's the Difference between B-Cells and T-Cells?" Cancer Treatment Centers of America. CTCA, November 18, 2019. https://www.cancercenter.com/community/blog/2017/05/whats-the-difference-b-cells-and-t-cells.

41   "10 Facts about the Microbiome." MyMicrobiome. Accessed September 22, 2020. http://www.mymicrobiome.info/10-facts-about-the-microbiome.html.

42   Keith Scott-Mumby, Fire in the Belly: the Surprise Cause of Most Diseases, Mental States and Aging Process (Reno, NV: Mother Whale, 2012), 42.

43   Lori Jo Berg and Steven Wright, "How to Overcome Chronic Pain Naturally," Healthy Gut Company, December 10, 2018, https://scdlifestyle.com/2017/04/how-to-overcome-chronic-pain-naturally/, 4.

44   Lori Jo Berg and Steven Wright, "How to Overcome Chronic Pain Naturally," Healthy Gut Company, December 10, 2018, https://scdlifestyle.com/2017/04/how-to-overcome-chronic-pain-naturally/, 4.

45   Cole, Will. "Exactly How To Fix Poor Gut Health." The Future of Natural Healthcare, September 14, 2020. https://drwillcole.com/4-tests-to-determine-if-you-have-a-leaky-gut/.

46   "The Brain-Gut Connection." Johns Hopkins Medicine. Accessed January 22, 2020. https://www.hopkinsmedicine.org/health/healthy_aging/healthy_body/the-brain-gut-connection.

47   Ibid.

48   Ibid.

49   Cross, Maria. "Heal Your Gut, Heal Your Mind." Better Humans. Medium, April 5, 2018. https://betterhumans.coach.me/heal-your-gut-heal-your-mind-fbef62fd61e5.

50   "Varatharaj, Aravinthan, and Ian Galea. "The Blood-Brain Barrier in Systemic Inflammation." Brain, Behavior, and Immunity. Academic Press, March 16, 2016.

51   King, Bailey. "New Study Identifies Gut-Brain Connection in Development of Parkinson's." PhillyVoice, June 26, 2019. https://www.phillyvoice.com/parkinsons-disease-gut-brain-connection-study/.

52   Cole, Will. "Exactly How To Fix Poor Gut Health." The Future of Natural Healthcare, September 14, 2020. https://drwillcole.com/4-tests-to-determine-if-you-have-a-leaky-gut/.

53   Massachusetts General Hospital. "Researchers Provide Evidence Linking 'Leaky Gut' to Chronic Inflammation." Medical Xpress, April 20, 2017. https://medicalxpress.com/news/2017-04-evidence-linking-leaky-gut-chronic.html.

54   Keith Scott-Mumby, Fire in the Belly: the Surprise Cause of Most Diseases, Mental States and Aging Process (Reno, NV: Mother Whale, 2012).

CHAPTER 9
DEDICATED TO DETOXING

As you become more aware of how what you put into your body, affects your body in both positive and negative ways, you will become more aware of toxins. Essentially, toxins are any substance that can cause harm to the body. When toxins accumulate in your body over time, they become a "toxic load" that burdens your body's systems and organs. Excessive exposure to toxins can leave the body tired, bloated, out of balance, and weak. Toxins can be inhaled in the air we breathe, ingested through the food we eat, absorbed when something is applied to our skin, or even produced from within when we dwell in destructive emotions.

YOU WERE DESIGNED TO DETOX

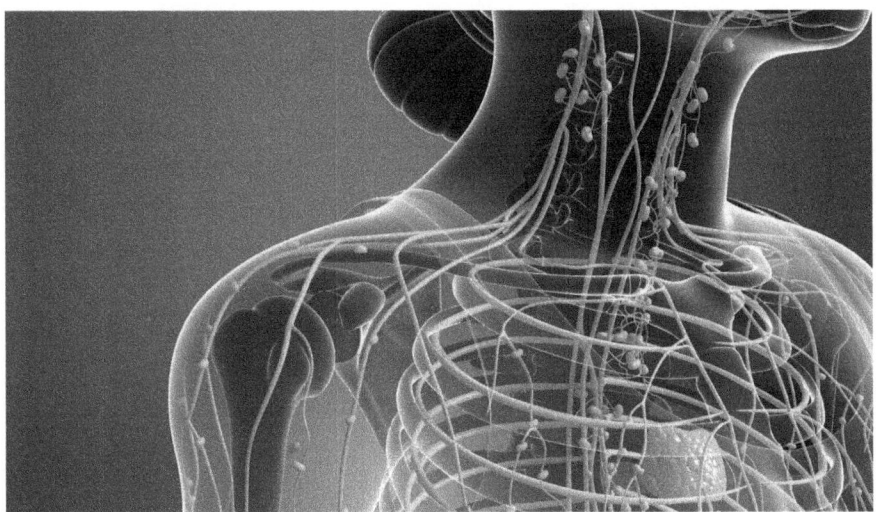

Toxins are a natural part of life, and it is highly unlikely that you will be able to avoid them all. But don't worry — God was prepared for that when He designed our bodies. You have a built-in, God-given detoxification system, working for you all day every day. In fact, your body has not one, but six organs that help with removing toxins: the lymphatic system, colon, liver, kidneys, lungs, and skin.

These organs are constantly working to keep your body clean and functioning well. If we take their work for granted, and overload them with additional toxins in our food, cosmetics, medicines, and processed foods, they simply can't keep up, and waste can re-circulate in the blood or become stored in the body, leading to all sorts of unwanted symptoms. Amie Valpone, author of the bestselling book Eating Clean, explains that when your major organs become overloaded, your body turns to your mucous membranes to try and excrete the overload, but this causes symptoms like:[55]

- Diarrhea

- Sneezing

- Coughing

- Excessive Urination

- Runny Nose and/or Lung Congestion

- Vomiting

These may seem like common symptoms, but pay attention to them because they may have significant implications. If toxicity continues to build, and these secondary mucous membranes cannot eliminate the toxins fully, your body begins to store the toxins in your tissues because your body can't find a way to excrete them. When this happens, you may notice:[56]

- Acne

- Rashes

- Memory Loss

- Fatigue

- Arthritis and Gout

- Depression

- Eczema

We must do our best to support our body's God-given function of detoxification, and reduce our toxin intake. Here is a brief overview of how your organs are working together to help you detox:

- **The lymphatic system** - made up of lymph nodes (or little collections of tissue) found in chains throughout the brain and body, parallels your red blood circulation. Lymph nodes require movement to flush out infection, bacteria, viruses, and other pathogens from the circulation.[57]

- **The large intestine or colon** - where much of your good and bad bacteria live. The colon's job is to take water from waste, create stool, and then get rid of it, so that chemical waste is not recirculated into the bloodstream.

- **The liver** - the heavy-lifter, performing over 500 functions, sorting through different compounds to remove anything toxic or unwanted from the body. When the liver becomes overloaded, it is forced to find somewhere else to put the toxins that can't remain in the bowel. Usually they end up in the bile, but this makes the bile toxic, which causes a release of damaging free radicals. When the liver is overworked its processes become sluggish, significantly affecting our metabolism, and the mucous membrane can become injured triggering Leaky Gut. If we don't overload our liver with toxins, and maintain good blood circulation, it can effectively perform its role in detoxification by transforming all toxins into a water-soluble form, so they can be excreted.

- **The kidneys** - begin to do their job, once the liver has made the toxins water-soluble, by creating urine. The kidneys are major regulators and act as a massive filtration system. In fact, the kidneys receive and filter about 1200ml of blood per minute, or about a quarter of our total blood volume.[58]

- **The skin** - acts as a helper to the liver and kidneys relieving their burden by sweating out heavy metals and toxic chemicals through your skin's surface.

- **The lungs** - manages any airborne toxins, filtering out fumes, mold, carbon dioxide, etc.

Isn't that amazing! God has masterfully designed six different parts of your body to work together to protect you from harm. He is such a good Father! He knows the challenges you are going to face and equips you in advance to handle them and remain in good health. This inspires me to want to serve Him, by treating my body well, and helping it do its job without overloading it with too many toxins!

HOUSE CLEANSING

When I think of creating a toxin free life for myself, I realize that I can't control too much in the general atmosphere, but I can control what goes on in my home and in my office. When I was struggling with allergies, I was determined to do whatever it took to get well. I began to notice how dust settles on surfaces and gets stuck in the carpet. I began to wonder about the air quality coming out of my air conditioner. But no more! I invested in the Rainbow Cleaning System. It creates a healthier living space using "The Power of Water" as it purifies the air. It has made a huge difference in the air quality in my home. And what about my cleaning agents? Whatever I sprayed, I would breathe in! There were invisible environmental toxins all around me that I was exposing myself to without even realizing it! Satan wants to blind us to these risks, and then overwhelm us with them, but God has not given us a spirit of fear (2 Tim. 1:7). As we increase our awareness of healthy solutions, we will learn that God has prepared good things for us, in advance. There are many natural alternatives to common toxin-filled products. We don't have to become inundated with harmful substances and live in sickness and ignorance. God's got a solution. Here are some of the alternatives He has shown me:

How to remove 10 toxic materials in your home with better natural alternatives:

1. Replace antibacterial soap with natural soap and water

Natural soap contains plant-based ingredients and is free of toxic chemicals. By using antibacterial soap you could be wreaking havoc on your hormones. The antimicrobial chemical "triclosan" found in many antibacterial soaps, body washes, toothpastes and some cosmetics may disrupt your thyroid function and hormone levels. In fact, the U.S. Food & Drug Administration has ruled to ban the sale of many antibacterial soaps, concluding that the risks outweigh the benefits.[59]

2. Remove furniture with flame-retardants, or dust and vacuum frequently

Furniture purchased in the 70's had flame-retardants added to their material to decrease the risk of house fires. These chemical substances flake off, constantly being expelled as little dust particles that end up on the floor (where children play), or on your hands. Then when you eat something they are transmitted into your body. Make sure you vacuum frequently to collect any fallen substances, or replace your furniture. The most harmful flame-retardants are PBDE's (polybrominated diphenyl ethers) which have been shown to lower cognitive function, and are also linked to fertility problems and lower birth weights.[60]

3. **Replace Teflon pans with cast iron, glass, or copper cookware**

Non-stick cookware can be a real life-saver for cleanup, but the toxic fumes released from Teflon pots and pans at high temperatures can kill pet birds and cause humans to develop flu-like symptoms. The non-stick coating of Teflon pans contains perfluorinated chemicals (PFCs) in very large doses. When cooking, these harmful chemicals leach into your food, and become airborne. Studies have shown that they may cause infertility, low birth weight, elevated cholesterol, abnormal thyroid hormone levels, liver inflammation and a weakened immune system.[61] A far better alternative is using cast iron, glass, or copper cookware. Although they are more difficult to clean, you'll be protecting your health in the long run.

4. **Replace plastic containers and water bottles, with glass jars and stainless steel bottles**

According to research, more than 90% of us have BPA (Bisphenol A) in our bodies right now.[62] BPA is a chemical used to harden plastic, and we are exposed to it when we eat foods that have been stored in plastic containers, or drinks from plastic bottles. Canned goods also contain BPA's as a preservative. New research is showing potential effects on the brain and behavior in fetal development, as well as male impotence, heart disease and other conditions.[63]

5. **Replace vinyl shower curtains with curtains made of cotton, polyester or nylon**

You know that distinct smell of a new shower curtain? What you're smelling is as many as 100 toxic chemicals being released into the air. Vinyl curtains often contain high levels of phthalates, which are used to soften the material. Breathing in the toxins from PVC shower curtains may contribute to respiratory irritation, damage to the central nervous system, liver and kidneys, or cause nausea, headaches and loss of coordination.[64]

6. **Replace cheap pressed wood furniture with 100% hardwood furniture (and/or add plants to rooms with pressed wood)**

Formaldehyde is a toxin used in many manufacturing processes;

it is most commonly found in particle-board products, foam insulation, wallpaper and wall paint, some synthetic fabrics and even some cosmetics and personal products. Short-term exposure may result in immediate symptoms, including eye, nose and throat irritation, coughing, headaches, dizziness and nausea. Long term exposure may cause some types of cancer.[65]

7. **Get rid of synthetic bug-spray and use natural pest repellents instead**

If it can harm a pest, chances are it can harm you too! Researchers have linked pesticides to various forms of cancer, including non-Hodgkin lymphoma. Insecticides have also been connected to brain damage in children.[66] God has given us many natural repellants, including: cedar (which repels moths), citrus peels (which repel spiders), and lemon or eucalyptus oil (which repels mosquitos).

8. **Check your cosmetics for toxic ingredients**

It's ironic that we use beauty products to look youthful, while these same toxic products are damaging our health on the inside! Cosmetics such as make-up, moisturizers, shampoo and conditioner, hair color, and sunscreen often contain cancer-causing agents, reproductive toxins, hormone disruptors along with a range of other nasties. In fact so many companies were using cheap chemicals without consideration of the health risks, that an act was written called the Safe Cosmetics and Personal Care Products Act (2013) to keep companies accountable.[67] To be a responsible consumer, I recommend using a couple of easy online tools to help you navigate all those 12 letter chemical names! Environmental Working Group (EWG),[68] or Decode INCI[69] allow you to either search by product or brand for a detailed assessment, or take a picture of the ingredient list while you are shopping, and it will interpret it for you and inform you of any risks.[70]

9. **Toss your chemical-filled cleaning agents, and cleanse your house naturally**

Choose plant-based products, or consider making your own. You'd be surprised how you can clean just as effectively with vinegar and baking soda![71] Natural products keep your air cleaner and your surfaces safer for pets and kids. Switching to natural laundry detergent is a simple way to save money, and reduce your exposure to toxins.

10. **Purify your air with essential oils and toxin-removing plants**

Stop using perfumed air fresheners and start diffusing natural essential oils. Artificial fragrance sprays often contain toluene which is known to damage the nervous system, and can slow brain development in newborns.[72] But the oils extracted from plants are incredibly healing and naturally fragrant. Many essential oils contain antiviral, anti-fungal, and anti-bacterial properties that kill active cells in dust particles, bacteria, allergens, mold, and airborne viruses.[73] You just use a few drops in a water diffuser, and within fifteen minutes your house can smell beautifully clean with 100 percent natural substances with healing properties. Consider any of these oils for air purification: spearmint, peppermint, eucalyptus, rosemary, cypress, lemon, tea tree, lavender, lemongrass, or cedarwood.

If you don't want to use oils, you can just use the plants themselves! In His wisdom, when God created the earth, He created certain plants that had the unique ability to remove toxins from the air. As they breathe in and breathe out, they purify and filter the air for humans and animals. Air purifying plants are excellent additions to any home or office environment. In 1989, NASA conducted a Clean Air Study to identify the most effective household plants for purifying the air of harmful pollutants. These pollutants are things such as benzene, formaldehyde, trichloroethylene, xylene, and ammonia, and can come from press-wood furniture, paint, plastics, cleaners, etc. If you notice that you experience headaches, dizziness, or have eye irritation and other adverse health effects, it could be airborne toxins. According to NASA's comprehensive research, one plant can purify 100 square feet! They listed the Florist's Chrysanthemum plant, and the Peace Lily as the most effective. But found that many other plants such as the Snake Plant and English Ivy were also quite effective for air purification.[74]

If making these changes feels a bit overwhelming for you, let me encourage you. You are not doing this by yourself! God will guide you. Talk to Him about it! Ask Him what you should focus on. Either He will speak directly to you, or He'll bring certain people across your path with confirmation, or expose you to more information that will guide your path. **You don't have to drive yourself crazy trying to change everything at once. Just start somewhere.** When you complete one area, then you can get excited about the next phase of transformation. God's grace is sufficient for us to take one step at a time.

DETOXIFICATION STRATEGIES

Getting rid of toxins in your home environment is a big part of moving into a more naturally healthy lifestyle. The unfortunate reality is that when we leave the house, we will inevitably still be exposed to harmful substances. In a world bombarded by harmful chemicals at every turn, daily detoxification strategies are a must! Adding these practices into your self-care routine will go a long way to supporting your body's natural purification processes:

- **Hydration**

  Staying hydrated is an important practice to cleanse your body of built up toxins. But proper hydration is not simply infusing your body with water, it's about getting the water inside your cells. God directed me to an 88 day program called "Energized Health" (www.energizedhealth.com) to better understand intracellular hydration. They taught me about optimal health at the cellular level. Intracellular hydration is essential for life. Here's how it works. Mitochondria is the "energy powerhouse" found in every human cell, which uses hydrogen molecules from water to make adenosine triphosphate (ATP). ATP is the basic energy that our cells need to function optimally. Healthy mitochondria pulls the water into the cells for proper hydration. But certain things like emissions from wireless technology, and dehydration, can interfere with this process. In a dehydrated state, for example, toxins are accumulated due to a lack of this electrical energy flow. If you are taking supplements and don't have the electrical charge across the membrane, the supplements won't go where they need to be in the body. However if you have intercellular hydration, it will lessen your chances of developing chronic diseases because you are getting water inside the cell, and ridding the cell of toxins.[75]

  Tips on how to increase water absorption in the cells:

  1. Drink spring water or filtered water with trace minerals or a pinch of high-quality salt, to help transport water into the cells.

  2. Sip your water throughout the day instead of chugging it down.

3. Drink water at room temperature as it boosts your metabolism and improves digestion.[76]

- **Fasting**

Fasting is taking a break from eating and relying only on water or clear liquids such as broth. It gives your gut a rest from digesting, and allows your body to use other energy sources for food, like body fat. This shift, strengthens your gut lining, supports heart health, and promotes self-cleansing detox processes which are helpful in preventing cardiovascular disease and Parkinson's disease.[77] Just extending the natural hours of fasting you do while you sleep to 12-16 hours before your next meal, is a form of intermittent fasting and is very strengthening for your body. Fasting also offers mental clarity and spiritual sensitivity. Look at this chart from Amchara health with a summary:

I try to fast once a week. Fasting removes those dirty toxins from my body naturally, and it is a great spiritual discipline. When I'm not eating, I am reminded that Jesus is the "Bread of Heaven." Eating this kind of bread won't give you digestive issues! In fact, it will make you whole. His sacrifice is our nourishment. Jesus says: *"I am the living bread that came down from heaven. Whoever eats this bread will live forever. This bread is my flesh, which I will give for the life of the world" John 6:51 NIV.*

Jesus is the bread of life. This gives such incredible meaning to the words of the Lord's prayer: *"Give us this day our daily bread" (Matthew 6:11).* More than physical food, communing with Jesus, and reading the word of God is spiritual food that nourishes your soul in more ways than you can imagine.

Don't let the word fasting turn you off, making you think you're going to fast for days at time and starve! Just ask God what you should fast from. It might be one meal a week, it might be TV in the evenings; God will tell you how He wants you to start.

For me, I have noticed that fasting renews my mind, and trains my ears to hear God's voice. Fasting helps detox thoughts and emotions and restores balance in life. Fasting takes self-control but it produces humility in my walk with God, which is very valuable in itself! When my flesh wants to indulge, I have to humble myself and submit my choice to God. James 4:6 says, *"God resists the proud but gives grace to the humble" (CSB).* I know I need His grace, so I have got to stay humble! Fasting keeps God in His rightful place: first amongst my priorities. Maintaining a hunger for Him is a significant priority to live a healthy life.

- **Regular Exercise**

  Cardio exercise has many benefits for detoxing. Just 20 minutes of aerobic exercise a few times a week will provide a myriad of benefits for your body! Exercise gets your heart pumping to increase blood flow and provide better circulation. This moves white blood cells through your body helping your organs cleanse themselves. Exercise flushes out the lungs, and your body sweats out toxins through your skin.[78] Every time you feel like groaning about exercise, just imagine the incredible gifts you are giving your body!

  I resisted exercise for a long time. I knew it was a healthy choice, I just didn't want to do it. Eventually, I realized no one was going to do this for me. I had to take responsibility for my life. So, I began to seek out information with the help of the Holy Spirit to get a clearer perspective on the benefits of exercise. I had to strengthen my motivation if I was going to be successful; I had to stay on the journey and not quit. I started to try different methods: an all-ladies gym and personal trainers, but they didn't feel like my niche. I realized I liked being outside. So I joined a fitness boot camp and found that I really enjoyed running. I began running with others and eventually built my endurance to be able to run 5k races.

From resistance to racing, I know the battle you may face to get there, but you can do it too! Just start. Move! Go for a walk! Begin with what you know how to do. Then, start dreaming — build your motivation — think about all the benefits you will have when you feel healthy. Just get started and keep going until you find your niche. Then stick with it! The benefits of exercise go far beyond weight loss and heart health. It will improve your brain health, increase your energy level and even help you to be happier.[79]

- **Over the Counter Cleanse Kits**

You can buy quality cleanse kits from natural health stores or your local apothecary. They generally encourage a restricted diet for 7-14 days, while taking herbal supplements to purge your body of toxins. You can buy cleanses that target your area of concern, be it the kidneys, or the colon, etc. Warning: the enemy loves to stir up deceptive products with rising trends; just because it's labeled, "natural cleanse kit" doesn't mean it's free of chemicals. So, check and ask questions to knowledgeable staff about good ingredients.

- **Infrared Sauna**

These wooden saunas penetrate heat directly into your body tissue through electromagnetic radiation.[80] This allows you to stay in the sauna for a longer time (20-30 minutes) as the temperature is lower than traditional saunas, providing you with enhanced health benefits. They have been shown to reduce inflammation, aid muscle recovery, provide deep relaxation, offer better sleep and give the skin a healthy glow, potentially supporting collagen production.[81] You'll feel both relaxed and energized after this self-care treatment.

- **Colon Hydrotherapy**

If you're feeling draggy, have brain fog, or just want to give your gut a good clean up, colonics can really lighten your load! Colonic hydrotherapy is somewhat like a glorified enema. During the treatment, water flows all the way up to your colon (large intestine) and cleans off any fecal matter that has hardened to the surface of the walls. Old fecal matter harbors parasites and pathogenic gut flora.

When I was first introduced to colonics, I did them weekly for three months to get myself cleaned out. Now, for basic maintenance, if I'm feeling stressed, or if I eat poorly, I will book myself an appointment and get one done. I feel so much better afterwards. Though, you should know going in, that if you are quite toxic, you may feel worse before you feel better. But, over time, as your body gets rid of all those latent toxins, you will feel cleaner than ever, and it will show!

- **Detox Foot Baths**

This is another health treatment, where you place your feet in warm water, salt, and an electrical current. The combination generates negative ions by separating oxygen and hydrogen from the water, neutralizing charged particles in the body and drawing toxins containing the opposite charge out. The bottom of your feet is a great portal for detoxification. This process can rid the body of heavy metals, reduce inflammation, support cardiovascular health, and reduce acidity in the body.[82] You can do foot detoxes at a spa or use detox packets at home.

- **Clay Baths**

A clay bath is similar to a facial mask, but over your whole body. You sit in a tub where the water is mixed with bentonite clay which has a negative charge, and as you relax it gently pulls toxins (which have a positive charge) out of your body like a giant magnet.[83] It may sound a bit crazy to sit in a tub of clay, but when I was sick, I was trying everything! I enjoyed the assurance of knowing that heavy metals were being pulled out of my body, although it was a messy process.

- **Dry Skin Brushing**

Dry skin brushing strengthens the lymphatic system while also encouraging soft healthy skin. The bristles on a dry brush massage the skin and stimulate the tiny capillaries, and the interstitial fluid near the surface of the skin.[84] Brush towards the heart to better drain the head, limbs, and body cavity walls. Dry brushing is a convenient detoxing habit before you shower, but should be used in conjunction with exercise or other methods that reach deeper-lying toxins.

- **Oxygen Steam Cabinet or Ozone Sauna**

  Dr. Otto Warburg, a two-time Nobel Prize winner in medicine, claimed the root cause of all degenerative disease is a condition called hypoxia (oxygen starvation at the cellular level). Oxygen therapy is used to open your skin's pores so it can release toxins and receive an abundance of oxygen. You wrap your body in a towel and sit in a steam cabinet, where your head is out so you can sip on water. After thirty minutes you can see toxic residue on the towel. Oxygen therapy is a gentle detox that removes toxins, improves circulation, boosts the immune system, and relaxes and rejuvenates your body.[85]

These detoxing strategies are excellent supplements (not replacements) for your healthy lifestyle. Eating poorly without exercise, and then going for a sauna treatment isn't going to cut it. But gradually involving detoxification practices into your routine is a healthy choice to care for your body and encourage its natural cleansing processes.

SLOW DOWN. BREATHE.

Let's talk a little more about oxygen. Oxygen is very healing to our bodies, and the practice of stopping to remember to breathe deeply not only benefits our bodies, but slows down our frantic pace of life. Stressed and rushed lifestyles can cause us to breathe shallow, tight breaths, robbing our lungs of this valuable detoxing tool. By inhaling deeply, we take in more oxygen which cleanses the body, and by exhaling deeply, we eliminate more waste in carbon dioxide; both actions have an overall detox effect on the body. If we don't breathe deeply, or have a good cardio routine that pushes us to suck in oxygen regularly, our lymphatic system will slow down and block waste from exiting our bodies. This can result in high blood pressure, heart problems, weight gain, and inflammation.[86]

Simple practices, like pausing to consciously take a few deep breaths before eating, help your body *rest and digest.* This state helps your body to absorb vitamins, nutrients and minerals much more efficiently.

Beginning or ending your day with deep focused breathing also stimulates your lymph nodes and increases the elimination of toxins as much as 15 times![87] To practice deep breathing, imagine your lower belly, rib cage, and then upper chest filling up sequentially like a balloon. Hold your breath at the top, and then forcefully but steadily release the air from each cavity.

A GLOBAL PAUSE

In 2020, the year this book was written, the entire planet slowed its pace, at the outbreak of a global pandemic. I don't think the world will ever forget "COVID-19," or the Coronavirus. It halted the activity of every nation on earth. Everyone was told, "Stay home, or risk contamination." Businesses closed. Schools were shut down. The whole planet took an extended rest. Did you know that it even allowed creation to rest? After Covid-19 broke out, environmentalists observed lower carbon emissions, and less air pollution. The skies became noticeably clearer from a lack of smog.[88] Environmentalists said, "this is the best quality of air in decades!"[89] They also noticed unexpected benefits of the reduction in noise pollution. Smaller earthquakes and storms from the other side of the world have been picked up by instruments because there is less noise. The oceans even became quieter, decreasing the stress hormone levels in marine creatures which can affect their reproductive success.[90] The coronavirus allowed wildlife to re-emerge, re-populate, and roam free.

This is a foreshadowing of the final day when all creation will become free: *"The creation itself will be set free from its bondage to decay and brought into the glorious freedom of the children of God. We know that the whole creation has been groaning together in the pains of childbirth until the present time" Rom. 8:21-22 BLB.*

This glimpse of global restoration helped us to realize that our busy industrial lifestyle was literally running God's creation in the ground. Including ourselves! When we slow down, we begin to notice where God is working, and where He is blessing us. We have clearer minds, and a more balanced body.

The Message translation says it this way: *"Slow down. Take a deep breath. What's the hurry? Why wear yourself out? Just what are you after anyway?" Jer. 2:25a MSG*

> Simplicity = Be still & know that I am God (Ps. 46:10)

God didn't mean for us to be in a constant state of busyness. He didn't intend for stress to define the rhythm of life. For myself, it wasn't until this mandated pause that I realized what was really important in life. I can sum it up in one word: SIMPLICITY! I forgot what it was like to take a walk, take a nap, ride my bicycle and talk to my neighbors! In the midst of all the hustle and bustle I couldn't see it. Now, I see the small things. **Slowing down helps me to partner with Him.** My spirit is more sensitive. My flesh is not so wrapped up in the world. I'm more calm. I've learned to stop to smell the roses. It was as if heaven cried out, "Slow down. Breathe. Be thankful."

A big part of living a healthy and rested lifestyle is making sure you are getting enough sleep. I used to be a workaholic. I have since learned that sleep changes everything! Sleep helps the brain commit new information to memory.[91] Sleep keeps our hormones in balance, so when we don't sleep well, our hormone balance is thrown off, and our natural appetites actually increase resulting in weight gain.[92] Sleep loss interferes with our body's natural healing processes. Our bodies can't build up our immune system or repair blood vessels without enough sleep.[93] Of course, we all know that lack of sleep can make someone a bear to be around: irritable, impatient, clumsy, with an inability to concentrate and just generally moody. When you're building a healthy life, proper rest is a must!

What's the rhythm of your life — what's your pace?

When we give ourselves the gift of slowing down, we detox from stress and distractions; our brain fog clears and we can ponder how we actually want to live. When we sleep well, we feel refreshed. **Choosing a less hurried pace means we begin to live by design and not by default.**

LIVING JOYFULLY

Life is too serious. Don't you think so? We can get so bogged down with problems. Sometimes, we have to detox our emotions and take a break from all of the worrying and complaining. Living a joyful life can seem elusive, but let me tell you: it is your birthright. If you aren't living joyfully, then begin to detox your heart, because God has greater things in store for you!

God created you for joy. Jesus said to His disciples: *"I have loved you even as the Father has loved me. Remain in my love. When you obey my commandments, you remain in my love, just as I obey my Father's commandments and remain in His love. I have told you these things so that you will be filled with my joy. Yes, your joy will overflow!" John 15:9-11 NLT.*

It takes a choice and some simple tricks to focus on the positive and enjoy the life God has given. Here are my suggestions:

- Choose to start a daily habit of remembering what you are thankful for.

- Be grateful for the simple things. Don't let worry rob you.

- When stress comes knocking, don't sweat the small stuff because the King is in control!

- Worship to remove stress from your body![94]

- Humble yourself before the Lord — this is a pathway to joy.

- Less demands for control over things and more letting go.

- Spend time with the Lord throughout the day communing with Him.

- Laugh throughout the day — it feels great!

Becoming more aware of the toxins in our environment and in our bodies can be overwhelming. The enemy may have an agenda to poison us and burn us out, but God's design for us is life abundantly (John 10:10). He has given our bodies systems to naturally cleanse out harmful substances, and He has inspired many practitioners to develop methods of renewal. As we follow God's lead into detoxifying our bodies, minds, and emotions by embracing a lifestyle of natural living, restful trust, and joyful perspectives, we are well on our way to experiencing life to the fullest.

ENDNOTES

55   Valpone, Amie. "The Healthy Apple." The Healthy Apple Symptoms That Show Your Body is Toxic Comments, March 19, 2014. https://thehealthyapple. com/symptoms-that-show-your-body-is-toxic/.

56   Ibid.

57   Lytle, Millie. "A New Way To Detox: Eat To Support 6 Organs Of Elimination." mindbodygreen. mbg health, February 6, 2020. https://www. mindbodygreen.com/0-27004/a-new-way-to-detox-eat-to-support-6-organs-of-elimination.html.

58   "Your Detoxification Pathway Explained." Artemis. Accessed January 18, 2020. https://www.artemis.co.nz/blogs/blog/your-detoxification-pathway-explained.

59   Militza. "5 Safe & Natural Alternatives to Antibacterial Soap." Little Green Dot, March 23, 2020. https://littlegreendot.com/antibacterial-soap-has-been-kicked-to-the-curb/.

60   "Gross, Liza. "Flame Retardants in Consumer Products Are Linked to Health and Cognitive Problems." The Washington Post. WP Company, April 15, 2013. https://www.washingtonpost.com/national/health-science/flame-retardants-in-consumer-products-are-linked-to-health-and-cognitive-problems/2013/04/15/f5c7b2aa-8b34-11e2-9838-d62f083ba93f_story.html.

61   Webster, Glenys. (2010). Potential human health effects of perfluorinated chemicals (PFCs). Blood. 4. https://www.researchgate.net/publication/266439138_Potential_human_health_effects_of_perfluorinated_chemicals_PFCs.

62   Brennan, Dan. "The Facts About Bisphenol A, BPA." WebMD, December 10, 2019. https://www.webmd.com/children/bpa.

63   Brazier, Yvette. "Bisphenol A: Hazards and Sources." Medical News Today. MediLexicon International, May 25, 2017. https://www.medicalnewstoday.com/articles/221205.php.

64   Cowan, Shannon. "How To Reduce Exposure To Indoor Toxins." Eartheasy Guides & Articles. Accessed March 3, 2020. https://learn.eartheasy.com/guides/how-to-reduce-exposure-to-indoor-toxins/.

65   Martin, David S. "5 Toxics That Are Everywhere: Protect Yourself." CNN. Cable News Network, May 31, 2010. http://www.cnn.com/2010/HEALTH/05/31/chemical.dangers/index.html.

66   Levin, Sam. "Largest Maker of Pesticide Linked to Brain Damage in Kids to Stop Producing Chemical." The Guardian. Guardian News and Media, February 6, 2020. https://www.theguardian.com/environment/2020/feb/06/chlorpyrifos-pesticide-corteva-trump-administration.

67   Schakowsky, Janice D. "H.R.1385 - 113th Congress (2013-2014): Safe Cosmetics and Personal Care Products Act of 2013." Congress.gov, July 8, 2013. https://www.congress.gov/bill/113th-congress/house-bill/1385.

68   "EWG Skin Deep® Cosmetics Database." EWG. Accessed August 18, 2020. https://www.ewg.org/skindeep/.

69   "Decode INCI." Ingredients explained. Accessed August 18, 2020. https://incidecoder.com/decode-inci.

70   Nora. "3 Easy Tools to Check the Safety of Cosmetic & Skincare Ingredients." Sugar & Spice, July 22, 2019. https://www.sugarandspice.com.sg/post/3-easy-tools-to-check-the-safety-of-cosmetic-skincare-ingredients.

71   Wells, Katie. "Natural Cleaning Tips & Recipes: Wellness Mama." Wellness Mama®, July 30, 2019. https://wellnessmama.com/6244/natural-cleaning/.

72   Iyer, Yuvika. "Top 15 Essential Oils to Purify Air in 2020 (How-to-Checklist+Air Purifying Kit!)." FreshOAir, November 22, 2019. https://www.freshoair.com/wellness-archive/essential-oils-to-purify-air/.

73   Aspen. "My Top 7 Essential Oil Diffuser Blends for Clean Air." The Miracle of Essential Oils, January 8, 2018. https://www.themiracleofessentialoils.com/essential-oil-diffuser-blends-for-clean-air/.

74   "NASA Reveals A List Of The Best Air-Cleaning Plants For Your Home." Bored Panda, 2017. https://www.boredpanda.com/best-air-filtering-houseplants-nasa/.

75   "The Mighty Mitochondria: Importance of Cellular Hydration for Health and Longevity." Aqua New. Accessed on May 6, 2022 at: https://aquanew.com/blog/the-mighty-mitochondria-importance-of-cellular-hydration-for-health-and-longevity/.

76   Thompson, Malia. "Hold Your Water! The Importance of Cellular Hydration". Colorado School of Clinical Herbalism. February 2, 2016. https://clinicalherbalism.com/hold-your-water-the-importance-of-cellular-hydration/.

77   Rose, Kelly. "The Physical Health Benefits of Fasting." Amchara Health Retreats. Accessed March 20, 2020. https://www.amchara.com/diet-fasting/the-physical-health-benefits-of-fasting.

78   "Benefits of Exercise During Your Detox I The LifeCo." The LifeCo: Detox and Wellness Centers, January 14, 2020. https://www.thelifeco.com/en/blog/benefits-of-exercise-during-your-detox/.

79   Oaklander, Mandy, and Heather Jones. "7 Surprising Benefits of Exercise." Time. Time, September 1, 2016. https://time.com/4474874/exercise-fitness-workouts/.

80   Lindberg, Sara. "Is an Infrared Sauna Better Than a Traditional Sauna?," May 29, 2018. https://www.healthline.com/health/infrared-sauna-benefits.

81   McCoy, Jenny. "6 Benefits Of Infrared Sauna Therapy." mindbodygreen, February 14, 2020. https://www.mindbodygreen.com/0-12265/6-benefits-of-infrared-sauna-therapy.html.

82   Group, Edward. "Foot Detox: Know the Facts, Top Benefits, and Recipes." Dr. Group's Healthy Living Articles, April 5, 2018. https://globalhealing.com/natural-health/foot-detox-know-facts-top-benefits-recipes/.

83   Penman, Tash. "Clay Baths Are Powerful Medicine." Holistic Health Herbalist. Tash, September 30, 2019. https://www.holistichealthherbalist.com/clay-baths-are-powerful-medicine/.

84   Penman, Tash. "7 Ways to Maintain a Strong Lymphatic System." Holistic Health Herbalist. Tash, September 30, 2019. https://www.holistichealthherbalist.com/7-ways-maintain-strong-lymphatic-system/.

85   "Ozone Sauna Therapy: The LifeCo." The LifeCo: Detox and Wellness Centers, August 10, 2020. https://www.thelifeco.com/en/ozone-sauna/.

86   eal_sales. "How to Breathe Deeply to Detox the Body." Expand a Lung, September 4, 2017. https://expand-a-lung.com/how-to-breathe-deeply-to-detox-the-body/.

87   Brunner, Kathrin. "Diaphragmatic Breathing for Detoxification." For the Love of Body, February 18, 2013. http://www.fortheloveofbody.com/blog/371.

88   Gardiner, Beth. "Pollution Made COVID-19 Worse. Now, Lockdowns Are Clearing the Air." Pollution made the pandemic worse, but lockdowns clean the sky, April 8, 2020. https://www.nationalgeographic.com/science/2020/04/pollution-made-the-pandemic-worse-but-lockdowns-clean-the-sky/.

89   Pereira, Ivan. "Cleaner Air Due to Coronavirus Pandemic Makes Earth Day 50th Anniversary Celebration Bittersweet for Environmentalists." ABC News. ABC News Network, April 22, 2020. https://abcnews.go.com/Health/cleaner-air-coronavirus-precautions-makes-earth-day-celebration/story?id=69923658.

90   Schuster, Kathleen. "Coronavirus Lockdown Gives Animals Rare Break from Noise Pollution." DW.COM, April 16, 2020. https://www.dw.com/en/coronavirus-lockdown-gives-animals-rare-break-from-noise-pollution/a-53106214.

91   Welch, Ashley. "Research Reveals How Sleep Helps 'Hit the 'Save Button' on Your Memories.'" CBS News. CBS Interactive, December 14, 2017. https://www.cbsnews.com/news/research-reveals-sleeps-impact-on-memory/.

92   "Why Skimping on Sleep Each Night Can Cause a Case of the Munchies." Sleep Foundation, July 28, 2020. https://www.sleepfoundation.org/articles/connection-between-sleep-and-overeating.

93   Watson, Stephanie. "11 Effects of Sleep Deprivation on Your Body." Healthline. Healthline Media, May 15, 2020. https://www.healthline.com/health/sleep-deprivation/effects-on-body.

94   Patterson, Jim. "Worship Is Good for Your Health: Vanderbilt Study." Vanderbilt University, May 31, 2017. https://news.vanderbilt.edu/2017/05/31/worship-is-good-for-your-health-vanderbilt-study/.

CHAPTER 10
THE ATTACK ON FOOD

The city of Almolonga, Guatemala was trapped in extreme poverty, alcoholism and idolatry, until God spoke to local pastor Mariana Riscajche and gave him prayer strategies to take the city for the Lord. He gathered a group to pray, but as they had no building to gather in, they went up on the surrounding hills and prayed and fasted, doing spiritual warfare for days at a time. As they obeyed the leading of the Lord, the power of God transformed their city. Revival fell in healing miracles and 90% of the city were saved, pubs and prisons closed down due to decreased crime, and God blessed the land itself to produce crops that were incredibly large in size — enough to attract American agriculturists to go and study the phenomenon. Today, this small city is exporting vegetables both to their nation and internationally![93]

This is God's desire: to bless our land and provide abundant life to all those who live in it. We see this in the Old Testament: *"The Lord will*

grant you abundant prosperity—in the fruit of your womb, the young of your livestock and the crops of your ground—in the land He swore to your ancestors to give you" Deut. 28:11 NIV.

The enemy's desire is exactly the opposite. He desires to destroy our lives, break our relationship with God, and restrict our fruitful production. So how does he do that? If we look back to Genesis chapter 1, the very first conversation God had with Adam, was to give him instructions on what to eat and what not to eat. And Satan's first attack was to lure us to eat something that wasn't intended for us. What we choose to eat is an important issue! So what did God say?

> **"Then God said, "I give you every seed-bearing plant on the face of the whole earth and every tree that has fruit with seed in it. They will be yours for food.** And to all the beasts of the earth and all the birds in the sky and all the creatures that move along the ground—everything that has the breath of life in it—I give every green plant for food." And it was so"* Genesis 1:29-30 NIV.

There was also a tree that was restricted from man:

> *"And the Lord God commanded the man, "You are free to eat from any tree in the garden; but **you must not eat from the tree of the knowledge of good and evil, for when you eat from it you will certainly die"** Genesis 2:16-17 NIV.*

I think of this tree like a tree of sugar-coated donuts. So desirable, yet so harmful! Why is it that every food that is bad for us comes with an element of temptation to eat it anyway? Can I hear an amen? Although God warns Adam and Eve, with good intent to protect them from harm, the enemy plants doubt in the mind of man, and lures Eve into eating from the forbidden tree anyway, thereby disobeying God's commandment. The enemy says:

> **"You will not certainly die," the serpent said to the woman. "For God knows that when you eat from it your eyes will be opened, and you will be like God, knowing good and evil"** *Genesis 3:4-5 NIV.*

It's as if he's saying, "eat as much sugar and white flour and fatty oils as you like; it won't harm your body one bit!" And what's the result of this deception? Unfortunately, disobedience added more than a few pounds to our waistlines, it came with a lot of health problems! Disobedience always comes with a curse. When Adam and Eve disobeyed, the ground was cursed: <u>the same ground that would produce their food.</u> God says:

> "And to the man He said,"Since you listened to your wife and ate from the tree whose fruit I commanded you not to eat, **the ground is cursed because of you.** All your life you will struggle to scratch a living from it. It will grow thorns and thistles for you, though you will eat of its grains" Genesis 3:17-18 NLT.

Guess what? This is the same earth that we continue to grow food on! Satan's scheming and mankind's sin has caused a curse from the ground itself, to the food it produces. We can see from the story in Guatemala that this curse on the land can be overcome! For those alerted to the strategies of the enemy, equipped with prayer and weapons of warfare, we can take back God's intended blessing. Satan is well aware that if he continues to destroy our food supply, he will poison our daily sustenance. What an effective strategy against mankind! If we look with spiritual sight, we can see the curse on food continuing throughout history until today. Satan's deception has blinded our society to the point that we don't even remember what real food is! We know how to microwave processed meals that pose as food, but what we are putting in our body lacks nutrition and contains all sorts of additives and chemicals that do our body harm! We know how to go through a drive-through and feel full after a burger and fries, but we've forgotten that being full isn't the goal. We are blinded to the consequences of the recycled oils, the hormone filled meats, the nutritionally empty white bun and the sugar filled condiments.

God gave us real food to eat. It was blessed. It was for our benefit. We had a beautiful garden. But now, the garden of earth has become compromised. As we choose our food, we must be aware of the enemy's agenda. **He is out to destroy us, and one of his greatest targets is the source of our life: our food supply.**

THE ORIGINAL GREEN DIET

What is food? Today there are so many trendy diets: "clean eating," "paleo," "gluten-free," "vegan," "flexitarian"... what does this even mean? We are told not to eat *processed* foods, but what does that mean? Afterall, frozen spinach is "processed." Is that bad for us too? Let's go back to the very beginning and understand what God intended for us.

Genesis 1:29-30 *"I have given you every herb that yields seed which is on the face of the earth, and every tree whose fruit yields seed; to you it shall be for food. And every beast of the earth, every bird of the air, to everything that creeps on the earth in which there is life, I give every green herb for food and it was so" (NKJV).*

At the very beginning, God gave us trees and herbs to eat from. He packed a ton of nutrition into those little leaves in order to sustain every living thing. Let's take a closer look at the wonder of greens...

Through photosynthesis, plants drink in the rain, breathe in the carbon dioxide in the air, and through the power of the sun, transform both into nutrients as food! Then, they release oxygen which sustains human and animal life. What wonderful things plants are! Chlorophyll, held in the green pigment of plant leaves, is the ingredient that converts sunlight into oxygen. Interestingly, it is referred to as the "green blood" of plants and is very similar in chemical structure to the part of human blood that carries oxygen through our bodies![94] God has given us plants not only as oxygen producers, but also for food. When we ingest chlorophyll, we receive nutrients that build and sustain our blood. Marilyn Gemino, from Garden of Life, explains that chlorophyll, 'stimulates red blood cells' quality and quantity, supports healthy oxygenation, detoxifies the liver, boosts energy levels, cleans the digestive tract and is a powerful antioxidant that fights off free radicals. Greens also have a strong alkalizing effect on the body."[95] Now I know why mom used to say, "Eat all your greens!" I've also learned you have to be careful not to overcook your vegetables or you'll cook this powerful nutrient right out of your food!

Did you know you might have a superfood growing in your own backyard! They have little yellow flowers and spread voraciously. Can you guess what it is? Dandelions! We kill dandelions and spray them with pesticides but dandelions are a powerful food. In herbal medicine, its root is used for tea that aids liver function, and its leaves are full of nutrients and minerals. Dandelion greens are an excellent source of vitamin A, folate, vitamin K, and vitamin C (in its raw form), and a good source of calcium and potassium.[96]

If you have a hard time getting greens into your diet, one ounce of wheatgrass juice is like a daily blood transfusion. Wheat grass is simply the young grass of the wheat plant. You can ingest it as a juice, or mix its powder in smoothies, or take it as an oral supplement. It is known to be anti-inflammatory and a powerful antioxidant having many benefits including slowing the growth of cancer cells.[97] Traditional medicinal benefits of wheatgrass include:

- Improved digestion

- Lower blood pressure

- Removal of heavy metals from the bloodstream

- Balance of the immune system

- Relief from gout

Wheatgrass contains ample nutrients, as do wheat berries. Wheat berries are the whole kernels of wheat at the top of the stem, and they are packed with fiber, protein and iron.[98] When ground into flour and mixed with water, they can be fermented to make sourdough which has less gluten and is good for your gut. In fact, one of the key ways that we benefit from greens is how they bolster our immune systems, starting with the gut. God has given us green plants to be a blessing to us in so many ways. They provide balance to our bodies, and support to our environment.

Did you know that there is a Bible character who only ate vegetables? And He was found to be one of the healthiest men amongst all the king's servants. Can you guess who it is?

Daniel! Daniel is one of my favorite role models in the Bible. His life exemplifies the ideal lifestyle that God presented in the garden of Eden: fellowship, obedience, and healthy eating. Daniel lived prayerfully and ate carefully — truly a man after my own heart! Daniel and his God-fearing friends were forced to live in Babylon, far from home and far from the land they loved, Jerusalem. What happened was, in 605 BC the Babylonians had exiled a group including Daniel and his three friends, best known by their Babylonian names: Shadrach, Meshach, and Abednego. Though they were young, they were committed to serving God no matter what the foreign king insisted upon. It all began with Daniel's decision not to compromise how he was going to eat. He and his friends resisted the temptation of the King's delicacies and remained faithful and obedient to the laws of God to not eat unclean food. After choosing a diet of strictly vegetables for ten days, they were assessed as healthier and better nourished than any of the other young men in the king's service. Eating your greens pays off! Daniel excelled, not only in physical health, but also spiritual health. His character displayed God's light in Babylon despite being under one of the harshest rulers. Even under great pressure Daniel remained calm and respectful. He spoke words with kindness and honor to those in authority. God gave Daniel favor, skill, and wisdom to solve problems. He was able to unlock revelation, visions and dreams, and was given prophetic insight into the future. The book of Daniel makes it clear that Elohim, the one true God is the supreme ruler over heaven and earth (Daniel 4:17). Each of the first six chapters testifies with a unique example of how these young men stood firm in their faith, time and time again. I don't know about you, but I strive to live up to Daniel's example: healthy eating + healthy spirit + healthy relationships = anointed lifestyle!

THE ATTACK ON FOOD TODAY

Daniel's example of using discernment to evaluate whether food will compromise or benefit his health is just as relevant now, as it was thousands of years ago. Our busy lifestyles have encouraged a diet of convenience: fast food, chemical laden food, boxed and packaged and renamed. No wonder our bodies are breaking down! The enemy loves to create confusion, and deception. If we are going to regain our health, we've got to take back what the enemy has stolen and regain clarity and truth about what we are meant to eat. Eating whole, clean, or real food means eating what God created for us to eat in the very beginning. It refers to plant foods that are not packaged in a factory, or prepared with additives. God did not create processed foods, pre-packaged food, junk food, soda, and artificial sweeteners. That was man's idea. Real food is primarily unprocessed.

WHAT IS PROCESSED FOOD?

By definition, "a processed food is a food item that has had a series of mechanical or chemical operations performed on it to change or preserve it."[99] Processed foods typically come in a package (a box or bag) and contain more than one item on the list of ingredients. Not all processed foods are unhealthy — like frozen organic spinach, organic nut butters, organic bone broth, etc. But watch out for the hidden ingredients in highly-processed foods that require a lab and many additives to produce a longer shelf life including: high-fructose corn syrup, hydrogenated oil, monosodium glutamate, soy protein isolate, or aspartame. Things like condiments, cereals, and anything with a long ingredient list! Dr. Fabrizio Mancini, the author of *The Power of Self Healing,* estimates the average American takes in about five pounds of additives a year through processed foods. He explains, "Food additives are substances that do not occur naturally in food. They may be 'direct' additives that are introduced intentionally into foods to enhance flavour, improve texture, or prevent spoilage. Others are 'indirect' additives; these include pollutants that come into contact with food from the environment, during growing, processing, or packaging."[100] Anything that God did not create for us, poses a threat. The body was not built to process unnatural products, and has a hard time digesting the preservatives and nitrates in processed foods. This means they end up accumulating in our bodies, becoming carcinogens (cancer-causing agents). Anything that dwells in the body that can provoke cancer cells is bad for you! Studies have found that a 10 percent increase in eating ultra-processed foods was associated with a 12 percent increased risk of cancer, and an 11 percent increased risk of breast cancer.[101] Eating heavily processed foods, even just a couple times a week, could increase your risk of dying prematurely.[102]

FOOD ADDITIVES

It's hard to know who to trust anymore! Marketing ads, especially for health products, can be very deceptive and misleading by claiming to be organic while only one ingredient may be organic, and the rest full of trans fats, food coloring and all sorts of nasty additives and preservatives. To be a discerning shopper, you must look at the ingredient lists, and not just the health claim on the front of the box. "This faulty advertising has become so common, it is now known as the 'health halo' effect, it is the act of overestimating the healthfulness of a certain product based on a single claim."[103] For example, "all natural" claims that synthetic ingredients aren't used, however that doesn't mean it's healthy for you! Mac and cheese, potato chips, and fried chicken are technically 'all natural' as they can be produced without any synthetic ingredients.[104] According to the Grains and Legumes Nutrition Council, for a product to rightfully claim the term "whole grain" they only have to ensure a minimum of 8g is made with whole grains.[105] Each serving may also contain refined sweeteners, refined grains, saturated fats, and high amounts of sodium.

The FDA (Food & Drug Administration) is the governing body meant to do assessments and safety checks on proposed food additives before they are released. Sadly, their system of checks and balances has been highly compromised. In 2016 the FDA approved a final ruling on GRAS ingredients. These additives are "Generally Regarded As Safe" which has created a huge loophole for food manufacturers to put whatever they deem is safe into food. The manufacturers themselves are responsible to decide whether or not it is safe for the public, and have the option to voluntarily inform the FDA. The FDA may put out guidelines to food manufacturers as to their process, but compliance and reporting is voluntary.[106] This allows the FDA to pass the blame if something bad ever happens with the consumers. For example, Lupin is an ingredient found in baked goods, and was approved as GRAS but later discovered to react badly with those who had peanut allergies. The FDA recommended to the manufacturer who had voluntarily sent a notice that Lupin was GRAS, to include warning labels on their goods, and to include Lupin on their ingredient list (because it wasn't previously included!).[107] What would have happened if that company hadn't volunteered to let the FDA know what they were putting in their foods? The bottom line is, the FDA is not doing due diligence to protect the general public. We cannot trust that the food on our shelves has been 'approved' by any scientific body with our best interest in mind. We have to do our own research as to what is healthy, and what is not. It is the simplest and healthiest solution to avoid processed food with names of ingredients you don't recognize. Stick to whole foods, and whole ingredients, not chemical derivatives with questionable side-effects.

Food companies spend millions of dollars lobbying government officials to influence votes on laws, rules and regulations. These powerful corporations also become major influences on mainstream media. The truth is that our attitudes, opinions and beliefs are greatly shaped by what we allow into our minds. After all, they don't call it TV *programming* for no reason. When we don't think for ourselves, our minds become enslaved to lies and fear. The mainstream media desperately does not want you to learn for yourself what true healthy food is. They don't want you to look at 'the man behind the curtain.' They just want you to stay plugged into the programming that they are feeding you, no questions asked. The media is a subtle brainwashing machine. We need to listen with *ears* to hear and shop with eyes to see to understand what is really going on.

KRAFT-HEINZ

We presume that manufacturers have our best interest at heart and the food is safe to eat; but we are being duped! Kraft-Heinz and other mega food corporations are feeding dangerous ingredients to many families. Prior to 2015, artificial dyes were present in more than 30 percent of Kraft macaroni and cheese products. These food dyes were made from petroleum which can cause allergic reactions and may be tainted with carcinogens (substances that cause cancer)! For the European market, Kraft reformulated mac and cheese without artificial dyes and replaced them with natural ingredients, but they didn't bother to do so in the United States because it wasn't required. It took a massive petition to convince them to do the same for Americans and eliminate the double standard. Finally, by 2015 they listened and agreed to make changes. Again in 2017, Kraft-Heinz was under scrutiny as another petition rose to remove phthalates (like DEHP) from many of their cheese products.[108] Phthalates are chemicals used to soften plastic, and have endocrine/hormone disrupting properties. This is especially tragic as children depend on hormones for proper development, and they also depend on their mac and cheese! Phthalates are linked to impaired brain development, lower IQ scores, and higher incidences of autism spectrum disorders. They also act as anti-androgens that block the male hormone testosterone, and may be related to infertility. We certainly cannot rely on our favorite brands to look out for our health and keep our best interests in mind! Kraft's history certainly proves it.

The reality of dangerous food additives proves that we as a nation have lost the plot! The enemy has twisted our priorities as a human race. Instead of looking out for one another to promote health and well-being, we are secretly trying to introduce harmful ingredients in order to make more money. Food companies spend millions of dollars lobbying government officials to influence votes on laws, rules and regulations, and little to no research is being carried out to ensure that what they are introducing is actually safe. Dawn Undurraga, a nutritionist from the Environmental Working Group, confirms that the current policy on food additives was written in 1958, "and has been completely co-opted by food and chemical companies."[109] A 2019 article in EcoWatch reveals that the FDA allows thousands of chemicals to go untested before they are added into processed foods. In fact, they have, instead, allowed companies to "voluntarily notify the agency about food chemicals and to allow companies to summarize the industry science supporting their conclusions."[110] Isn't the FDA supposed to be protecting our food supply? We can no longer blindly trust our favorite brands, or our governments to make decisions based on the health of the people. We've got to educate ourselves to be wise consumers.

PESTICIDES ON PRODUCE

Food additives are not the only thing to be concerned about. As farmers aim to mass produce fruits and vegetables quickly and cheaply, heavy pesticides are used which contain dangerous ingredients for human consumption. A large body of evidence[111] points at pesticides as a major cause of chronic diseases including: Cancer, diabetes, neurodegenerative diseases such as Parkinson's, Alzheimer's, and ALS, birth defects and reproductive disorders, asthma, COPD, and more. Nearly 70 percent of the produce sold in the U.S. comes with pesticide residues, according to the Environmental Working Group's (EWG) analysis of test data from the Department of Agriculture.[112] In order to support shopper awareness, each year the EWG puts out a list of the produce containing the highest residues of pesticides, called the "Dirty Dozen."

EWG'S DIRTY DOZEN

1. Strawberries

2. Spinach

3. Kale

4. Nectarines

5. Apples

6. Grapes

7. Peaches

8. Cherries

9. Pears

10. Tomatoes

11. Celery

12. Potatoes

They also produce a "Clean Fifteen" list of the produce containing the least amount of pesticide residue. Seventy percent of the produce on this list contained no pesticide residue at all!

EWG'S CLEAN FIFTEEN

1. Avocados

2. Sweet corn

3. Pineapples

4. Frozen sweet peas

5. Onions

6. Papayas

7. Eggplants

8. Asparagus

9. Kiwis

10. Cabbages

11. Cauliflower

12. Cantaloupes

13. Broccoli

14. Mushrooms

15. Honeydew melons

Using this list while you're shopping can help you evaluate what's worth spending extra for organic (really as much as you can), or which regular produce to include more often in your diet. The other thing you can do, is make sure you clean your produce well! According to Food Revolution, studies have shown that putting your produce under running water for 30 seconds can remove 9 out of 12 common pesticides.[113] However, it is even more effective to let your veggies soak in water with some baking soda in it. This solution was shown to remove pesticides on and under the skin of apples!

THE WAR ON WHEAT

Nowadays, wheat is getting a bad rap as gluten intolerance is on the rise. I, myself, used to have an allergic reaction whenever I ate wheat. I loved bread, and was so devastated that I had to give it up. It wasn't until many years later that I found out it wasn't actually the wheat I was allergic to, it was the chemicals used in the processing. Due to mass production, today's farmers use many chemicals to manage vast crop yields. High doses of radiation help crops become more resistant to disease. But these chemicals actually change the molecular structure of the grain, creating carcinogens and chemical toxicity. Also, to get rid of pests, sixteen different pesticides are used on wheat, the most common is Malathion (a neurotoxin); this is serious stuff![114] Farm workers are, of course, most at risk of exposure, but unwashed grains may still carry traces of this toxic chemical. The Agency for Toxic Substances and Disease Registry in Atlanta Georgia warns:

"Malathion interferes with the normal way that the nerves and brain function. Exposure to very high levels of malathion for a short period in air, water, or food may cause difficulty breathing, chest tightness, vomiting, cramps, diarrhea, blurred vision, sweating, headaches, dizziness, loss of consciousness, and death."[115]

The enemy has a war on wheat to destroy a God-given grain, meant for our sustenance. Wheat is talked about a lot in the Bible, as it was a common crop for the Israelites. In biblical times, bread was the main source of nourishment, accompanied by wine and olive oil. It became such a staple that wheat was the first cereal grain to be cultivated in history.[116] Today, wheat is one of the most widely grown crops on the face of the earth. In the past ten years, the US alone has planted 59 million acres of wheat, which is equivalent to about 44 million football fields![117]

In biblical times, agriculture was a trade that acknowledged dependence upon God for success and prosperity. The fertility of the land was not automatic. The ground was tilled manually and farmers prayed for good weather and protection from pests. However, today, farmers are under pressure to produce larger crops faster. Most modern day wheat has been bred to yield greater quantities. They use a hybridization process, where they take two different strains of wheat, and encourage cross-fertilization, to create a hybrid.[118] Today's wheat has large grain heads, and short stalks which soak up less sun, and shallow root systems which extract fewer minerals. As a result, both the mineral and vitamin content of harvested wheat has decreased. The new hybrids also have more gluten proteins, and can cause inflammation in the gut.[119] There's a reason gluten sensitivity is on the rise! Gluten is like a glue that holds bread together giving it elasticity, but it can also cause damage to the intestinal villi and block our nutrient absorption.

When I was battling my allergies, I was so scared I'd have to give up bread for good. But thankfully, wheat itself is not the problem. You just have to be aware of what you're buying. I discovered a baker who made organic sourdough bread from wheat flour. The fermentation process made such a difference for me. No more allergic reactions - my rashes, and stomach issues cleared right up. If you notice yourself reacting to eating wheat, organic sourdough fermented bread is a great alternative to the chemical laden, gluten heavy bread that is more commonly sold.

SUGAR: THE SWEETEST DECEPTION

As we grow in our awareness about the state of our food and fight to take back our health, we must be on guard not to miss a small but great danger right in front of our faces. One cunningly "sweet" way the enemy has deceived us is by luring us into an addiction to one of the most toxic substances of all: **sugar**.

We all know it's bad for us, but why is it so hard for us to stop eating it? The first reason is, we eat sugar to feel better. When I was going through my dietary changes, I used to love Baby Ruth candy bars, Kit Kats, Oreos, cakes and cookies! If I was having a bad day, a handful of candy or anything sweet would put my mood in a better place. Sugar makes you feel good (at least that's what you think). At the other end of that insulin high, you crash and begin craving more sugar to get you up again. The second reason we can't stop is because this is an addictive cycle. The British Journal of Sports Medicine has demonstrated that sugar has a similar effect on the brain and our behavior to mirror powerful illegal drugs and can be as addictive as cocaine! Cutting out sugar causes you to act just like an addict on withdrawal: cravings, binges, agitations, etc.[120] Sugar and cocaine share a very similar chemical makeup and, therefore, cause our bodies to react similarly. We crave sugar, and get restless and anxious when we are deprived of it. Studies have shown that when given the option, 94 percent of rats who are addicted to cocaine will choose sugar instead for the euphoric mood boost![121] Sugar is responsible for a myriad of health issues.

Health Problems Related to the Intake of Refined Sugar

- ADHD

- Acne

- Alcoholism

- Allergies

- Anxiety

- Binge Eating, Bloating

- Bone loss

- Candidiasis

- Depression

- Difficulty Concentrating

- Eczema

- Edema

- Emotional problems

- Fatigue, Insomnia

- Food cravings, Sugar addiction

- High LDL Cholesterol

- Hormonal problems

- Hyperactivity, Behavioral problems

- Memory issues

- Menstrual difficulties, Mood swings

- Mental illness

- Premature aging

- Psoriasis

- Tooth decay

Many parents dealing with hyperactive kids fear their children may have ADD (Attention Deficit Disorder), and put them on Ritalin to calm them down. But more and more, kids are being misdiagnosed.[122] Before you turn to drugs for your kids, just take them off sugar. Get them real food that supplies what their bodies need. Several years ago, there was a massive push for schools in the US to remove vending machines, getting rid of sugary sodas and chocolate bars and replacing them with fruit and vegetables, water and milk. A study was done comparing student behavior before and after sugar intake had decreased, and, sure enough, students were more frequently on time for class, and less likely to be referred to the principal's office for behavior problems.[123]

The truth is, "refined sugar is 99.4 - 99.7% pure calories with no vitamins, minerals, fats, or proteins."[124] Refined sugar is a pure carbohydrate that spikes your blood sugar, causing an insulin response which then crashes your energy and gives you a craving for more sugar. According to Laura Nunes at BrainMD.com, refined sugar "interferes with the actions of calcium and magnesium, increases inflammation, increases erratic brain cell firing, and has been implicated in aggression, and feeds cancer cells."[125]

I remember when I stopped drinking soda. I loved Coke for the carbonated caffeine boost! Taking it out of my routine was a real shift for me, because soda was a regular pick-me-up. But taking it away made me irritable and moody, making me realize how dependent I was upon it. I had to detox from it! It takes the body a few days to adjust; your system almost begins to panic because it's not getting its 'drug boost.' But the cravings did subside as I learned to replace it with other things. A bowl of fruit is a much healthier way to enjoy sugar naturally. And, as I relied less on the refined stuff, fruit began to taste even sweeter! Breaking my sugar addiction meant removing items with artificial sweeteners, and high-carbohydrate items like french fries, crackers, and cookies. I learned there are many other ways to enjoy treats. Do you have to give up brownies? Absolutely not! Brownies can be made with black beans instead of white flour. You can make cheesecake with ground nuts for the crust instead of sugary graham crackers. Cutting down on sugar doesn't mean you are only eating lettuce and celery. God gave us natural sugars to enjoy in limited portions. **There are many ways to be creative and healthy in eating if you take back the power to choose, instead of being driven by addictions and cravings.**

My other book, *Eat Well - Live Raw Food Preparation Using Pure Therapeutic Grade Essential Oils,* is full of nutritious and delicious recipes. If you like brownies and blueberry cheesecake, there is a way to make them both healthy and tasty. Even desserts like chai lattes, mojitos, carrot cake, and ice cream - they can all be made from whole food that will nourish your body and restore your health. The enemy is a copycat, and he has tricked us into believing these foods must be made with white flour and white sugar and all kinds of preservatives and dyes. God has a better way! We just have to choose to make the change.

As you increase your awareness, you will grow in your ability to make wiser, healthier choices. If you have love for God, you can love the body He has given you by treating it well. Use self-discipline and God's sufficient grace to get you through. *"For God has not given us a spirit of fear and timidity, but of power, love, and self-discipline"* 2 Tim. 1:7 *NLT.* **Eating responsibly will make you feel so much better!** You'll get rid of that brain fog, that hyper-anxiety, and those depressive lows. It's all about beginning to think about your choices, because when you are not thinking, the enemy can just pick you off, and start breaking down your body and emotions one bag of chips at a time.

WHAT SHOULD I BE EATING?

1. **Eat whole, natural, plant-based foods** - as close to their freshly-picked state as possible.

2. **Eat animal products (if you are not vegetarian) that have been raised well** - livestock fed with healthy feed, not supplemented with hormones or antibiotics. You can still eat burgers, but choose quality, grass-fed beef.

3. **Eat probiotic rich foods** - kefir, sauerkraut and kimchi can cause your gut and your mood to thrive. They support nutrient absorption and support your immune system.

4. **Limit gluten intake** - choose breads that have been made using traditional methods like soaking, sprouting and souring the grains. Sourdough is much easier on your gut to digest than whole wheat or other mass produced varieties. When I began my health journey, I actually stopped eating bread for over 10 years! But as I got my health together, I now enjoy fermented bread, like sourdough, without the effects of gluten intolerance.

5. **Eat healthy fats** - a balance of Omega-3 & 6 are essential for brain development. If you notice your brain struggling with attention and cognition deficits, depression, or anxiety, make sure you are nourishing your brain! Malnutrition can also cause a decrease in brain volume, the number of neurons, synapses, dendrites and reactive zones which affects cellular communication, performance, and social/emotional development.[126] Make sure you are getting enough calories and use oils like olive oil which includes a high amount of antioxidants that protect your cells from damage. Olive oil also acts as an anti-inflammatory to improve memory and cognitive function. Fatty fish, walnuts, and flaxseed are other great Omega-3 sources.

6. **Choose healthier dairy substitutes** - for everything you want to eat, there is a healthy alternative. Dairy has been shown to cause inflammation and a host of other problems, so try an alternative. Afterall, you are not a cow or a goat, so your body wasn't designed to ingest that type of milk. The media has convinced us we need dairy milk to get our vitamins. God created other ways. Try almond milk — it's not that bad and very good for you. If you want something creamier, try coconut milk or homemade cashew milk.

7. **Consider a healthy diet plan** - there are many healthy diet plans available online these days depending on what your body needs: mediterranean, paleo, keto, gluten-free, anti-inflammatory, etc. As for me, I became infatuated with the raw food diet. I decided that eating raw whole foods was the closest to what God created for me to eat, held the highest nutritional value, and held the least risk of affecting my body negatively. I loved what I was eating! But once my health stabilized, I took classes from many chefs, and learned how to prepare cooked food well. I collected many recipes and began to love wild salmon and cod, organic steamed broccoli, and quinoa. You can create food simply, healthily, and deliciously, once you understand what you are eating.

It took me a long time to establish healthy eating habits, but now that I understand what my body needs, I get to reap the benefits. I finally have energy and vitality! My eyes are bright and clear. I have healthy skin and nails. My mind feels clear, and I can concentrate. My body is lean and trim. I feel great! You can too. The more you understand your body, and how it is affected by different foods, the more you can create a nutrition plan best suited for you.

While the above guidelines are effective strategies to give you a running start, just begin with the first step. Don't get tangled up in too many rules. I used to live by my own food laws: "I can't have this," "I can't eat that." I felt like I was getting legalistic about how I was supposed to eat. I realized it was all based on fear coming from, you know who: the devil! The Lord told me, "It doesn't have to be as structured as you're making it." My legalistic rules were a trap of the enemy that I didn't see until later. I was so scared of getting sick again! I felt I had to have such a restrictive diet to stay well. God shifted my mindset similarly to when He spoke to the apostle Peter on the rooftop and gave him a vision of eating unclean foods (Acts 10). At first, Peter resisted, but then he had to choose to trust the voice of the Lord, that what God said was clean, was clean. Now I realize, I can put aside my rigid laws, and use the wisdom God gives me. Really, you just have to be balanced in your emotions, stay close to Jesus, and eat responsibly. God desires for you to prosper and for your soul to prosper. It's not just about the food, it's about your mind, body and spirit. Now, I can finally say I have experienced my breakthrough in healing!

HOW SHOULD I BE EATING?

Regardless of what you eat, these tips on how to eat, will aid your body:

1. **Eat slow, be relaxed, and chew your food well** - digestion actually starts in the mouth — not in the stomach. Chewing stimulates the brain and helps food to move smoothly through your system. Because saliva contains enzymes that contribute to the digestive process, the work of absorbing your dinner has in fact already started before you have even swallowed! Chewing well is important because it helps to relax a muscle in your lower stomach called the pylorus. Distracted eating, such as eating in front of the TV or computer, has been shown to send your blood and energy to other parts of your body, rather than to the task of digesting, which negatively affects digestion and causes weight gain.[127]

2. **Take digestive enzymes with your meals to aid nutrient absorption** - you aren't only what you eat, but you are what you digest! Make sure your body is breaking down the nutrients you are feeding it.

3. **Take a good friendly-bacteria supplement (probiotic)** - this supports your gut, helps reduce gas and any substances rotting in the bowel.

4. **Don't overeat** - control your portion sizes by eating slowly and being aware that it can take 10-15 minutes for your body to feel full. Use smaller plates to avoid the visual pressure of covering a large plate with food. Restaurants often serve portions larger than your body needs. Consider taking half of it home, or sharing an order with a friend.

5. **Prepare healthy snacks in advance** - feeling rushed is one of the biggest reasons people turn to fast or processed foods, so be prepared! Cut up some veggies or fruit on the weekend to have throughout the week, make nut-based snacks like trail mix, granola bars or powerballs for when you're feeling munchy, or kale chips when you desire that crunch!

6. **Stay hydrated** - our bodies are made up of mostly water. We need to drink clean, filtered water to replenish the water we lose in normal, daily activity. The rule of thumb is to drink between half an ounce to one ounce of water per pound of body weight per day.[128] For example, if you weigh 130 lbs, then your minimum daily water intake should be roughly 2 quarts (8 cups). Weight isn't the only factor in determining how much water to consume. When we are born, we are made up of over 75 percent water but our water level goes down considerably as we age.[129] Gender and health can also influence the ideal amount of water you should be drinking to maintain optimal hydration. In 2020, the Mayo Clinic suggested the adequate daily fluid intake is: 3.7 litres for men (125 fluid ounces/15.5 cups) and 2.7 litres for women (91 fluid ounces/11.5 cups). About 20% of this amount would also include foods that contain water like fruits and vegetables.[130] When calculating your hydration level, make sure you measure your intake of pure water, not tea, coffee, soda, alcoholic drinks, wine, or energy drinks. Your body intakes each of these differently. If you struggle with a weak immune system, opt for distilled water as it is the purest form of water available. However, remember that if you choose distilled, you'll need to get your minerals elsewhere as the distillation process removes all bad contaminants as well as mineral content.[131] An adequate daily intake of high quality water is of paramount importance to slow signs of aging that come with dehydration.

7. **Combining foods for optimal digestion** - when you are meal planning, be intentional to pair foods that work well together to promote better nutrient absorption, rather than causing malabsorption or inflammation. Meat requires an acidic environment to be digested well, and carbohydrates require an alkaline environment. So, no more steak and potatoes! Some rules of thumb: eat your meat with vegetables, eat your carbs with vegetables, eat fruit alone.[132] Drink between meals, not while you eat, as this also can affect how well your body absorbs the nutrients in the food, and may result in indigestion.[133]

When you learn to eat and drink well, you will feel incredible! The devil may try and pull the wool over our eyes until we're feeling so sick we can't figure out why, but when you really see what's going on, and begin to make empowering choices, you'll never want to go back! I feel like I'm a walking billboard for people. When I tell them my age, they can't believe how young and vibrant I look. I don't say that to boast, but to give God glory; He's the one who designed us to eat this way! We don't have to carry bags under our eyes and excessive wrinkles, be fatigued and undernourished. He created, for us, a glorious earth, with endless amounts of healthy food to eat. If we are willing to pay the price of time and effort to remove all the poison and artificial impacts of man, we can feel and look fantastic, day in and day out!

ENDNOTES

93   Robinson, Marv. "Stories of Transformation - Almolonga." Go and Proclaim Ministries. Accessed July 13, 2020. http://www.goandproclaim.co.za/transformation_in_almolonga.php.

94   Gemino, Marilyn. "Chlorophyll, Alkalizing Effects and Gut Immune Health Benefits from Greens." Garden of Life, March 24, 2015. https://www.gardenoflife.com/content/chlorophyll-alkalizing-effects-gut-immune-health-benefits-greens/.

95   Ibid.

96   "Dandelion Recipe & Nutrition: Precision Nutrition's Encyclopedia of Food." Precision Nutrition, July 4, 2019. https://www.precisionnutrition.com/encyclopedia/food/dandelion.

97   Villines, Zawn. "Wheatgrass Benefits: Nutrition, Side Effects, and Warnings." Medical News Today. MediLexicon International, October 17, 2019. https://www.medicalnewstoday.com/articles/320210.php.

98   White, Dana Angelo. "Meet This Grain: Wheat Berries." Food Network. Accessed November 7, 2019. https://www.foodnetwork.com/healthyeats/healthy-tips/2009/02/meet-this-grain-wheat-berries.

99   Fry, Sidney. "What Is a 'Processed' Food?" Cooking Light, June 3, 2015. https://www.cookinglight.com/eating-smart/smart-choices/what-are-processed-foods.

100   Mancini, Fabrizio. "The Truth about Food Additives: How They Threaten Your Health." The Ecologist, January 18, 2012. https://theecologist.org/2012/jan/18/truth-about-food-additives-how-they-threaten-your-health.

101   Milan, Jaime. "There's a BIG Reason to Avoid Ultra-Processed Food." Cooking Light, February 20, 2018. https://www.cookinglight.com/news/can-ultra-processed-foods-cause-cancer.

102   Milan, Jaime. "Yes, Ultra-Processed Foods Are Probably Killing You, Study Says." Cooking Light, May 30, 2019. https://www.cookinglight.com/news/processed-packaged-food-killing-you.

103   McCoy, Jenny. "Beware of These 4 'Healthy' Buzzwords While Grocery Shopping." Cooking Light, February 13, 2018. https://www.cookinglight.com/eating-smart/unhealthy-healthy-grocery-store-food-labels.

104   Ibid.

105   "Whole Grain Ingredient Content Claims." Grains & Legumes Nutrition Council. Accessed February 12, 2020. https://www.glnc.org.au/codeofpractice/whole-grain-ingredient-content-claims/.

106   Markey, Edward J. "Food That Is 'Generally Recognized as Safe' Is Not Good Enough." STAT, September 23, 2016. https://www.statnews.com/2016/09/23/fda-gras-rule-harmful/.

107   Markey, Edward J. "Food That Is 'Generally Recognized as Safe' Is Not Good Enough." STAT, September 23, 2016. https://www.statnews.com/2016/09/23/fda-gras-rule-harmful/.

108   Fahy, William. "Op-Ed: Calling on Kraft-Heinz to Find and Remove Dangerous Phthalates." EHN. EHN, August 28, 2019. https://www.ehn.org/phthalates-in-macaroni-and-cheese-2640037202.html.

109   Truthout. "There Are 2,000 Untested Chemicals in Packaged Foods - and It's Legal." EcoWatch, November 19, 2019. https://www.ecowatch.com/chemicals-packaged-foods-2641391530.html?rebelltitem=4.

110   Ibid.

111   Mostafalou, Sara, and Mohammad Abdollahi. "Pesticides and Human Chronic Diseases: Evidences, Mechanisms, and Perspectives." Toxicology and applied pharmacology. U.S. National Library of Medicine, February 9, 2013. https://www.ncbi.nlm.nih.gov/pubmed/23402800.

112   Group, Environmental Working. "EWG's 2020 Shopper's Guide to Pesticides in Produce™." Shopper's Guide to Pesticides in Produce. ewg, March 25, 2020. https://www.ewg.org/foodnews/summary.php.

113   Honeycutt, Emily. "How to Wash Vegetables and Fruits to Remove Pesticides." Food Revolution Network, December 1, 2017. https://foodrevolution.org/blog/how-to-wash-vegetables-fruits/.

114   Network, Pesticide Action. "Pesticides on Wheat Flour." What's On My Food. Pesticide Action Network North America. Accessed July 17, 2020. http://www.whatsonmyfood.org/food.jsp?food=WF.

115   "Malathion." Toxic Substances Portal. Agency for Toxic Substances and Disease Registry, September 2003. https://www.atsdr.cdc.gov/toxfaqs/TF.asp?id=521&tid=92.

116   Gascoigne, Bamber. "History of the Cultivation of Plants." HistoryWorld, 2001. http://www.historyworld.net/wrldhis/PlainTextHistories.asp?ParagraphID=ayp.

117 "Wheat 101: Key Facts About the World's Essential Grain." Wheat World. National Association of Wheat Growers, 2016. https://www.wheatworld.org/wp-content/uploads/2016/12/wheat-101.pdf.

118 Anderson, Jane. "Is GMO Wheat Increasing Celiac Disease and Gluten Sensitivity?" Verywell Health, September 24, 2020. https://www.verywellhealth.com/is-gmo-wheat-causing-increases-in-gluten-issues-562530.

119 "11 Ways Gluten Can Damage Your Health: Paleo Leap." Paleo Leap, June 6, 2020. https://paleoleap.com/11-ways-gluten-and-wheat-can-damage-your-health/.

120 Nunes, Laura. "Sugar vs. Cocaine: The Science Behind Why Sugar Is So Bad For You." BrainMD Health Blog, August 31, 2018. https://brainmd.com/blog/what-do-sugar-and-cocaine-have-in-common/.

121 Stein, Amy. "Sugar Vs Cocaine." Visual.ly, January 3, 2020. https://visual.ly/community/Infographics/health/sugar-vs-cocaine.

122 Lotter, Eugene. "5 Conditions That Could Be Mistaken for ADHD." Health24, September 20, 2019. https://www.health24.com/Medical/ADHD/News/5-conditions-that-can-be-mistaken-for-adhd-20170623.

123 Price, Joshua. "De-Fizzing Schools: The Effect on Student Behavior of Having Vending Machines in Schools." Agricultural and Resource Economics Review, April 2012. https://pdfs.semanticscholar.org/c477/105ae3b58501e4ec3c2a60d6ec0b808b2b5f.pdf.

124 Nunes, Laura. "Sugar vs. Cocaine: The Science Behind Why Sugar Is So Bad For You." BrainMD Health Blog, August 31, 2018. https://brainmd.com/blog/what-do-sugar-and-cocaine-have-in-common/.

125 Ibid.

126 Epstein, Iris. "Giving The Brain The Fuel It Needs." Body & Soul, January 28, 2019. http://www.bodyandsoulheals.com/latest-news/2019/1/28/giving-the-brain-the-fuel-it-needs.

127 "Distracted Eating Can Spell Trouble for Digestion." Real Food Whole Health. Accessed February 19, 2020. https://www.realfoodwholehealth.com/2010/12/distracted-eating-can-spell-trouble-for-digestion/.

128 Shaw, Gina. "How Much Water Do You Need? Can You Drink Too Much?" WebMD. WebMD, July 7, 2009. https://www.webmd.com/diet/features/water-for-weight-loss-diet.

129 Thompson, Malia. "Hold Your Water! The Importance of Cellular Hydration". Colorado School of Clinical Herbalism. February 2, 2016. https://clinicalherbalism.com/hold-your-water-the-importance-of-cellular-hydration/.

130   "Water: How Much Should You Drink Everyday?" Mayo Foundation for Medical Education and Research. Healthy Lifestyle: Nutrition & Healthy Eating. October 14, 2020. https://www.mayoclinic.org/healthy-lifestyle/nutrition-and-healthy-eating/in-depth/water/art-20044256#:~:text=The%20U.S.%20National%20Academies%20of,fluids%20a%20day%20for%20women.

131   Kubala, Jillian. "Purified vs Distilled vs Regular Water: What's the Difference?" Healthline. Healthline Media, March 1, 2018. https://www.healthline.com/nutrition/purified-vs-distilled-vs-regular-water.

132   Leonard, Katherine. "10 Food Combinations to Improve Digestion." mindbodygreen, October 11, 2019. https://www.mindbodygreen.com/0-6851/10-Food-Combinations-to-Improve-Digestion.html.

133   Eckelkamp, Stephanie. "The Surprising Reason You Shouldn't Chug Water with Your Meals." Prevention, October 18, 2016. https://www.prevention.com/food-nutrition/healthy-eating/a20456813/why-you-shouldnt-drinking-water-with-meals/.

CHAPTER 11
KEEPING YOUR MOUTH HEALTHY

YOUR DENTIST - A MEDICAL DOCTOR

When I chose to study dentistry, I wasn't sure if it was the right career for me. There were some unexpected twists and turns in the road along the way, but now, it has formed the better part of my life. After deciding I didn't want to be a general dentist, I found myself applying to grad school to specialize in Endodontics and got in by the grace of God! After graduating, I began a teaching career at Howard University School of Dentistry in Washington D.C., and stayed there for 11 years. Then, God gave me the courage to open my own private practice in Maryland, as an Endodontist (Root Canal Specialist) which I ran for 15 years. I've learned that dentistry is a lot more than caring for your teeth!

Dentists are medical doctors. Professionally, we are considered doctors of oral health, but to care for your oral health, we must also advise you about eating habits and nutrition, and be knowledgeable about the bacteria in your mouth and how it can affect the health of your whole body! Often dentistry does not get the full recognition it deserves as a medical science, despite the professional titles, such as: Doctor of Dental Surgery (DDS) or Doctor of Medicine in Dentistry (DMD) or Doctor of Dental Medicine (DDM). Many people think the mouth is simply the doorway for food to enter the body, be broken down by the teeth, swallowed, and digested. But the mouth is a significant digestive organ which can affect the health of your whole body. The truth is, your mouth holds many different types of bacteria. Some are beneficial to your dental health, but others are harmful. For example, *Fusobacterium nucleatum,* is the name of a stealthy bacteria, commonly found in the mouth, that opens up blood vessels, making them permeable for other bacteria and substances to sneak into the bloodstream. Once in the bloodstream, bacteria can cross all sorts of cellular barriers such as the blood-brain barrier and the placental barrier that guards a growing fetus.[132]

A good dentist can spot early warning signs in the mouth that may indicate symptoms of systemic disease. Did you know that if your immune system has been compromised by disease or medical treatments, bacteria from the mouth can cause infection in other parts of the body?[133] Studies have shown that periodontal disease from unhealthy teeth and gums may be linked to cardiovascular disease, stroke, diabetes and low-birth weight babies.[134]

To protect the rest of your body, keeping your mouth healthy is a big deal. What does this mean? Let's take a history lesson from Dr. Weston A. Price (1870-1948), a Cleveland dentist, who has been called the "Isaac Newton of Nutrition."[135] He travelled around the world studying patterns of tooth decay and observed how isolated, native populations who primarily fed on a traditional diet of growing or hunting their food, had consistently strong bodies, straight teeth without decay, and were resistant to disease. Whereby, those who lived a more urban lifestyle, with modern day convenience-eating, high carb, high sugar, and chemical additives had crooked, awkwardly spaced teeth, and were more susceptible to disease. He observed that the food of the indigenous peoples provided at least four times the calcium and other minerals, and at least ten times the fat-soluble vitamins from animal foods such as butter, fish, eggs, shellfish and organ meats. What you eat matters!

Based on his findings, and modern research, I recommend eating foods that are high in nutritional value, and avoiding processed fast foods. And avoid refined sugars! Sugar acts like a magnet for bad bacteria, and together, they form acids that strip minerals from tooth enamel, which, over time, weakens the enamel and forms cavities. It's also wise to prioritize dental coverage, and keep regular hygienist and dental visits twice a year. When you get older, you will be thankful you maintained strong, healthy teeth so you can keep your own teeth longer!

FACTS ABOUT FILLINGS

I worked hard in dental school to do the best I could with hopes to make a decent living in a reputable career. But along the way, I could tell something wasn't quite right. I remember one day in the lab, there was a liquid mercury spill and all the students were ushered out. Poison control arrived completely covered with protective space-suits in order to enter the lab and clean up the spill. Evidently, mercury is highly hazardous! It struck me, why on earth would I place mercury in people's teeth to fill a cavity, if it's so dangerous? Why would the industry encourage me to do this? Something didn't add up.

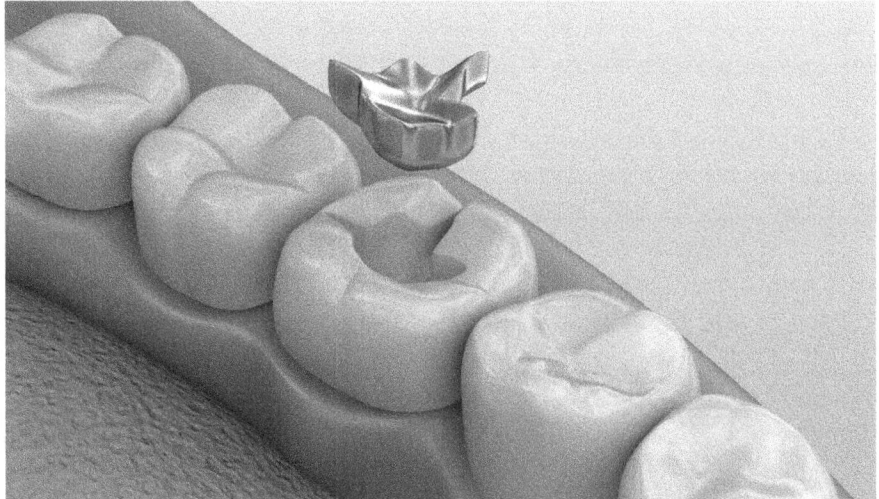

In the early days of the dental profession, fillings were made of gold, but by the time the first dental college opened in 1840, placing mercury fillings were less technically difficult to place than gold fillings. But at what long term cost? Fast forward to today, when we have discovered that even simple brushing can release a mercury vapor level that is above the safe limit.[136] To date, 28 countries have banned mercury amalgam use in dentistry for children under the age of 15 and for pregnant, or nursing mothers. Despite this, the USA refuses to comply, and continues to declare it a safe treatment. When questioned, the leaders of the American Dental Association (ADA) stated: "There are benefits and drawbacks to all dental materials, but dental amalgam is *more affordable* and offers longer lasting results than the alternatives."[137] What they failed to mention is that the ADA holds two patents for mercury amalgam, so they are personally invested.[138] If you have to get a filling, I'd recommend getting a composite, or white filling. It may not be as durable as mercury, but you can be confident it's not releasing toxins into your bloodstream.

THE TRUTH ABOUT TOOTHPASTE

People think that keeping their mouths healthy is all about using the right toothpaste. Wrong! As a dentist for 28 years, this deception around the health benefits of toothpaste hits close to my heart. You don't actually need all the many choices of toothpastes that are marketed by your dental hygienist, or the media, in order to remove bacteria and prevent cavities. Toothpaste is filled with harmful additives and doesn't provide much benefit at all! The promotion of toothpaste is basically propaganda and simply causes confusion. First of all, when you eat responsibly you lessen your chances of getting cavities. Not letting food settle around your teeth by brushing after each meal, rinsing with mouthwash, and daily flossing, will, of course, promote good dental health, but you don't need chemical filled products to do it! You can even make your own!

Recipe: Homemade Baking Soda and Peppermint Toothpaste

- Mix all the following ingredients in a bowl until a paste is formed:
  - 1 tsp baking soda
  - 1 drop peppermint or lemon essential oil
  - A few drops of water
  - Stevia as a sweetener (optional)

Recipe: Dentist-recommended Matcha Tea mouthwash[139]

- Combine all of the following in a jar with a lid and shake to mix.
  - 1 cup of water
  - 1 teaspoon matcha powder
  - ½ tsp calcium carbonate
  - ½ teaspoon L-Arginine
  - ¼ teaspoon baking soda
  - ½ -1 tablespoon of xylitol

- Swish one tablespoon of mouthwash in your mouth for 30 seconds - 1 minute

- Mixture will keep for two weeks - shake before use.

You might wonder if it's worth the effort to make your own health products. I mean, how bad can "reliable" brands like Colgate or Crest be? Let's take a closer look at the development, ingredients, and risks associated with toothpaste, and then you can decide for yourself.

COLGATE-PALMOLIVE

Colgate toothpaste hit the market in 1873. The recipe began with soap which was later replaced with Sodium lauryl sulfate which is still currently in use. Sodium lauryl sulfate is added as a detergent and cleansing agent. It interferes with the function of your taste buds and has been linked to the formation of canker sores and is registered as an insecticide. It may also affect your immune system and cause inflammation.[140] Remember, anything that goes into your mouth could have a free pass into your bloodstream, so you must be on guard! Read those labels! Colgate is also famous for standing by Triclosan as a key ingredient. According to the US Environmental Protection Agency (EPA) triclosan has been registered as a pesticide since 1969.[141] The

FDA banned triclosan in soaps in 2016, but it has taken until 2019 to finally have Colgate concede and choose an alternate ingredient.[142]

CREST

In the early 1940's, Procter and Gamble began a research program to find ingredients that would become Crest toothpaste. In 1960, the ADA confirmed that Crest effectively prevents tooth decay. By 1962, Crest had become the best selling toothpaste brand in the United States. Since then, it has been exposed for including unnatural and harmful ingredients. Simply for aesthetic value, they inserted polyethylene plastic microbeads, made out of the same plastic as non-degrading grocery bags. Since the microbeads are not considered to be an active ingredient in toothpaste, the FDA had not been monitoring this ingredient. Thanks to growing public concern about the beads' effects, Procter & Gamble, the maker of Crest, agreed to eliminate it.[143] But many dangerous substances remain. Check your ingredient list for:

- **DEA** - Consumers find diethanolamine, or DEA in products that foam including toothpaste. DEA disrupts hormones and forms cancer-causing nitrates.

- **Propylene glycol** - an active ingredient in antifreeze, propylene glycol acts as a wetting agent and surfactant in toothpaste. A build up in the body can cause rashes, vertigo, shortness of breath, heart attacks, and brain problems. Though it is deemed to have low toxicity, it is risky for those with kidney or liver disease, pregnant women and children.[144]

THE TRUTH ABOUT FLUORIDE

Toothpaste was actually developed because of the discovery of sodium-fluoride in water. It was discovered as a water contaminant, but as it seemed to be present in areas where people had less cavities, it was quickly promoted. **The truth is that sodium-fluoride is an industrial waste product, a byproduct of aluminum production.**[145] But before it was properly tested, many municipalities began to add a non-pharmaceutical grade of sodium-fluoride to the water supply in hopes it would strengthen teeth, and then later created topical applications of it in toothpaste. Though small amounts of fluoride have been seen to strengthen tooth enamel, it is not a safe substance. Fluoride is an endocrine disruptor that can affect your bones, brain, thyroid gland, pineal gland, and even your blood sugar levels.

Many municipalities in America still fluoridate the tap water, and nowadays, fluoride is added to almost everything: common pesticides on our food (including herbicides, miticides, and fungicides), contain sodium fluoride as their active ingredient, as well antidepressant drugs like Prozac and Paxil.[146] Though we are getting fluoride from many sources, according to the American Association of Poison Control (AAPC), toothpaste ingestion is still the main source of fluoride toxicity. [147] And where dentists used to assert that fluoride reduced decay by over 60 percent, today, they claim a more modest 25 percent, which some suggest may still be inflated.[148]

WHAT'S IN YOUR WATER?

Unless you live near a well or spring, you likely have to pay for purified, clean water because our water system is tainted. What's really going on here? When we look with the eyes of the Spirit, we can see that the enemy knows how badly we need clean water and has, therefore, found means to contaminate our water supply. He is out to destroy it. The story of Newark, New Jersey, is a clear illustration of the enemy's work:[149]

Newark is a very poor town suffering from years of contaminated water. Carcinogens (cancer-causing agents) had been discovered in the water, so the city added a chemical to deal with the problem, but neglected to acknowledge the consequence of raised acidity levels. The problem compounded because the city's old infrastructure used lead pipes, which hadn't been maintained, nor had residents been informed of the risks of the lead currently leaching into their water supply.[150] After much finger-pointing, city and state officials decided to add a chemical to stop the corrosion, but the high acidity levels in the water made the lead protectant ineffective. However, the enemy wasn't done yet. The city tried handing out water filters for home use, but many were not installed or maintained properly, and when residential water was tested, only two out of three actually filtered the lead properly![151] Newark residents were literally being poisoned at three times the federal action level for lead exposure. When it comes to lead exposure, experts agree that, "Pregnant women and children are most at risk: Even low lead levels are associated with serious, irreversible damage to developing brains and nervous systems. Lead exposure is also linked to fertility issues, cardiovascular and kidney problems, cognitive dysfunction, and elevated blood pressure in otherwise healthy adults."[152] Almost half of Newark's public and charter schools were affected, and over 22 thousand homes. While the officials debated about who deserved to receive bottled water, the enemy was having a hayday. Human negligence, cover-up, and corruption wove their way through this story, while innocent people suffered.

The attack on water goes far beyond this one town. From a broader view, the EWG (Environmental Working Group) did a 5-year study looking at the quality of US tap water, revealing over 500 different contaminants supplied to each of the 50 states. "The disturbing truth shown from the data is that when most Americans drink a glass of tap water, they're also getting a dose of industrial or agricultural contaminants linked to cancer, harm to the brain and nervous system, changes in the growth and development of the fetus, fertility problems and/or hormone disruption."[153] To add to the list, the World Health Organization has announced that the frequent use of pharmaceuticals (both prescribed and over the counter) has resulted in a relatively continuous flow of pharmaceuticals into the wastewater.[154] It is released through the sewage of people who have ingested these drugs, and also runoffs from livestock manure who have been given antibiotics. If you are concerned about the purity of water in your area, I highly recommend a quality filtration system! There are some home-based filtration systems that use processes such as reverse osmosis, which remove more than 99% of large pharmaceutical molecules.[155]

All over the world, the enemy is targeting our water sources; they have been neglected, tampered with, compromised by disease pathogens, infiltrated with chemical residues, or leached with heavy metals and toxic chemicals while transporting it. We must open our eyes to see, and our spirits to understand what we are ingesting. **The enemy has an agenda, but with the wisdom of God, we will prevail.**

When the Israelites wandered in the wilderness, they also struggled to find pure water that was suitable to drink. The story of the bitter water at Marah, demonstrates that the Lord has sovereign wisdom that can guide and provide for us. He alone is our healer.

"Then Moses made Israel set out from the Red Sea, and they went into the wilderness of Shur. They went three days in the wilderness and found no water. When they came to Marah, they could not drink the water of Marah because it was bitter; therefore it was named Marah. And the people grumbled against Moses, saying, "What shall we drink?" And he cried to the Lord, and the Lord showed him a log, and he threw it into the water, and the water became sweet.

There the Lord made for them a statute and a rule, and there He tested them, saying, "If you will diligently listen to the voice of the Lord your God, and do that which is right in His eyes, and give ear to His commandments and keep all His statutes, I will put none of the diseases on you that I put on the Egyptians, for I am the Lord, your healer" Exodus 15:22-26 ESV.

God is the answer to all we need. He's just waiting to help us with our problems. God understands the struggles we will face in this fallen world no matter how insignificant they seem. There is no need to murmur and complain, because God already has the best solutions for your every need prepared in advance. He is our Father ready to take care of ANY issue we, His kids, face. So, let's start relying on our Daddy God, and ask Him to lead us to pure sources of water. The enemy may have a strategy to contaminate the nation, but God will always provide a way out. Like Jesus says, *"If you only knew the gift God has for you and Who you are speaking to, you would ask Me, and I would give you living water" John 4:10 NLT.*

ENDNOTES

132   Gould, S.E. "How Bacteria Sneak into Your Blood through Your Mouth." Scientific American Blog Network. Scientific American, January 4, 2012. https://blogs.scientificamerican.com/lab-rat/how-bacteria-sneak-into-your-blood-through-your-mouth/.

133   "Links between Oral & General Health." Dental Health Foundation, April 30, 2020. https://www.dentalhealth.ie/your-oral-health/the-healthy-mouth/links-between-oral--general-health/.

134   Periodontology, American Academy of. "Periodontal Disease and Systemic Health." Periodontal Disease and Systemic Health | Perio.org. Accessed May 4, 2020. https://www.perio.org/consumer/gum-disease-and-other-diseases.

135   "Weston A. Price, DDS." The Weston A. Price Foundation, January 1, 2000. https://www.westonaprice.org/health-topics/nutrition-greats/weston-a-price-dds/.

136   Panahpour, Alireza. "28 Countries Ban Mercury 'Silver' Fillings for Children and Pregnant Mothers." The Systemic Dentist, February 26, 2018. https://www.systemicdentist.com/pdf/28-countries-ban-mercury-amalgam-for-children-why-not-in-north-america.pdf.

137   Garvin, Jennifer. "Dental Amalgam Is Safe and Reliable." ADA News. ADA, November 18, 2018. https://www.ada.org/en/publications/ada-news/2019-archive/november/ada-testifies-that-dental-amalgam-is-safe-and-reliable.

138   Panahpour, Alireza. "28 Countries Ban Mercury 'Silver' Fillings for Children and Pregnant Mothers." The Systemic Dentist, February 26, 2018.

139   Burhenne, Mark. "DIY Matcha Green Tea Mouthwash to Beat Bad Breath, Gingivitis, and Cavities." Ask the Dentist, June 26, 2020. https://askthedentist.com/diy-matcha-green-tea-mouthwash/.

140   "Sodium Lauryl Sulphate." Healthy Choices.

141   "Triclosan Facts." EPA. Environmental Protection Agency, March 24, 2010.

142   Kary, Tiffany. "Colgate Total To Relaunch Without Triclosan Ingredient." Bloomberg.com, January 15, 2019. https://www.bloomberg.com/news/articles/2019-01-15/colgate-total-toothpaste-to-relaunch-this-time-sans-triclosan.

143   Carroll, Linda. "Plastic Beads Being Removed from Toothpaste: Safe to Brush?" TODAY.com, September 17, 2014. https://www.today.com/health/microbeads-toothpaste-safe-brush-1D80157769.

144   Mandl, Elise. "Propylene Glycol in Food: Is This Additive Safe?" Healthline.

Healthline Media, March 2, 2018. https://www.healthline.com/nutrition/propylene-glycol.

145   "Toxic Treatment: The Story of Fluoride." Origins. Accessed June 16, 2020. https://origins.osu.edu/article/toxic-treatment-fluorides-transformation-industrial-waste-public-health-miracle.

146   Ullah, Rizwan, Muhammad Sohail Zafar, and Nazish Shahani. "Potential Fluoride Toxicity from Oral Medicaments: A Review." Iranian journal of basic medical sciences. Mashhad University of Medical Sciences, August 2017. https://www.ncbi.nlm.nih.gov/pmc/articles/PMC5651468/.

147   Ibid.

148   "Toxic Treatment: The Story of Fluoride." Origins. Accessed June 16, 2020. https://origins.osu.edu/article/toxic-treatment-fluorides-transformation-industrial-waste-public-health-miracle.

149   Corasaniti, Nick, Corey Kilgannon, and John Schwartz. "Tainted Water, Ignored Warnings and a Boss With a Criminal Past." The New York Times, August 24, 2019. https://www.nytimes.com/2019/08/24/nyregion/newark-lead-water-crisis.html.

150   Anselm, Bryan. "Newark Drinking Water Crisis." NRDC, January 2020. https://www.nrdc.org/newark-drinking-water-crisis.

151   Corasaniti, Nick, Corey Kilgannon, and John Schwartz. "Tainted Water, Ignored Warnings and a Boss With a Criminal Past." The New York Times, August 24, 2019. https://www.nytimes.com/2019/08/24/nyregion/newark-lead-water-crisis.html.

152   Anselm, Bryan. "Newark Drinking Water Crisis." NRDC, January 2020. https://www.nrdc.org/newark-drinking-water-crisis.

153   "The Dirty Secret of Government Drinking Water Standards." EWG Tap Water Database, October 2019. https://www.ewg.org/tapwater/state-of-american-drinking-water.php.

154   "Information Sheet: Pharmaceuticals in Drinking-Water." World Health Organization, August 29, 2016.

155   Ibid.

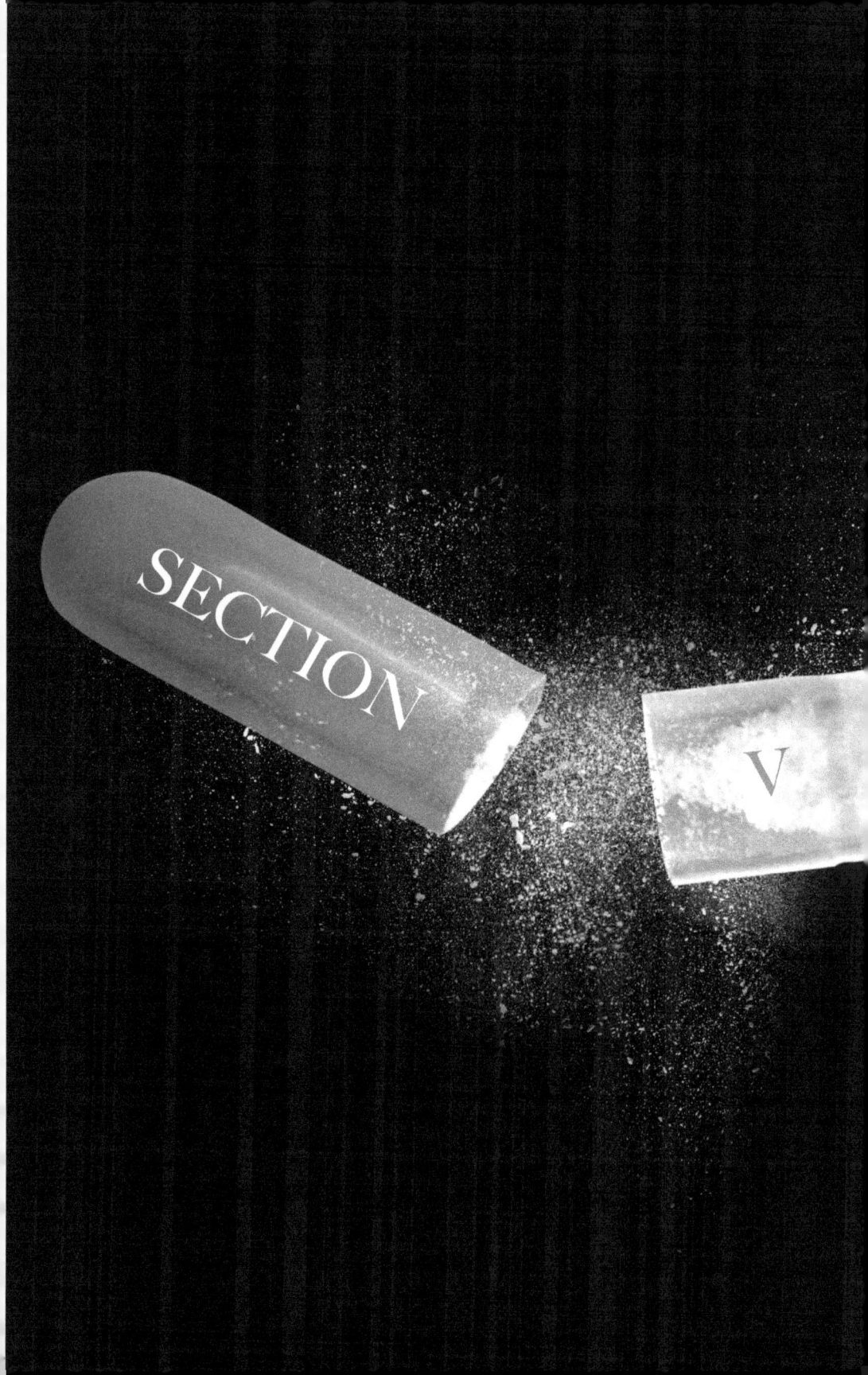

SECTION

V

LIVING WITH YOUR EYES OPEN

The Bible says, *"Your enemy the devil prowls around like a roaring lion looking for someone to devour"* 1 Peter 5:8 *NIV*. Satan establishes his rule by prowling around looking for individuals to be the leaders of his government on earth who will create structures and laws that will keep the rest of humanity in bondage. In America, Satan has found several key people who have, one generation after the other, built structures upon corruption and greed, enslaving the people to lies and fear. The trouble is, many don't see the chains, because they don't see the strings being pulled behind the scenes. In this section, I'm pulling back the curtain. We must be aware of the enemy's schemes operating within our medical system, so that we don't get blindsided. Are you ready to see?

CHAPTER 12
A NATIONAL STRATEGY AGAINST WELLNESS

Have you ever wondered:

- Why doctors mainly target symptoms rather than trying to correct what caused the illness in the first place?

- Why effective natural healing modalities aren't covered by insurance companies?

- Why there is so little yearly coverage for most dental insurances?

- Why medical insurance premiums keep going up and up?

- Why, despite advances in understanding health, people seem to be getting sicker and sicker?

I have felt so frustrated by these questions. Doesn't the world seem backwards in its thinking? But when I opened my spiritual eyes to see what was going on behind the scenes, everything became a lot clearer. Satan has existed since before the creation of the world. He has seen history repeat itself and has learned a lot about humankind. Satan's agenda goes beyond attacking individuals, and instead, focuses on long-term systemic control. He will infiltrate the government, the decision-making bodies, the media, and the mass public for his own gain. When we look back through American history, we can observe how the enemy has infiltrated our medical system from the very beginning, starting with a man named John D. Rockefeller.

WESTERN MEDICINE IS ROCKEFELLER MEDICINE

The Rockefellers are one of the most richest and powerful families of the American elite. From one sector of society to the next, they have used their wealth and influence to pressure and manipulate agendas for their own gain. Their power-hungry agendas make them no less than tyrants with the intent of dominating the world. They are key puppets in Satan's kingdom-building strategy. They started with monopolizing oil; today, they dominate the United Nations, the World Health Organization, the Council on Foreign Relations, the Trilateral Commission, Planned Parenthood and many, many other organizations that either govern or influence culture to a large extent. Let's take a closer look at how these seeds were planted.

Satan began his agenda with William Avery Rockefeller (John Rockefeller's father) who was a con artist. He worked as a traveling snake-oil salesman who posed as a deaf-mute peddler and hawked miracle drugs and herbal remedies. If a lifestyle of lies and deception isn't enough of a signature of Satan, William was even nicknamed "Devil Bill."[156] William had a son, John D. Rockefeller, who became the first billionaire of America by extracting oil from the ground and aggressively monopolizing the industry. He plotted with the railroads to restrict oil delivery, forcing competitors to be bought out or forced to pay scandalous shipping costs that would drive them out of business. The ones who stubbornly insisted on fairness were bludgeoned with price wars. The result was, by 1890, Rockefeller controlled approximately 90 percent of the oil production in America.[157] Rockefeller believed, "competition is sin."[158] He wanted complete power. Sound familiar? Despite his wealth, he began looking for more ways to monetize his oil products. He began using derivatives of petroleum (coal tar) to produce drugs and topical skin treatments despite their effects on the mind, body and nervous system. Rather than curing illness, these drugs masked symptoms (and have since been found to be full of carcinogens).[159] But he needed a channel to sell his chemicals nationally, so he went big, and targeted the American Medical Association (AMA).

THE AMERICAN MEDICAL ASSOCIATION

You might be familiar with the symbol of the AMA — a staff with one or two serpents wrapped around it. This dates back to the days of Moses:

"So the Lord sent poisonous snakes among the people, and many were bitten and died. Then the people came to Moses and cried out, "We have sinned by speaking against the Lord and against you. Pray that the Lord will take away the snakes." So Moses prayed for the people. Then the Lord told him, "Make a replica of a poisonous snake and attach it to a pole. All who are bitten will live if they simply look at it!" So Moses made a snake out of bronze and attached it to a pole. Then anyone who was bitten by a snake could look at the bronze snake and be healed" Numbers 21:6-9 NLT.

The people were complaining and whining about their struggles in the wilderness. So God sent snakes to remind them that they were being influenced by Satan (the serpent from the garden). God tells Moses to put the snake on the pole as if to say, "Look at the bronze snake long enough to face the fact that you are listening to the devil, not to me. If you look at it long enough, you'll get it, and your repentance will be heartfelt and your bodies will be restored."

Though the medical symbol kept this imagery, they missed the point that it's meant to restore our relationship to God as the one we obey and receive healing from. Wouldn't it be amazing if our medical symbol was Jesus on the cross, reminding us to lift our eyes to Him for our healing? When I see the medical caduceus, still exalting the snake on the pole, it reminds me of how the medical profession is bound together with Satan. Sadly, all medical professionals, dentists and physicians take an oath and, unknowingly, make a covenant using this double serpent symbol to represent their allegiance. Satan has wound his way through the whole system, (the hospitals, pharmaceutical industry, the insurance companies) corrupting them from the inside out.

The American Medical Association has become a wealthy political group, using its profits to lobby the government for its own agenda. In essence, it is a research institution that educates people about health legislation and advocates for governing bodies to promote their views. But when the AMA began in 1849, it was a weak organization, until John D. Rockefeller and Andrew Carnegie "took on a 'philanthropic mission to help.'"[160] Rockefeller wanted to eliminate the alternatives to Western medicine (the only modality which would propose drugs and radiation as treatment, thus enriching Rockefeller who owned the means to produce these treatments). The Carnegie Foundation hired Abraham Flexner to visit medical institutions all over the country and write a report for Congress, which stated that all the natural healing modalities which had existed for hundreds of years were unscientific quackery, and called for a standardized approach where only AMA Medical institutions would be granted medical school licenses. These schools were then forced to comply by removing all other modes of healing from their curriculum, including herbs, plants, and nutrition; this meant they could only offer Rockefeller's allopathic methods: using drugs to suppress symptoms in the name of science. Granted, some level of standardization would benefit the nation, but the widespread elimination of all natural healing remedies was undoubtedly the devil's way of corrupting our perception of health and what 'medicine' really is. Now, when we don't feel good, we pop a pill because that's all we've been taught to do; meanwhile, God's natural healing remedies are all around us.

I don't know about you, but when I began learning about all this, I began to get so angry. And not only about the greed and corruption, but the impact on the next generation... what will they grow up believing about where healing comes from? Satan just wants to kill people off by getting them addicted to drugs. He wants to enslave them to more problems and get our eyes off of our loving God who has already provided so many natural healing remedies. God wants us to live in abundant freedom, but the devil is determined to steal our destiny: "Let's keep 'em weak and controlled so they never really find out who they are and I can stay in control." Let's allow a righteous anger to rise up inside until we can shout, "Enough is Enough!"

THE ROCKEFELLER FOUNDATION

Many call Rockefeller one of America's greatest philanthropists, but a closer look will show that his 'gifts' were often tied to his own agenda. His critics denounced his contributions as being made with "tainted money," as he only became wealthy by breaking the backs of the competition.[161] This unsurpassed wealth gave him the influence he needed to build his own kingdom. In 1913, he used $100 million to capitalize The Rockefeller Foundation, devoted primarily to public health and medical science.[162] The Rockefeller foundation insisted that medical schools place Rockefeller employees on their board of directors to ensure compliance. If they obeyed, huge grants (in the millions) were given, which was a lot of money in the early nineteen hundreds.[163] In his lifetime, Rockefeller gave a total of $530,853,632 to various institutions, primarily around the pursuit of knowledge. He saw everything through the lens of business. The New York Times quoted him as saying: "I investigated and worked myself almost to a nervous breakdown in groping my way, without sufficient guide or chart, through the ever-widening field of philanthropic endeavors. It was forced upon me to organize and plan this department upon as distinct lines of progress as our other business affairs."[164] His critics observed that his 'benevolent trusts' served only the privileged interests and promoted class education. For example, from 1919-1920 Vanderbilt Medical School was given $4,000,000, the University of Rochester $5,000,000, Johns Hopkins received over $2,200,000 and Meharry Medical College (primarily for African Americans and other minorities, and actually where I went to school), was only given $150,000. These larger donations allowed the ivy-league schools to excel in research, and, more importantly, maintain a prestigious status; but this status was dependent on coming under the guiding hand of Mr. Rockefeller. In reality, all of this philanthropic giving was building a kingdom where the leading institutions could be controlled to continue to promote his agenda of allopathic chemical-based healing.

By the early 1900s, the Rockefeller empire controlled virtually all medicine. He owned the lion's share of the chemical industry, which would later be called the pharmaceutical industry. Through the years, the fruit of this industry has remained true to the seed it started from: a way to make more money.

BIG PHARMA

I get why people take prescription medications; it's a quick fix to subdue immediate pain. It may seem like the only option. It's an easy route. But masking pain and symptoms never gets to the root of the problem. It appears like an immediate solution, but it can become an insistent addiction that, consequently, lines the pockets of pharmaceutical companies solely interested in increasing their profit margins. The cycle of pharmaceutical dependency is a horrible trap that leaves people sicker, poorer, and feeling helpless. If you're taking prescription medications, I encourage you to seek to understand the industry you're partnering with, and consider alternative solutions. Let's take a closer look.

"Big Pharma" is the nickname given to the world's pharmaceutical industry. Drug companies bring in billions of revenue each year, spending a large percentage on marketing their products to drive sales higher, and to influence doctors to promote their drugs over other brands. Big Pharma is a big business! In fact, major pharmaceutical companies make about twice as much in profit each quarter as they spend on research & development.[165] In 2014, the BBC published an article revealing that Johnson & Johnson made 71.3 billion dollars annually, of which only 8.2 billion was spent on research and development, giving them a hefty profit of 13.8 billion dollars. They spent more than double their research expenditures on sales and marketing (17.5 billion)! Other firms are similar. Pfizer made 22 billion annually, with only 6.6 billion used towards research and development, but 11.4 billion on sales and marketing. That's a 43 percent profit margin!

Major pharmaceutical companies also spend significant amounts on lobbyists pushing laws to approve new products,[166] and, at times, even bribing doctors to prescribe their products.[167] Rather than lowering prices to make health care affordable, these pharmaceutical companies go the extra mile to keep their prices high for as long as possible.

Imagine this classic scene: a child sitting on the couch at night watching TV; mom enters the room and says, "Jimmy, it's time for bed." Jimmy responds, "Aww mom, just five more minutes?" Five minutes later, mom returns and guess what Jimmy says? "Mom please, it's almost over. Just five more minutes?" Thirty minutes later, Jimmy is still not in bed. Pharmaceutical companies play the same game! But instead of manipulating mom, they manipulate their patents.

Did you know that cheaper generic versions of medicine are not allowed to be created for 20 years after the original brand's filing date? But, as the 20 year mark approaches, these crafty chemical giants have adopted a practice of making slight modifications, such as adding a stripe to a pill,[168] in order to preserve their patents for longer and delay any competition. Of course, they keep the price high, even though all the expensive research has already been reimbursed through 20 years of sales. A 2018 study in the Journal of Law and the Biosciences found that 78 percent of new drug patents awarded in the past decade went to drugs that already existed![169] And 50 percent of the best selling drugs extended their patents more than once.[170] These chemical giants are cutthroat and down-right dirty in their strategies to ward off competitive products. They will even go to the extent of submitting excessive patent applications (known as "thicketing") just to flood the U.S. Patent and Trademark Office to make it extra difficult for competing firms to secure patents.[171] So much for health care that is patient-focused and for the benefit of the public! Big Pharma is willing to do anything to preserve their monopoly and keep prices high.

According to National Health Expenditure data, Americans spent $333 billion on prescription drugs in 2017, which was a rise of 41 percent from 10 years earlier.[172] According to a study quoted on WebMD, 55 percent of Americans regularly take prescription medicine, and typically take four different types on average.[173] We are a drug addicted nation!

Let's back up for a moment. Can you see the enemy's agenda? Can you see how he has taken a grip on the entire industry, corrupting the leaders with greed and lust for power? And what is the result? For Big Pharma, there is no financial incentive to actually try to heal you because a patient cured is a customer lost! The bitter truth is that when you go to a Western doctor you are seen as a potential prospect for pharmaceutical sales. You end up suffering — not only financially but also physically. Western Medicine relies on Big Pharma's petroleum drugs (derived from fossil fuel) which the body can never ultimately assimilate, and that's why people who use them experience nasty side effects. As long as money rules the game, cures will be avoided. Why find a cure when you can make big bucks off medicine that doesn't make patients well, but keeps them chemically dependent? We have to open our eyes and ask the Holy Spirit to lead us to other solutions. God created a world full of healing agents. Chemical dependency from a corrupted system is far below our destiny.

WHO IS PROTECTING THE AMERICAN PUBLIC?

When I was young, I always wished I had a big brother to look out for me; you know, someone older, wiser, tougher, who would have my back. If I got bullied at school or felt sad, my big brother could be there to stand up for me, fight in my defense, and cheer me up, telling me things were going to get better. Sometimes, I even feel that as an adult! Who is looking out for me? Who has my back? The more

I glimpse the inside-scoop on American government institutions, the less confident I feel that someone really has my best interest in mind. But then I put on my spiritual glasses again, and I realize, I don't just have a good big brother; I have one who is the Savior of the whole world watching over me! Seriously, what would we do without Jesus?

THE FDA

But who is looking out for Americans? America does have a federal agency appointed to protect the health of Americans, but it's more like an overtasked and ill-equipped big brother. The FDA (Food and Drug Administration) is a federal agency of the United States Department of Health and Human Services that is supposed to investigate and regulate the safety of what is being released on the market. It began as the "Bureau of Chemistry." An agency formed to investigate the effects of adulterating food and drugs, which later became the FDA in 1913. Remember, this was the same year the Rockefeller Foundation was launched.

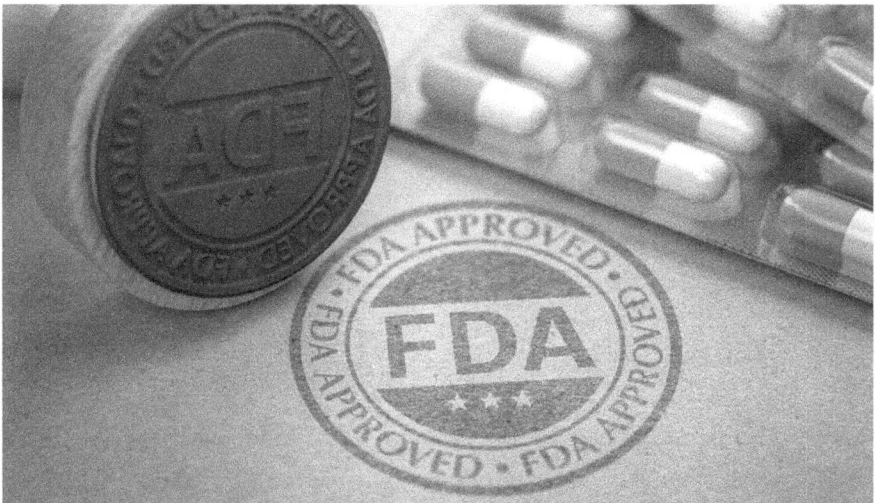

The FDA investigated the effects of the adulteration of food and drugs with the intention of protection. But just as the AMA received tremendous pressure from the heavy hand of Rockefeller back then, the FDA receives tremendous pressure from Big Pharma to approve whatever they want to sell now — even if it's harmful. In 2006, the Union of Concerned Scientists (UCS) took a survey, and of the almost 1000 FDA scientists who responded to the survey, nearly one-fifth (18.4 percent) said that they "have been asked, for non-scientific reasons, to inappropriately exclude or alter technical information or their conclusions in a FDA scientific document."[174] What happened to the honest, transparent, scientifically-based organization created to look out for the health of the public? Sadly, even its core structure has become twisted, lacking quality control and accountability. Now, over a century since its establishment, the FDA gets 75 percent of their budget from drug companies[175] so, how likely are they to discourage the use of the drugs those companies are producing? In reality, its current job seems to be to approve and sanction products from the chemical industry and legally shield the chemical industry from repercussions when the American people discover the drugs aren't safe. In 1995, the FDA approved the sale of a high strength addictive narcotic pill, OxyContin, as "safer and more effective" than other painkillers as per the manufacturer, Purdue Pharma.[176] But the FDA didn't require clinical trials, and tens of thousands were killed through overdosing. When rebuked, the FDA didn't pull it from the shelves, but offered poorly planned training events for physicians, with little effort and no guarantee that there would be safer usage moving forward.

The chair of the FDA's opioid advisory committee, Dr. Raeford Brown, later exposed the corruption that happened behind closed doors. He accused the FDA of putting the interests of narcotics manufacturers ahead of public health, and even allowing manufacturers to pay to attend advisory meetings in order to influence the criteria for approving the prescription. Brown is quoted as saying, "The lack of insight that continues to be exhibited by the agency is in many ways a willful blindness that borders on the criminal."[177] Even the FDA's operating procedures are poorly formulated as the final decision makers are not even legally required to follow the decisions of its advisory committees. Brown claims the committees are just a cover. When asked why the FDA would overrule the decision of an advisory committee, Dr. Bob Rappaport, head of the agency's opioid approval division, insisted that there be "a level playing field for business"![178]

David Graham, who works in the FDA's Office of Drug Safety, accuses the FDA of being partially responsible for the death of 60,000 patients who were taking Vioxx, a drug the FDA approved.[179] The other responsible party, a major pharmaceutical producer called Merck, introduced Vioxx as a "safer" alternative to pain killers for those with osteoarthritis. Despite early warning signs that there was significant cardiovascular risk, Merck obscured the reports to the FDA, showing tests that minimized cardiovascular assessment,[180] Billions of dollars were on the line, and the FDA was also gripped by corporate influence. [181] Thirty thousand lawsuits knocked on Merck's door, when the true lack of safety of this drug came to light.[182]

Donald W Light from Harvard University's Center for Ethics reports the following stats:[183]

- Newly released prescription drugs have a 1 in 5 chance of causing serious reactions even after they have been approved.

- Even properly prescribed drugs (aside from misprescribing, overdosing, or self-prescribing) cause about 1.9 million hospitalizations a year.

- 840,000 hospitalized patients are given drugs that cause serious adverse reactions.

- About 128,000 people die annually from drugs prescribed to them.

- Prescription drugs rank 4th (along with strokes) as a leading cause of death.

Why is all of this happening? For the love of money. The Bible warns us, *"For the love of money is a root of all kinds of evil" 1 Tim. 6:10 NIV. And unfortunately, these roots keep spreading so that the corrupt tree grows bigger and bigger. The Bible confirms it: "Evildoers and impostors will go from bad to worse, deceiving and being deceived" 2 Tim. 3:13 NIV.*

We see this progression in the FDA. From releasing unsafe drugs to make a profit, to even creating diseases in order to sell vaccines. In April 2009, the H1N1 Swine Flu pandemic was announced by the World Health Organization (WHO) saying, "As many as 2 billion people could become infected over the next two years — nearly one-third of the world population.[184] The WHO contemplated 4.9 billion vaccine doses, and national governments ordered millions of doses of the swine flu vaccine from Big Pharma, which evidently constituted a multi-billion corporate bonanza for the pharmaceutical companies. After the initial scare, the reality of media disinformation, political lies and fabrications began to surface. The reality was, there were only 148 laboratory confirmed cases worldwide of the swine influenza, including 8 deaths. Nowhere near a pandemic![185] Epidemiologist Wolfgang Wodarg, declared that the H1N1 "false pandemic" was "one of the greatest medicine scandals of the century."[186]

PHARMAKEIA

What is going on in this world? We live in this very progressive country with supposedly amazing education, freedom to be creative, and wealth to be obtained from honest work. We live in the land of opportunity! We could have an amazing country! Every nation looks to America as a global example, as a beacon of light. But it's been taken captive by greed and power. What has become of our great nation?

Maybe the primary question is: what is going on in the spiritual world? The reason I ask is because whatever we see with our natural eyes, it happens in the spiritual realm first. There is a spiritual realm beyond what we see, but it affects everything around us. Let's begin to look at these pharmaceuticals with eyes of the Spirit to discern who and what is really crafting this agenda.

"The thief comes only to steal, kill, and destroy..." John 10:10a NIV.

Did you know that the biblical word for sorcery or witchcraft is "Pharmakeia" in Greek? It translates as a form of idolatry through the use of administering drugs, sorcery, or witchcraft. The related word, "pharmakeus" means magic, one who prepared a spell-given potion, a druggist, or a poisoner. I fear that half of all Americans today are unwittingly participating in pharmakeia, by turning to the pharmacy, taking their 'poison' and putting their faith and trust in magic pills! The pharmaceutical industry is a modern day cauldron of pharmakeia.

The Bible says, "Thus says the Lord,
"Stand by the roads and look; ask for the ancient paths,
Where the good way is; then walk in it,
And you will find rest for your souls" Jeremiah 6:16 ESV.

What are the "ancient paths" of medicine? Hippocrates is known as the "Father of Medicine." Born on the Greek island of Kos around the year 406 BC, he based his medical practice on the observation of the body as a whole. He believed that health was a harmonious balance between body parts, and disease resulted from disharmony and imbalance in the body. Therefore, you could not just treat the area showing symptoms, but the whole body must be treated. In Hippocratic medicine, diet, sleep, work, and exercise were all seen as important factors in reversing illness.[187] Diseases were allowed to run their natural course alongside treatment with specific herbal medicines. Surgery was seen as a last resort.

Can you imagine if our medical care system followed this example? We would have saved ourselves much grief. Today, God's natural remedies have been devalued in exchange for man-made chemical blends that alter our body's chemistry in harmful ways. "Medicine" is defined in Oxford Learner's Dictionary as "a substance that you take in order to cure an illness,"[188] but pharmaceuticals, though we consider them medicine, often don't prevent or cure the disease itself; they simply cover up the symptoms. This is a form of deception. We take medicine thinking these pills promote good health, but they just dull our awareness of the painful need for deeper healing! Think about it: if you take a Tylenol or Advil for pain relief, does it heal your problem? No, it just buys you time to feel like you're healed, when really, it's adding another layer of confusion. Before you know it, you develop a chemical dependence on pills to function through pain. It doesn't help you understand the root of your pain or resolve the underlying issue. In fact, it may even cause more problems. Why take a laxative that will mess with your gut health, when a magnesium supplement will do the same thing and bring you additional benefits?[189]

Pharmaceuticals really do steal, kill and destroy. Your gut microbiome is very delicate, and very important to your overall health as it protects your immune system. When you take antibiotics excessively, all the bacteria in your gut (both good and bad), are wiped out. This increases your risk of disease. That's why they are called "anti"-biotics. Anti means against. Biotics are living organisms in an ecosystem. So at the end of the day, you are taking a drug that's actually weakening your body's defense system. How many doctors do you know who advise you to take probiotics (pro-life) after the antibiotics in order to restore your gut bacteria? Do you see the enemy's agenda here? The more pills, the more disease, then more pills, then more dependency and then chemical addiction. Pharmakeia often functions by providing a smokescreen, an environment like 'smoke and mirrors' that causes mental confusion and the inability to discern truth, making it difficult or even impossible to recognize. Lord, please give us eyes to see!

PILLS OR NO PILLS?

Ask yourself: what are your habits? Would you rather keep popping pills on autopilot, or seeking God to get to the root of your issue so you can actually be healed? Did you know that tylenol is one of the most dangerous drugs for liver damage?[190] Why not pursue a natural alternative? Did you know that ginger has proven to be superior to Advil or Tylenol for joint inflammation and helps with pain relief?[191] If you are not a fan of ginger, you can take it in capsule form, or try magnesium. Magnesium helps curb migraine headaches and muscle and nerve pain, including fibromyalgia. Don't let the routine of drug-taking cloud your mind. Think about what will actually bring healing and restoration to your body and pursue that first. Search out the natural solutions. So much information is available to us online. It's a good idea to see a natural medicine or holistic doctor for advice. If you've always taken aspirin, look for another path. Believe it or not, the bark from willow trees has been used for centuries as a natural remedy that works in a similar way to aspirin.[192] God has thought of everything! Be determined to renew your mind, obtain the mind of Christ, and break your chemical dependency. You may have to work with a doctor to wean yourself off of the pharmaceuticals. But be warned, a Western doctor will likely try to put fear in you because they have been conditioned to believe that chemical medications are the only solution. They may also be getting a kick back! So, we have to think! You will almost never leave a doctor's office without a prescription. They have to give you something. But, you have the choice and the wisdom to discern whether or not that is the best course of action for you. Sometimes, we need to make a real change in our lifestyle in order to attain the health we are searching for. Pharmaceuticals are often a crutch to make a way for us to do what we have always done. Yes, it takes time for your body to be re-programmed, and none of us feel we have the time. We just want it fixed, now! But, is what we are prioritizing more important than our body's physical ability to function?

Restoration takes effort and time. For me, I had to make the time to figure it out. I had to take time to get my gut back into alignment so my body didn't react to everything I ate as an allergen. I had to restore nutrition and take probiotics and rebuild from the inside out. Restoring your health is worth the sacrifice. Once you figure it out, you'll never go back to taking drugs for a temporary fix. Anybody can do it. It's just about changing your lifestyle.

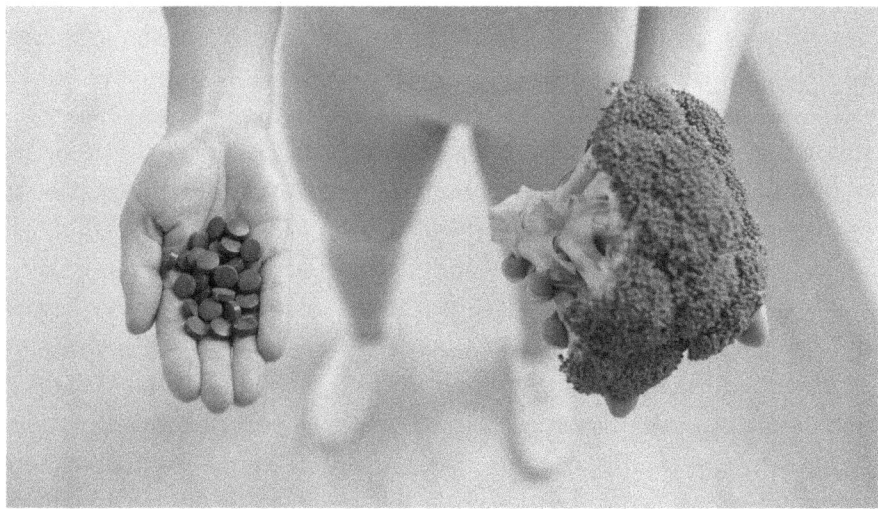

It really is possible to live more naturally. Personally, I don't take any medicine. I don't take any kind of drugs. If I have a headache, I take Arnica (a homeopathic medicine). If another need comes up, I go to a nearby apothecary and ask for a natural solution. I believe God has created all that we need to manage our health, on earth, from the earth. But first, we have to wake up to see the system that opposes our dependence on God. The more you choose to submit yourself under the deceptive influence of pharmaceutical drugs, the more your emotions and thoughts are going to go all over the place. Up one day and down the next. That pill can create anger. It can release emotions that make you depressed or suicidal. It can destroy your brain cells. It can cause hallucination, which adds another layer of deception and paranoia. When under the drug's influence, you are subject to all of the ways it affects your body's functions, including your metabolic processes, your hormones, and your stamina.

How many people in America are feeling depressed, or tired all the time just as a side effect of their daily pills? Satan will use anything he can to cloud your mind and transfer your dependency to his vices instead of on the Lord. It's easier to take a pill than to seek the Holy Spirit's guidance, but to choose the influence of the pill over the leadership of the Holy Spirit is pure foolishness, and our bodies will bear the consequences. We must not follow the ways of the world into a medicated existence. We are people of the Spirit of the Living God! We must follow Him and allow our minds, emotions and bodies to be transformed. Remember God designed people in His image to possess and enjoy a spirit-filled life!

"Those who live as their human nature tells them to, have their minds controlled by what human nature wants. Those who live as the Spirit tells them to, have their minds controlled by what the Spirit wants. To be controlled by human nature results in death; to be controlled by the Spirit results in life and peace. And so people become enemies of God when they are controlled by their human nature; for they do not obey God's law, and in fact they cannot obey it. Those who obey their human nature cannot please God" Romans 8:5-8 GNT.

EARTHLY VS. HEAVENLY WISDOM

The Prince of the Air rules this world, and when we rely on worldly wisdom to heal us, we are missing out on the heavenly wisdom and the heavenly healing that Jesus paid for on the cross. We have to reactivate our dependence on God. We need to come to the end of ourselves and admit that we need God. He has the best help for us. God desires to remove chaos and restore His order. He designed you with a lively body, an ability to maintain a clear mind, with balanced emotions and energy. Why trade that in for a chemical addiction? That muscle relaxant, that pain killer, that high cholesterol medicine, none of them have any comparison to the healing power of Jesus Christ. Don't let drug usage dull your sensitivity to the work the Lord wants to do in your life.

So what should you do? If you realize you have opened a door to pharmakeia, or find yourself defaulting to drugs when dependency should be on the Holy Spirit, stop and repent. Come back to the feet of your Savior, Jesus. Allow yourself to feel the urgency of developing a deeper relationship with Him. Pursue His insight into your healing. Choose to bow your knees to His ways.

Now, don't misunderstand me — I'm not suggesting you stop all your current medications immediately. Choose to work with a doctor who will respect your values to help you to transition. If a medical issue arises, ask God if you should take medication, or go for medical treatment. He will lead you. More and more cancer patients are refusing chemotherapy, and opting for natural strategies like green juice, a very restrictive but healthy diet and a range of other alternative treatments.[193] And guess what, their bodies are recovering! But God uses different strategies for different people. If you're depressed, God may say to one person "Start taking this specific herb," and to another, "Start exercising everyday" and to another He might say, "continue taking your antidepressants for one month while you adjust your diet to rebalance your body." The answer is not the same for every situation. My plea is just that you open your eyes and ears to the Lord's wisdom for your health, and don't be blind to the enemy's strategy working through pharmakeia. Ask God what He is saying about your situation, He is listening. He has all the answers and He cares for you.

ENDNOTES

156   Klein, Christopher. "10 Things You May Not Know About John D. Rockefeller." History.com. A&E Television Networks, September 1, 2018. https://www.history.com/news/10-things-you-may-not-know-about-john-d-rockefeller.

157   "John D. Rockefeller." Encyclopædia Britannica, July 4, 2020. https://www.britannica.com/biography/John-D-Rockefeller.

158   Eschner, Kat. "John D. Rockefeller Was the Richest Person To Ever Live. Period." Smithsonian.com, January 10, 2017. https://www.smithsonianmag.com/smart-news/john-d-rockefeller-richest-person-ever-live-period-180961705/.

159   Bickers, David R., and Attallah Kappas. "Human Skin Aryl Hydrocarbon Hydroxylase." Journal of Clinical Investigation 62, no. 5 (November 1, 1978): 1061–68. https://doi.org/10.1172/jci109211.

160   Montague, Tigger. "Down the Rabbit Hole: The Rise of Western Medicine." BioStar US, September 24, 2016. https://blog.biostarus.com/rise-western-medicine/.

161   "Rockefeller Gifts Total $530,853,632." The New York Times. The New York Times on the web, May 24, 1937. http://www.nytimes.com/books/98/05/17/specials/rockefeller-gifts.html.

162   Ibid.

163   Montague, Tigger. "Down the Rabbit Hole: The Rise of Western Medicine." BioStar US, September 24, 2016. https://blog.biostarus.com/rise-western-medicine/.

164   "Rockefeller Gifts Total $530,853,632." The New York Times. The New York Times on the web, May 24, 1937. http://www.nytimes.com/books/98/05/17/specials/rockefeller-gifts.html.

165   Kuchler, Hannah. "Why Prescription Drugs Cost so Much More in America." Financial Times, September 18, 2019. https://www.ft.com/content/e92dbf94-d9a2-11e9-8f9b-77216ebe1f17.

166   Freeman, Makia. "Western Medicine Is Rockefeller Medicine – All The Way." The Freedom Articles, October 17, 2014. https://thefreedomarticles.com/western-medicine-rockefeller-medicine/.

167   Engelberg, Joseph, Christopher A. Parsons, and Nathan Tefft. "Financial Conflicts of Interest in Medicine." Rady School of Management, January 2014. https://rady.ucsd.edu/faculty/directory/engelberg/pub/portfolios/DOCTORS.pdf.

168   Meller, Abbey, and Hauwa Ahmed. "How Big Pharma Reaps Profits While Hurting Everyday Americans." Center for American Progress, August 30, 2019. https://www.americanprogress.org/issues/democracy/reports/2019/08/30/473911/big-pharma-reaps-profits-hurting-everyday-americans/.

169   "How Big Pharma Plays Games with Drug Patents and How to Combat It." USA Today. Gannett Satellite Information Network, July 18, 2019. https://www.usatoday.com/story/opinion/2019/07/18/big-pharma-plays-games-drug-patents-you-pay-editorials-debates/1769746001/.

170   Robin Feldman, "May Your Drug Price Be Evergreen," Journal of Law and the Biosciences 5, no. 3 (December 2018): pp. 590-647, https://doi.org/10.1093/jlb/lsy022.

171   "Meller, Abbey, and Hauwa Ahmed. "How Big Pharma Reaps Profits While Hurting Everyday Americans." Center for American Progress, August 30, 2019. https://www.americanprogress.org/issues/democracy/reports/2019/08/30/473911/big-pharma-reaps-profits-hurting-everyday-americans/.

172   Campbell, Kevin. "Why Are Prescription Drug Prices Rising?" U.S. News & World Report, February 6, 2019. https://health.usnews.com/health-care/for-better/articles/2019-02-06/why-are-prescription-drug-prices-rising.

173   Preidt, Robert. "Americans Taking More Prescription Drugs Than Ever." WebMD, August 3, 2017. https://www.webmd.com/drug-medication/news/20170803/americans-taking-more-prescription-drugs-than-ever-survey.

174   "Survey: FDA Scientists (2006)." Union of Concerned Scientists, July 11, 2008. https://www.ucsusa.org/resources/survey-fda-scientists.

175   LaMattina, John. "The Biopharmaceutical Industry Provides 75% Of The FDA's Drug Review Budget. Is This A Problem?" Forbes. Forbes Magazine, June 28, 2018. https://www.forbes.com/sites/johnlamattina/2018/06/28/the-biopharmaceutical-industry-provides-75-of-the-fdas-drug-review-budget-is-this-a-problem/.

176   Goodnough, Abby, and Margot Sanger-katz. "As Tens of Thousands Died, F.D.A. Failed to Police Opioids." The New York Times, December 31, 2019. https://www.nytimes.com/2019/12/30/health/FDA-opioids.html.

177   McGreal, Chris. "FDA's Opioids Adviser Accuses Agency of Having 'Direct' Link to Crisis." The Guardian. Guardian News and Media, January 24, 2019. https://www.theguardian.com/us-news/2019/jan/24/fda-opioids-big-pharma-prescriptions.

178   Ibid.

179   Herper, Matthew. "David Graham On The Vioxx Verdict." Forbes. Forbes Magazine, August 19, 2005. https://www.forbes.com/2005/08/19/merck-vioxx-graham_cx_mh_0819graham.html.

180   Krumholz, Harlan M, Joseph S Ross, Amos H Presler, and David S Egilman. "What Have We Learnt from Vioxx?" BMJ (Clinical research ed.). BMJ Publishing Group Ltd., January 20, 2007. https://www.ncbi.nlm.nih.gov/pmc/articles/PMC1779871/.

181   Herper, Matthew. "David Graham On The Vioxx Verdict." Forbes. Forbes Magazine, August 19, 2005. https://www.forbes.com/2005/08/19/merck-vioxx-graham_cx_mh_0819graham.html.

182   Krumholz, Harlan M, Joseph S Ross, Amos H Presler, and David S Egilman. "What Have We Learnt from Vioxx?" BMJ (Clinical research ed.). BMJ Publishing Group Ltd., January 20, 2007. https://www.ncbi.nlm.nih.gov/pmc/articles/PMC1779871/.

183   Light, Donald W. "New Prescription Drugs: A Major Health Risk With Few Offsetting Advantages." Edmond J. Safra Center for Ethics. Harvard University, June 27, 2014. https://ethics.harvard.edu/blog/new-prescription-drugs-major-health-risk-few-offsetting-advantages.

184   Chossudovsky, Michel. "Remember the 'Fake' 2009 H1N1 Swine Flu Pandemic: Manipulating the Data to Justify a Worldwide Public Health Emergency." Global Research, July 8, 2020. https://www.globalresearch.ca/the-h1n1-swine-flu-pandemic-manipulating-the-data-to-justify-a-worldwide-public-health-emergency/14901.

185   Chossudovsky, Michel. "April 2009, The H1N1 Pandemic: Political Lies and Media Disinformation Regarding the Swine Flu Outbreak." Global Research, April 17, 2016. https://www.globalresearch.ca/political-lies-and-media-disinformation-regarding-the-swine-flu-pandemic/13433.

186   Chossudovsky, Michel. "Remember the 'Fake' 2009 H1N1 Swine Flu Pandemic: Manipulating the Data to Justify a Worldwide Public Health Emergency." Global Research, July 8, 2020. https://www.globalresearch.ca/the-h1n1-swine-flu-pandemic-manipulating-the-data-to-justify-a-worldwide-public-health-emergency/14901.

187   "Hippocrates: Science Museum Group Collection." Hippocrates | Science Museum Group. Accessed May 5, 2020. https://collection.sciencemuseumgroup.org.uk/people/cp37445/hippocrates.

188   "Medicine." Oxford Advanced Learner's Dictionary. Accessed May 5, 2020. https://www.oxfordlearnersdictionaries.com/definition/english/medicine.

189   O'Neill, Terri. "Magnesium for Constipation." Ann Arbor: University of Michigan, March 2017. http://www.med.umich.edu/1libr/MBCP/Magnesium.pdf.

190   Orrange, Sharon. "The 10 Worst Medications for Your Liver - GoodRx." The GoodRx Prescription Savings Blog, February 15, 2019. https://www.goodrx.com/blog/the-ten-worst-medications-for-your-liver/.

191   Ginger Better than Drugs for Pain?" HowStuffWorks, January 3, 2012. https://health.howstuffworks.com/wellness/natural-medicine/herbal-remedies/ginger-better-than-drugs-for-pain.htm.

192   Goldman, Rena. "Willow Bark: Nature's Aspirin." Healthline, February 14, 2017. https://www.healthline.com/health/willow-bark-natures-aspirin.

193   Quinn, Jessie. "Fighting Cancer Without Chemotherapy: 8 Alternatives to Chemo and Radiation." Showbiz Cheat Sheet, August 16, 2018. https://www.cheatsheet.com/health-fitness/fighting-cancer-without-chemotherapy-alternatives-to-chemo-and-radiation.html/.

CHAPTER 13
WHAT'S REALLY KILLING US?

A CLOSER LOOK AT CHOLESTEROL

Let's consider the biggest killer in America: Heart disease. What is the cause of heart disease? Was "high cholesterol" the first thing that came to your mind? If so, you may be the victim of, at best, misguided information, and more likely, deception in order to line someone else's pockets.

In his book, The *Cholesterol Myth,* Clinical Nutritionist Dr. Jack Tips says, it was late 1980 when cholesterol began getting blamed for every heart related illness because it appeared to be present in every heart patient. But the logic doesn't stand up. He says it's equivalent to saying, "Every time there's a fire, there are firemen around, so firemen must have caused the fire."[194] Every time there is heart disease there is cholesterol around, so we blame it! But, what if some of this cholesterol was actually attempting to naturally rectify the real problem? The truth is, cholesterol is produced for the benefit of the body. It supports the tissues, nerves, and immune system, and we couldn't live without it. Consider this list of benefits:[195]

- Cholesterol plays a vital structural role in the brain

- The liver makes cholesterol out of lipids (fatty acids) for the body's needs

- Conduction of nerve impulses is dependent on cholesterol

- Female and male hormones are made from cholesterol

- Cholesterol serves anti-inflammatory processes in the body

- Life-saving immunoglobulins are made from cholesterol

- Vitamin D in the body originates as cholesterol

- Bile, necessary for fat digestion, is made from cholesterol

So, if cholesterol is good for our body, why has it been framed as a bad thing? To get the answer, once again, we need to follow the money. Statins are the biggest selling class of pharmaceutical compounds of all time. Used to lower cholesterol for those concerned about a heart attack or stroke, statins have annual sales in excess of $22 billion, and estimated to reach 1 trillion USD in 2020.[196] What would you do to protect that kind of income? High cholesterol is big business! The media has promoted this 'fear cholesterol' messaging benefitting many players: the drug industry with their statins, the food industry selling fat free, and low fat products, and the medical industry offering cholesterol screening treatments. And what is the public left with? Increased health problems, confusion, and a pile of medical side effects that make the situation worse! According to Mayo Clinic, the side effects of statin drugs include muscle pain, weakness, liver damage, digestive problems, rashes and flushing, increased blood sugar, sexual dysfunction and neurological side effects such as memory loss or confusion.[197] Why are these statins the only option? Have you ever wondered, with over 35 million people in the US taking these medications, why heart disease never seems to decline?[198] Is cholesterol really the problem?

Dr. Dwight Lundell, a former heart surgeon, spent 25 years prescribing cholesterol-lowering drugs and recommending low-fat foods as per his medical training. After observing countless arteries, he began to change his opinion about what the best treatment actually was, and he gained insight into the true cause of heart disease.

He says "that every artery that has been damaged by chronic inflammation caused by the wrong diet looks the same: the artery's wall appears to have been scraped repetitively. To demonstrate how this actually happens, imagine using an aluminium sponge rubbing over your delicate skin. With continuous rubbing, your skin will eventually show signs of bruising. Now think of doing this to your skin every waking moment of your entire life. If this is done non-stop, your skin will become inflamed and wounded. With each repetition of the action, the status of your skin only gets worse. That is what happens when inflammation happens inside your body. And this is brought about by the wrong food that we eat over and over again that causes the body to react with inflammation."[199] Is the picture getting clearer? According to Dr. Lundell, the true cause of heart disease may not be cholesterol afterall, but the chronic inflammation that traps the cholesterol in the blood vessel walls, which then causes heart disease. When Dr. Lundell realized the error of his ways, he stopped conducting heart surgeries and dedicated his career to heart disease prevention. He concludes that recommending cholesterol-lowering drugs and low-fat diets is "no longer morally defensible."[200]

RETURNING TO GOD'S HEALTH PLAN

If we genuinely want to get healthy, then we must encourage our bodies to work the way they were designed to work. Inflammation is not necessarily our enemy. When our bodies are functioning healthily, the way God intended them to, inflammation will actually protect us by acting as a natural defense mechanism when bacteria or viruses need to be blocked out; and cholesterol will be produced to repair the damage. But when we sabotage our body with food it's not intended to digest, spiking our blood sugar, and overdosing on omega-6 oils, the body enters panic mode and inflammation goes into overdrive, the walls of our blood vessels harden trapping the cholesterol in.

Our diets are the real culprit. We are destroying ourselves from the outside in! We are becoming like the unbelievers who the Apostle Paul said are *"ruled by their bellies" (Phil. 3:19)*, instead of being led by the Holy Spirit's wisdom. We are not meant to make choices based on the cravings of our taste buds, or the common culture of our day. God has given us heavenly wisdom, that will free us from all bondage, including food addictions and all unhealthy habits.

Those who suffer from high cholesterol are often dependent on medications. Most people will default to taking LIPITOR or another statin drug, which alters the inflammatory cycle, so the cholesterol can be released; but this doesn't get our bodies any closer to functioning well! Statin drugs also block the inflammation that is supposed to protect us from viruses and bacteria - it is a natural bodily process that we still need to function. It gets worse: while taking these drugs, people keep eating the same bad foods, so more and more statins are prescribed, and this eventually causes the liver to stop working, followed by the weakening of our muscles and our memory. There's a better solution! Return to God's way of taking care of your body! Return to natural, living foods; turn away from processed foods and hydrogenated oils.

Dr. Lundell says the answer is clear: **"To heal the body from chronic inflammation, there is no other way but to return to the old ways of feeding our bodies** — back to natural and healthier produce, like fruits and vegetables and avoiding, at all costs, foods that are processed and are packed with sugars, simple carbohydrates, and omega-6 oils."[201]

Inflammation can be averted by diet change. There's no room for excuses. We hold the keys to our own health, and the health of our nation.

A CLOSER LOOK AT CANCER

It's a similar story in the fight against cancer. According to the Centers for Disease Control & Prevention (CDC), cancer is the 2nd leading killer in the United States.[202] Why is this? Is it that there are just more cancer cells in the world? Is it that we are creating environments for them to flourish? Are the treatments themselves simply ineffective? Or are the big-players keeping the business of illness running so they profit off a sustainable industry?

What we are told about cancer:

- It is passed down genetically

- Cancer drugs are expensive because of all the research needed to create them

- The only way to treat it is with chemotherapy and radiation

- You can't do much to prevent it

What is actually true about cancer:

- Genetic transfer? News flash! You cannot inherit cancer. During conception you receive genes from both your parents. If a parent has a faulty gene, you may receive that gene but that doesn't mean you get cancer. It just means you have a faulty gene that, if your body doesn't handle it, may increase your risk of getting cancer.[203] The American Cancer society confirms: "Most cancers are not clearly linked to the genes we inherit from our parents. Gene changes that start in a single cell over the course of a person's life cause most cancers."[204] The truth is, we all have faulty cells at all times. The good news is that God gave our bodies a very orderly system of discarding broken cells and reproducing new cells to replace them. Cancer only develops when this orderly process breaks down. It happens when abnormal, old, or damaged cells survive, that should have died, and new cells form and divide where they are not needed. These extra cells can divide without stopping, forming masses of solid tissue called tumors. Many cancers form within these solid tumors. But a healthy immune system finds these mutated cells and gets rid of them! When we keep our immune system strong, by God's amazing design, these bad cells will be eliminated!

- High drug prices, due to research? Newsflash! Profits might have more to do with it. A study published in the Journal of the American Medical Association (2017) shows it's a lot cheaper to develop cancer drugs than you think.[205] According to the data, the average cost of developing a cancer drug is about $720 million. The average annual revenue is about $2.7 billion. Dr. Brian Druker, director of the Knight Cancer Institute asks "If you are making $3 billion a year on Gleevec (a cancer drug), could you get by with $2 billion? When do you cross the line from essential profits to profiteering? "[206]

- Can't prevent cancer? Newsflash! You have the power to protect your own body! What we eat and drink is our body's fuel. It provides us the nutrients, minerals, enzymes, and energy to sustain health. Our immune system will work if we live in such a way that supports its optimal performance. Obesity and poor nutrition has been shown to increase the odds of developing cancer.[207]

What does this tell you? Your choices matter! Leafy greens, cruciferous vegetables, berries, whole grains and even green and black tea have all been shown to provide protection against various types of cancer. Harsh radiation is not the only way to kill cancer cells. Plants, like medicinal mushrooms for instance, boost the activity of your natural-killer cells.[208] When these cells are working full force, cancer doesn't stand a chance! God has given us what we need. Maintaining positive mental and emotional well-being along with obtaining the appropriate combination of vitamins and minerals along with a well-balanced diet can provide solid protection. A Cancer Foundation in Cameroon recommends the following for alternative treatments:[209]

- The Gerson Therapy / Juicing

- The Bud Wig Protocol

- Proteolytic enzyme therapy

- Vitamin-C chelation

- Frankincense essential oil therapy / Probiotic foods and supplements

- Sunshine & vitamin D3

- Turmeric & curcumin

- Oxygen therapy and hyperbaric chambers

- Prayer and building peace

The mainstream media and pharmaceutical industry promote the availability of cancer treatments, such as chemotherapy, in a positive light. But the hidden truth is that chemotherapy is often the cause of death itself. In Milton Keynes, just outside of London, 50 percent of their patient's deaths were assessed to be due to the cancer drugs themselves.[210] Also, in 2018 there were comprehensive clinical trials to study chemo on children; In 170 clinical trials, among 4,604 children who received chemo, there were 4,675 grade 3 and 4 adverse events. This means, on average, more than one severe, medically significant and potentially life-threatening incident occurred per child from the chemo itself! Among the 3,569 children who had solid tumors (as opposed to leukemia) the objective response rate (ORR) to the chemotherapy treatment, was only 3.17 percent. Three out of a hundred experienced some shrinkage of their tumor but almost all of them suffered severe side effects, from which 2.09 percent of them died.[211]

Even though natural methods have been shown to help cancer patients, there is evidence that some of these natural cures are being eliminated as part of unwanted competition. Laetrile, also known as amygdalin, a substance found in the pits of apricots was banned by the FDA during the early 1970s despite its efficacy. Dr. Ralph Moss, who worked with Memorial Sloan Kettering Cancer Center in New York, later spoke up about the conspiracy he witnessed. In Moss's own words:

> "Shortly after I went to work there I went to visit an elderly Japanese scientist, Kanematsu Sugiura, who astonished me when he told me he was working on Laetrile (B17), at the time it was the most controversial thing in cancer ... reputed to be a cure for cancer. We were finding this [Laetrile's efficacy] and yet we in public affairs were told to issue statements to the exact opposite of what we were finding scientifically, and as the years went by I got more wrapped up in this thing and 3 years later I said all this in my own press conference, and was fired the next day, 'for failing to carry out his most basic job responsibility' – ie to lie to the public about what goes on in cancer research. Dr Sugiura, never renounced the results of his own studies [proving laetrile halted cancer], despite the fact they put enormous pressure on him to do so. When I was at MSK, a lot of very weird things started to happen to me, there was this cognitive distance between what I was told, and was

writing about treatment, especially chemotherapy, and what I was seeing with my own eyes."[212]

Thankfully, the studies on apricot seeds have continued, revealing that their natural ingredients can weaken cancer cells' typical resistance to treatment, and can even kill the malignant cell directly.[213] The pharmaceutical industry still scoffs at their use as taking too many can be problematic, but researchers are seeing positive results.[214]

NUTRITIONAL NEGLIGENCE

Sadly, the effects of Rockefeller's insistence against natural cures has crippled our nation's understanding of wellness. Research conducted in 2015 on "the State of Nutrition Education in US Medical Schools," found that though the basic requirement is only 25 hours of nutrition education (over a four year degree), 71 percent of schools did not meet the minimum. In fact, 36 percent provided less than half that much![215] Even within that small amount, the majority of this educational content relates to biochemistry, not diets or practical food-related decision making.[216] Lifestyle changes like nutritious eating and exercise have the power to prevent life-threatening illnesses, but many doctors remain ill-equipped to give this life-saving advice.

> I heard the story of someone's father who was diagnosed with stage 4 colon cancer. During the six weeks between his colon resection and the start of heavy chemo and radiation, he went on a modified Gerson diet which is an organic, plant-based diet, that includes detoxification, and supplements. The change in his appearance, energy and overall well-being was amazing! He began to gain weight and look years younger. X-rays even showed shrinkage of the masses in his liver. The oncologists and radiologists explained this away as some sort of artifact or illusion. Being nutritionally ignorant, the oncologists started pushing him to go off the diet and eat carbs and sugars to bulk up for chemo. So, he followed their advice, went off the protective nutrition, and began to eat unhealthy food in order to gain weight for chemo. It was only a week or two into the chemo that he could

no longer eat or drink anything. It was a quick slide downhill, and within two months, he was gone. His son overheard the nurses whispering about the poor advice that was given to him about nutrition.

A lesson remains for all of us: without a healthy diet full of life-giving nutrients, our bodies will begin to die. Diet is arguably the single most important preventative measure for healthy aging. Eating nutritiously decreases the chances of developing various diseases, it boosts your immune system, helps you maintain a healthy weight, and increases your energy levels. Hippocrates said: "Let food be thy medicine;" it's so true.

This is why God said, *"I have given you every seed-bearing plant throughout the earth and all the fruit trees for your food" Gen. 1:29 NLT.* God knows how to guide you into homeostasis, living a balanced life, with proper nutrition. With His guidance, you can design your own nutrition-based eating plan. Think about what you're putting into your mouth and why. You'll learn the difference between eating something just to stimulate your taste buds, and eating food that actually satisfies your cells. When you start eating food that fuels you, you'll notice you won't need to eat huge portions. Your body will feel satisfied with less, because your cells have what they need. I remember when I used to eat McDonald's, I'd be hungry thirty minutes later. Now that I choose healthy foods, I'm satisfied and I'm not sleepy after I eat. We were designed for a nutritious diet. If you're not sure where to start, consult a naturopathic doctor who can help get you on the right track and educate you in developing a nutrition-based lifestyle. Simply changing this one part of your life, can dramatically heal your body, and prevent much harm.

ENDNOTES

194   Tips, Jack. The Cholesterol Myth: A Deception of Mammoth Proportion. Wellnesswiz. Austin, TX: Apple-A-Day Press, 2012. https://wellnesswiz.com/wp-content/uploads/2018/11/OBH-Cholesterol-Myth-v1.pdf, 2.

195   Ibid, 3.

196   Demasi , Maryanne. "Statin Wars: Secrecy and the World's Most Lucrative Drugs." Michael West Media, January 22, 2018. https://www.michaelwest.com.au/statin-wars-secrecy-and-the-worlds-most-lucrative-drugs/.

197   "Statin Side Effects: Weigh the Benefits and Risks." Mayo Clinic. Mayo Foundation for Medical Education and Research, January 14, 2020. https://www.mayoclinic.org/diseases-conditions/high-blood-cholesterol/in-depth/statin-side-effects/art-20046013.

198   Fookes, C. "Statins for High Cholesterol: Are the Benefits Worth the Risk?" Drugs.com, September 10, 2018. https://www.drugs.com/article/statins-benefits-and-risks.html.

199   "The True Cause of Heart Illness as Revealed by a Heart Surgeon." PatientStory.sg - Singapore Blog Reviews. Accessed October 12, 2019. https://patientstory.sg/true-cause-heart-illness-revealed-heart-surgeon.

200   Hamblin, James. "A Heart Surgeon's Viral Confession." The Atlantic. Atlantic Media Company, January 28, 2014. https://www.theatlantic.com/health/archive/2014/01/a-heart-surgeons-viral-confession/283413/.

201   "The True Cause of Heart Illness as Revealed by a Heart Surgeon." PatientStory.sg - Singapore Blog Reviews. Accessed October 12, 2019. https://patientstory.sg/true-cause-heart-illness-revealed-heart-surgeon.

202   "FastStats - Leading Causes of Death." Centers for Disease Control and Prevention, February 6, 2020. https://www.cdc.gov/nchs/fastats/leading-causes-of-death.htm.

203   "Family History and Inherited Cancer Genes." Cancer Research UK, September 3, 2018. https://www.cancerresearchuk.org/about-cancer/causes-of-cancer/inherited-cancer-genes-and-increased-cancer-risk/family-history-and-inherited-cancer-genes.

204   "Genetics and Cancer." American Cancer Society. Accessed September 9, 2019. https://www.cancer.org/cancer/cancer-causes/genetics.html.

205   Prasad, Vinay, and Sham Mailankody. "Cost of Developing a Single Cancer Drug." JAMA Internal Medicine. JAMA Network, November 1, 2017. https://jamanetwork.com/journals/jamainternalmedicine/fullarticle/2653012.

206   Pollack, Andrew. "Doctors Denounce Cancer Drug Prices of $100,000 a Year." The New York Times, April 25, 2013. https://www.nytimes.com/2013/04/26/business/cancer-physicians-attack-high-drug-costs.html.

207   Seiler, Annina, Michelle A Chen, Ryan L Brown, and Christopher P Fagundes. "Obesity, Dietary Factors, Nutrition, and Breast Cancer Risk." Current breast cancer reports. U.S. National Library of Medicine, January 19, 2018. https://www.ncbi.nlm.nih.gov/pmc/articles/PMC6335046/.

208   Chilkov, Dr. Nalini. "Six Cancer-Fighting Medicinal Mushrooms." HuffPost, December 7, 2017. https://www.huffpost.com/entry/cancer-foods_b_1192207.

209   "10 Natural Cancer Treatments." Z Cancer Foundation. Accessed November 9, 2020. http://www.zcancerfoundation.org/our-researches/10-natural-cancer-treatment.

210   Moss, Ralph W. "When Chemo Kills: The Inside Story." Moss Reports, February 26, 2019. https://www.mossreports.com/when-chemo-kills/.

211   Ibid.

212   Fassa, Paul. "The Seeds Banned by The FDA. Truth From a 40-Year-Long Cover-Up Revealed." "Global Possibilities". Accessed March 9, 2020. https://globalpossibilities.org/the-seeds-banned-by-the-fda-truth-from-a-40-year-long-cover-up-revealed/.

213   "Apricot Seed Extract Cancer Therapy: Oasis of Hope Tijuana, Mexico." Oasis of Hope Hospital, April 22, 2020. https://www.oasisofhope.com/cancer-therapies/apricot-seed-extract-cancer-therapy/.

214   Cassiem, Wagheda, and Maryna de Kock. "The Anti-Proliferative Effect of Apricot and Peach Kernel Extracts on Human Colon Cancer Cells in Vitro." BMC Complementary Medicine and Therapies. BioMed Central, January 29, 2019. https://bmccomplementmedtherapies.biomedcentral.com/articles/10.1186/s12906-019-2437-4.

215   Pierce, Shanley. "Food for Thought: Medical Schools Lack Adequate Nutrition Education." TMC News, September 25, 2019. https://www.tmc.edu/news/2019/09/food-for-thought-medical-schools-lack-nutrition-education/.

216   "What's at Stake in Nutrition Education during Med School." American Medical Association, July 23, 2015. https://www.ama-assn.org/education/accelerating-change-medical-education/whats-stake-nutrition-education-during-med-school.

CHAPTER 14
A CLOSER LOOK AT GMOS

"Then God said, "Let the land sprout with vegetation—every sort of seed-bearing plant, and trees that grow seed-bearing fruit. These seeds will then produce the kinds of plants and trees from which they came." And that is what happened" Genesis 1:11 NLT.

WHAT IS A SEED?

A seed is a container of the future. Whether big or small, it holds the potential for greater life to be produced. In the human body, sperm is a "seed;" when planted in a woman's egg, it contains genetic code for an entirely new human body to be formed. In this way, we are all a product of seed. In agriculture, seeds are planted by the farmer with hope to reap a harvest. When we tithe, we give our "seed" as a financial offering to God, trusting Him to multiply it for His kingdom's purposes. There are many examples of seeds in the Bible:

- The seeds of plants and trees (Gen. 1:11-12)

- The seed of a man - his sperm (Gen. 4:1)

- The seed of a woman - her children (Gen. 3:15)

- The seed of a man & woman - their offspring (Gen. 4:25)

- The seed of the word of God (Lk. 8:11)

- The seed of the Kingdom of God (Mark 4:31-32)

You can predict what the final product will look like based on the seed it started from. But what happens if you change the nature of the seed itself? When God created seeds, He intended that they would produce after their own kind.

"And God said, "Let the earth sprout vegetation, plants yielding seed, and fruit trees bearing fruit in which is their seed, each according to its kind, on the earth." And it was so" Genesis 1:11 ESV.

There was no mixing or cross-contamination. Moses even laid out rules about not letting different seeds fall too closely together for it might damage the entire crop.

"Do not plant two kinds of seed in your vineyard; if you do, not only the crops you plant but also the fruit of the vineyard will be defiled" Deuteronomy 22:9 NIV.

We know that God's plans for us are good. He gives us rules and guidelines to protect us. But the curiosity and greed of mankind has enabled Satan to corrupt God's good plan for our health through introducing genetic modification.

GOD'S INTENTION VS. MAN'S INVENTION

Today, seeds are being genetically modified in labs in order to create 'better' versions of the original. A GMO (genetically modified organism) is the result of a laboratory process where genes from the DNA of one species are extracted and artificially forced into the genes of an unrelated plant or animal.

Monsanto (an American agrochemical giant) was one of the largest producers of genetically engineered seed. They developed the powerful herbicide RoundUp, designed to kill any plant or insect it touches, and then, seeds that could resist the effects of RoundUp. These "RoundUp ready" seeds increased agricultural efficiency because farmers could spray their entire crop with the herbicide and their plants would remain alive, but all pests and weeds would die. This raised many environmental and health concerns, as upon harvesting, heavy doses of the toxic chemical remained on the plant.[217] While GMOs typically produce higher yields and are pest resistant, these production benefits come with a hefty price tag. Many health experts agree that reactions to genetic modification is the source of gluten intolerance and many other health problems.[218]

GMO foods can affect your health in a number of ways:

- Increased allergies

- Gluten disorders

- Increased toxicity exposure

- Decreased nutritional intake

- Antibiotic resistance

- Liver problems

- Infertility

- Autism

- Accelerated aging

What complicates the issue, is that the danger is invisible to the naked eye. Just as in Jesus' parable of the wheat, when weeds were scattered throughout the wheat fields to intermingle and grow up together, today, farmers are at risk of GMO seeds contaminating their pure crops, without their awareness. Seeds can be carried by the wind from neighboring fields, or a passing truck, and will grow up alongside the pure crops, reproducing their own seed. Monsanto commonly sues these farmers for 'stealing' their product.[219] GMO products have also been scattered throughout the marketplace, making it very difficult to identify which products are pure, and which have come from a genetically modified process. Can you believe that 70-80 percent of our foods in the US are genetically modified (most of them are processed foods)? Today, more than 90 percent of all soybeans grown in the USA are GMO, and more than 80 percent of all corn and cotton.[220] Genetically modified ingredients have contaminated everything from soups, to vodka, to lipstick and just about every piece of produce in the supermarket. More than 60 countries around the world, including Australia, Japan, and all of the countries in the European Union have acknowledged the health risks associated with GMOs, and have insisted on clear labeling of all GMO food. Sadly, North America has suppressed GMO identification. To guard their profit, many companies don't want you to know which foods contain them.

WHICH FOODS SHOULD I BE CAUTIOUS ABOUT EATING?

The Non-GMO Project is a non-profit organization driven to identify and protect a non-GMO food supply. They remain the educational leader for GMO avoidance and have published the following list of high-risk GMO foods:

Foods at high-risk of being genetically modified:[221]

- Alfalfa
- Canola
- Corn
- Cotton
- Papaya
- Soy
- Sugar Beet
- Yellow summer squash / zucchini
- Potato
- Animal products

Note: These high-risk GMO ingredients are also distributed in disguise, within commonly used packaged products such as: Amino acids, alcohol, aspartame, ascorbic acid, sodium ascorbate, citric acid, sodium citrate, ethanol, flavorings (both natural and artificial), high-fructose corn syrup, hydrolyzed vegetable protein, lactic acid, maltodextrins, molasses, monosodium glutamate (MSG), sucrose, textured vegetable protein (TVP), xanthan gum, vitamins, vinegar, and yeast products.[222]

WHERE DID GENETIC MODIFICATION COME FROM?

You might be able to guess... The Ford and Rockefeller foundations were heavily involved in the Green Revolution, bent on superseding organic farming with human-improvements on God's design. The Green Revolution, of the late 1960s, introduced technologies such as developing high-yielding varieties (HYVs) of cereals, especially dwarf wheats and rices, in association with chemical fertilizers and agro-chemicals, and with controlled water-supply (usually involving irrigation) and new methods of cultivation, including mechanization. All of these together were seen as a package of practices to supersede traditional technology and to be adopted as a whole.[223] What motivated this Green Revolution?

The Rockefeller brothers were responsible in the 1970's for a US Government top secret project directed by Rockefeller National Security Adviser Kissinger, NSSM-200 titled: "Implications of Worldwide Population Growth for US Security and Overseas Interests." It argued that high population growth in developing nations that supplied the US with strategic raw materials were a "national security threat" as increased population would cause them to use up their own resources internally, and effectively decrease the US's supply.[224] This made population reduction programs to developing countries a precondition of US aid.

The Rockefeller Foundation created the entire field of genetic manipulation through its ownership of Monsanto Corporation, and financing of university biology research, to create the "gene cannon" and other techniques to artificially alter gene expression of selected plants.

By controlling the makeup and distribution of GMO foods, Rockefeller would gain an upper hand in manipulating the entire human and animal food chain. Henry Kissinger, David Rockefeller's political adviser, summed up David Rockefeller's world strategy: **"If you control the oil, you control entire nations; if you control food, you control the people; if you control money, you control the entire world."**[225]

The clear strategy of Monsanto and the Washington government backing them, was to introduce the genetically modified seeds to every corner of the world. They were unleashed on unsuspecting farmers, and have now proven to be environmentally destructive, limiting biodiversity, and increasing social inequity. Scientists carrying out honest studies were slandered. Reputed scientific establishments were silenced or made to toe the line that was supportive of the Rockefeller's food control and depopulation agenda.[226] GMOs could rightly be called the world's largest biological experiment; and humans are the guinea pigs.

THE LINK TO EUGENICS

All these initiatives to corrupt the seed, have not been limited to agriculture. Research in eugenics (the belief that the human species could be improved by discouraging reproduction of those with less desirable traits, and encouraging reproduction of those with desirable traits)[227] was financially supported by the Rockefeller and other elite families, and was first tested on Jews in Nazi Germany.

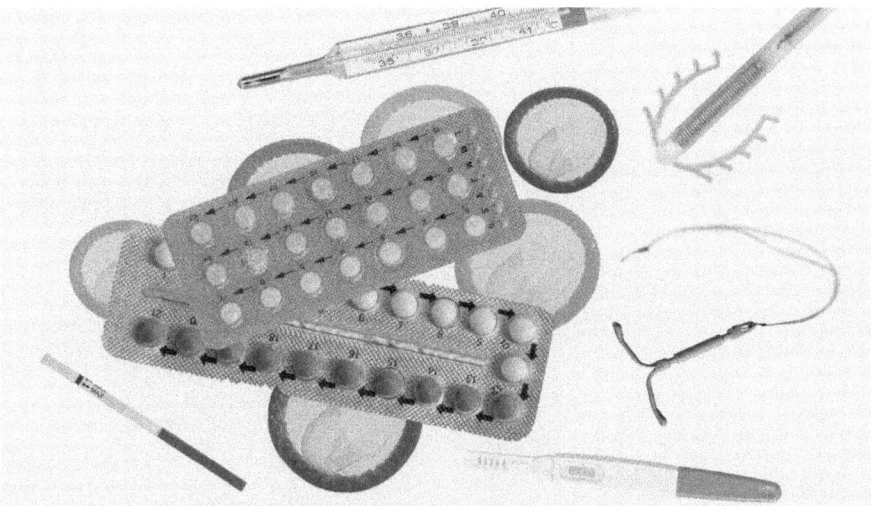

Before the war, Rockefeller purchased shares in what was to become a massive German chemical and pharmaceutical cartel: I.G. Farbenen. This conglomerate would invent, produce and distribute the Zyklon B used in Nazi concentration camps, producing enough to kill 200 million humans in gas chambers.[228] IG Farbenen built Auschwitz, and Rockefeller's company, Standard Oil supplied their oil needs and actually opened the American branch of IG Farbenen.

Up until 1939, the Rockefeller Foundation financed biological research at the Kaiser Wilhelm Institute, in Berlin, exploring how to breed a superior race and how to kill off or sterilize those they deemed "inferior."[229] In other words: Nazi Eugenics! After the war, the Rockefeller brothers secretly brought Nazi scientists to the USA and Canada, under new identities, to continue their eugenics research in the CIA's MK-Ultra project. In the 1950's, the Rockefeller brothers founded the Population Council to advance eugenics, disguised as population research into birth control.[230]

Does it surprise you that these initiatives have been going on behind closed doors in our own country all this time? It shouldn't! It is not man's agenda that is driving it — it is the enemy's. He uses the elites in his worldly kingdom to depopulate nations. The Eugenic Movement eliminates the weak and undesirable in order to 'improve' the genetic composition of the human race. It is truly the fulfillment of the enemy's mission to steal, kill, and destroy those whom God created and loves.

This is a heavy topic and it may leave you feeling like there is no hope. But, the Lord knew this narrative was going to play out from the very beginning of time. Although this sounds hopeless, we can believe for better days. Because God has the perfect plan. He is going to redeem everything the enemy has stolen. Our hope is in Jesus, and we can trust Him.

ENDNOTES

217   Funke, Todd, Huijong Han, Martha L. Healy-Fried, Markus Fischer, and Ernst Schönbrunn. "Molecular Basis for the Herbicide Resistance of Roundup Ready Crops." PNAS. National Academy of Sciences, August 29, 2006. https://www.pnas.org/content/103/35/13010.

218   Spector, Kaye. "Can Genetically Modified Foods Trigger Gluten Sensitivity?" Earth Island Journal, November 26, 2013. https://www.earthisland.org/journal/index.php/articles/entry/can_genetically_modified_foods_trigger_gluten_sensitivity/.

219   Horne, L.E. Trent. "Monsanto V. Schmeiser 20 Years Later: The Answer Wasn't Blowin' in the Wind." Lexology, August 5, 2020. https://www.lexology.com/library/detail.aspx?g=60688c01-6ea1-440f-bafb-e310025c2281.

220   Perkins, J.H. "The Rockefeller Foundation and the Green Revolution, 1941–1956." Agriculture and Human Values 7, no. 3-4 (June 1, 1990): 6–18. https://doi.org/https://doi.org/10.1007/BF01557305.

221   "What Is a GMO?" Non GMO Project. Accessed May 22, 2020. https://www.nongmoproject.org/gmo-facts/what-is-gmo/.

222   Ibid.

223   "Green Revolution." Wikipedia. Accessed September 5, 2019. https://en.wikipedia.org/wiki/Green_Revolution.

224   "Implications of Worldwide Population Growth For U.S. Security and Overseas Interests (The Kissinger Report)," November 26, 1975. https://pdf.usaid.gov/pdf_docs/Pcaab500.pdf.

225   Engdahl, William. "D. Rockefeller's Gruesome Legacy." Information Clearinghouse, March 31, 2017. http://www.informationclearinghouse.info/46776.htm.

226   "Independent GMO Research Is Trashed: Scientists Hounded & Silenced." Alliance for Human Research Protection, March 1, 2017. https://ahrp.org/how-independent-scientific-gmo-research-is-suppressed/.

227   "Eugenics." Dictionary.com. Accessed September 5, 2019. https://www.dictionary.com/browse/eugenics.

228   Montague, Tigger. "Down the Rabbit Hole: The Rise of Western Medicine." BioStar US, September 24, 2016. https://blog.biostarus.com/rise-western-medicine/.

229   Engdahl, William. "D. Rockefeller's Gruesome Legacy." Information Clearinghouse, March 31, 2017. http://www.informationclearinghouse.

info/46776.htm.

230   "Population Council." https://www.influencewatch.org/. Accessed November 14, 2020. https://www.influencewatch.org/non-profit/population-council/.

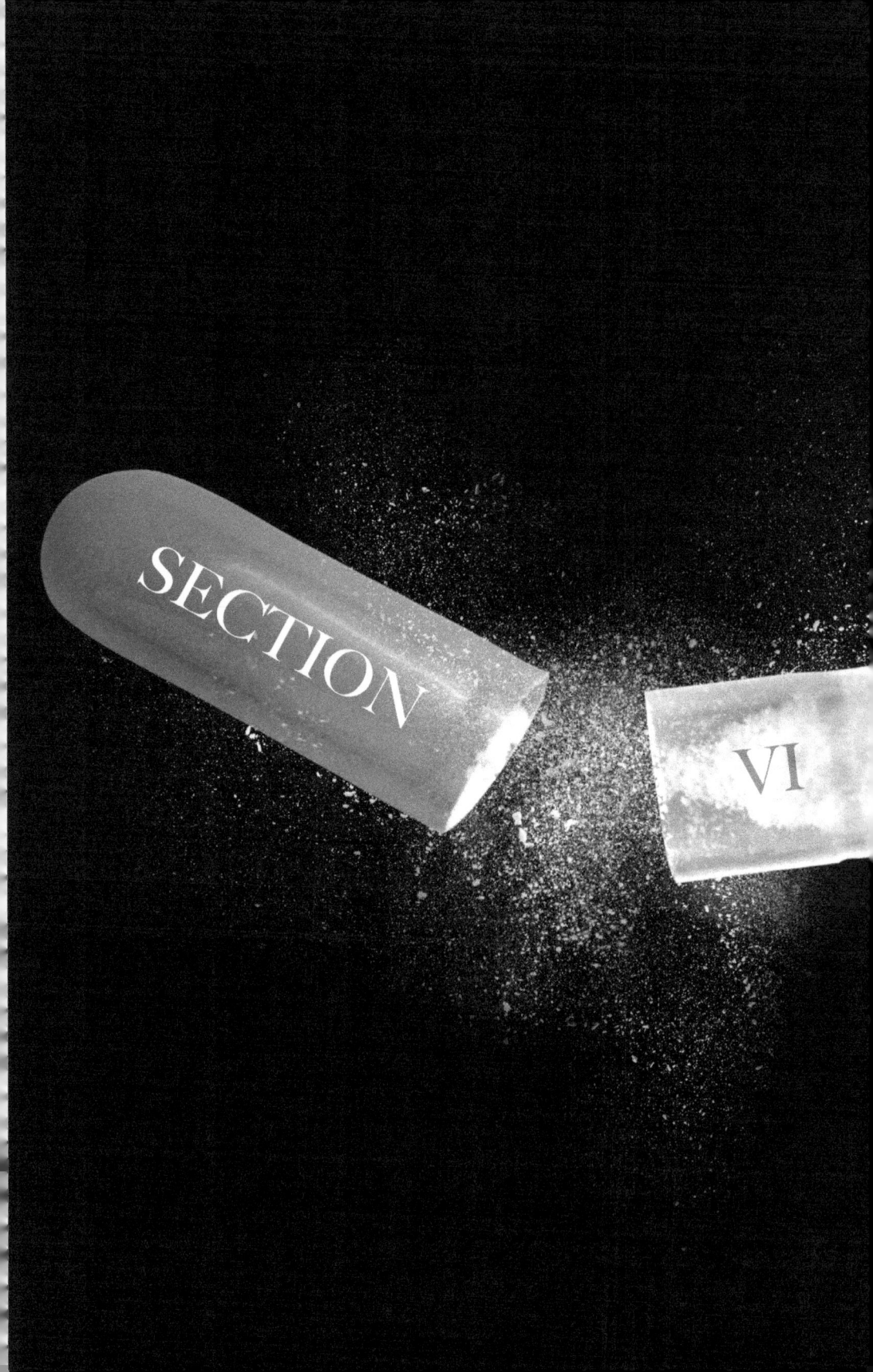

SECTION VI

FOR SUCH A TIME AS THIS

Have you ever wondered why you are here? Why were you born at such a time as this? Just as the enemy has been laying out his plans through our nation, how much more has our God; the Omniscient All-Powerful One, been preparing His plans since the creation of the world, to redeem and restore all that is His. The victory has already been determined! But guess what? You and I have an important role to play: to establish that victory on earth until He returns. In fact, you are His secret weapon, with a destiny written long ago.

CHAPTER 15
TAKING BACK THE LAND

After reading the previous section describing all the ways the enemy is attacking humanity, you may be feeling the painful reality that the truth hurts. But wouldn't you rather know the truth than live in darkness? The question that remains is what are we going to do about it? How should we respond to this? We can't just walk into the Rockefeller's house and say, "Stop what you're doing! You're a mean evil man!" But what do we do? What role do we have to play?

When the nation of Israel was moving out of slavery towards the promised land, they had to depend on the Lord for their food. It was manna from heaven, and it sustained them; at the same time, He was leading them to a land flowing with milk and honey. In this Scripture we see the true desire of God for His people:

"For the Lord your God is bringing you into a good land of flowing streams and pools of water with fountains and springs that gush out in the valleys and hills. It is a land of wheat and barley, of grapevines, fig trees, and pomegranates; of olive oil and honey. It is a land where food is plentiful and nothing is lacking. It is a land where iron is as common as stone, and copper is abundant in the hills" Deuteronomy 8:7-9 NLT.

The promised land was the Israelite's inheritance, but how were they to obtain it? **They first had to kick the enemy out.** The Canaanites lived in the land that God was going to give to Israel. So what did Israel do? They sent spies into the land to assess their enemies so they would know how to overtake them. God gives us promises as well, but there are also giants in our land of promise. The two spies who came back with a good report regarding the giants in their land are a great example to us. They were not afraid, because they knew their God would fight for them, and bring them safely into their promised land.

*"Joshua son of Nun and Caleb son of Jephunneh, who were among those who had explored the land, tore their clothes and said to the entire Israelite assembly, "The land we passed through and explored is exceedingly good. If the Lord is pleased with us, He will lead us into that land, a land flowing with milk and honey, and will give it to us. Only **do not rebel against the Lord. And do not be afraid of the people of the land,** because we will devour them. Their protection is gone, but the Lord is with us. Do not be afraid of them" Numbers 14:6-9 NIV.*

Here's the truth for us: **If we are going to take back our health for God, we need to spy on the enemy and understand his tactics, then be obedient to the Lord, refuse fear, and step forward in faith.** There are some giants that we need to overthrow to take back our land, but God has already prepared the way.

Remember, we don't win by fighting with earthly methods, in our own strength. We are battling an invisible spiritual enemy, and this battle belongs to the Lord. It will be won in the Spirit, by the Spirit, and through you! When you walk in the fullness of who God created you to be, knowing your identity as a son or daughter of God, co-heir with Christ, crowned with glory, given authority and dominion, filled with His Spirit — then your light will shine brightly and transformatively.

If you work in the medical system, or in any industry where you see the hand of the enemy moving, stand your ground, and remember who you are in Christ. And remember that you're not alone. You are walking with a whole army of light-bearers, as believers across the earth form one tribe — together we can take back the land. When the Lord leads us into battle, even one person can put 1000 to flight, and 2 people can put 10,000 to flight (Deut. 32:30). Don't give up! Look at the book of Acts: the apostles were determined to fulfill their destiny, even if they were imprisoned or beaten, they kept going. Don't let Satan burden you with heavy discouragement or being overwhelmed. You are a living and active part of God's story. God is not threatened by Satan's schemes. He is confident in His own plan. God sits in heaven and laughs:

"Why do the nations conspire
and the peoples plot in vain?
The kings of the earth rise up
and the rulers band together
against the Lord and against His anointed, saying,
"Let us break their chains
and throw off their shackles."
The One enthroned in heaven laughs;
the Lord scoffs at them.
He rebukes them in His anger
and terrifies them in His wrath, saying,
"I have installed my king
on Zion, my holy mountain" Psalm 2:1-6 NIV.

The strongest weapon we have against the enemy is God within us. We have a God-ordained destiny, and the sooner we awaken to who we are in Christ, the sooner the bright light of His Spirit can dispel the darkness in our land.

ROOTED ON THE ROCK

Your relationship with God is the bedrock of the rest of your life. It is your foundation and will affect everything else you do. Your relationship with God is the most important relationship in your life.

He has all the wisdom you will ever need, all the strength you long for, and deep love beyond what any other human can offer you. He will be your constant companion and ever-present help in time of need (Ps. 46:1). **To root yourself on the Rock, you must intentionally deepen this relationship.**

For relationships to work well, they require an investment of time, energy, and care. It's the same with God. It won't happen by default, or simply by attending church. It is a personal one-on-one relationship that grows through your commitment to meet with Him when no one else is around. God calls you to *"abide in Him" (John 15:5).* As your spiritual relationship grows, it will move beyond a daily appointment time with God, and spread throughout your whole day. You will be able to enjoy a lifestyle of continuous communion with Him, where you talk to Him throughout your day — ever aware of His nearness, His love, and His guidance. This is where true relational authority begins, and where your confidence grows to pursue His will despite the enemy's ploys.

To be truly rooted on the Rock, means to become unshakeable, to grow a solid conviction that will stand in the face of discouragement, tear down the enemy's lies, and share in the heart of God. Here are 5 principles that I believe are absolutely essential to build yourself a solid foundation:

1. **You must have faith that God's word works in your life when you apply it and it doesn't return void**

    "The Word of God is alive and active" Heb. 4:12 NIV. It works to accomplish things on earth. When God speaks, things begin to shift, to grow, to change. And His word never fails. It always accomplishes the purposes for which it was sent.

    > *"As the rain and the snow*
    > *come down from heaven,*
    > *and do not return to it*
    > *without watering the earth*
    > *and making it bud and flourish,*
    > *so that it yields seed for the sower and bread for the eater,*
    > *so is my word that goes out from my mouth:*
    > *It will not return to me empty,*
    > *but will accomplish what I desire*
    > *and achieve the purpose for which I sent it"* Isaiah 55:10-11 NIV.

    God says with authority, "It will accomplish what I desire." You can have that same confidence as you declare the Word of God over your life. Faith is the currency of heaven. If you don't believe what you are saying and reading, it's pointless. You must have confidence that what you are saying is going to come to pass. This is the power of faith that God has given you. You must build up your faith muscles. When the enemy tries to discourage you, you must be confident that His word will come to pass, and it will never return void.

2. **Believe that all of God's word is true, not just some of it**

    I used to pick out the parts of the Bible that made sense to me, or only focus on the verses that were easier to believe. Other parts I'd dismiss. The plagues in Egypt couldn't *really* have been true, right? Rivers turning to blood? But I have learned, it all has meaning, it is all relevant, and the more you understand it, the more you realize it is all true! Don't rob yourself of receiving deeper revelation by avoiding the parts you're not sure about. Dive in! Ask questions. Wrestle with it. Each word holds keys to who God is as well as keys to your own healing. To find your breakthrough, read the Bible with a hungry heart to unpack heaven's mysteries. Take the word of God as your spiritual food. Ask Him about what you read. You'll be amazed at what He'll reveal to you!

Maybe certain verses you want to believe, but can't find the faith. First, believe that all of God's word is inspired by the Holy Spirit (2 Timothy 3:16); for He is the Spirit of truth, who cannot lie. When you own this reality, the Bible will become a sword at your side, and you will wield it with great confidence and authority. Every word of the Bible is true, and is relevant for today.

> *"Indeed, if you call out for insight*
> *and cry aloud for understanding,*
> *and if you look for it as for silver*
> *and search for it as for hidden treasure,*
> *then you will understand the fear of the Lord*
> *and find the knowledge of God" Proverbs 2:3-5 NIV.*

3. **Accept that the ways of God's kingdom are totally different from what we are taught in the world**

The brain is an organ. It collects data through our five senses, and our mind tries to make sense of this data. Once we begin to renew our minds by the Spirit, we have to be prepared for an entirely new set of data, and it cannot be discerned by those same five senses! It may feel strange. The process of adapting our perception to discern by the Spirit is a journey. You have to prepare yourself to see the world in a whole new way. You will become spiritually-minded, and perceive things in a way that is completely opposite to what people in the world think. As you dive deep into the word of God for answers, and cultivate a deeper, intimate relationship with the Lord, you will be ready. Looking through a spiritual lens at the old sensory data, with the new understanding of how it all fits together, your whole life will begin to make sense.

Think about it. God's word tells you to praise your way through trials. You may say, "it doesn't make sense to sing songs of joy when I'm depressed." But praise won the battles in the Old Testament (2 Chron. 20:21-26). If God tells you to praise, there's a good reason! This is a kingdom principle that uses heavenly wisdom far beyond the understanding of the world: **persistent praise defeats the enemy.** Living by spiritual wisdom will increase your authority and your victories! Another example, the world says, when people mess with you, you have a right to be offended and demand your rights. But Jesus says, forgive those who keep hurting you (Matt. 18:22), even up to seventy- seven times! God knows, we were not designed to maintain a state of unforgiveness. It makes us ill and bitter, and causes us to lose the freedom He designed us to enjoy! God does things differently, but His way always works! Your life is going to operate on completely different principles than the kingdom of this world. Unbelievers may not understand, but you will be standing on truth and operating with divine wisdom.

4. Transform your mind into the mind of Christ, and your character to be like His character

Your goal is to think and act like Jesus. If you can fill your mind with His perspective, you have already won half the battle. When you live with the mind of Christ, your thoughts are aligned with a heavenly perspective — they are steady and full of truth. Things will be a lot clearer for you. The battlefield of the enemy is our mind, and he fights with confusion, doubt, fear and accusation. But if you see things through Jesus' eyes, and respond with His character you are well on your way to victory! Making Christ-likeness your goal, aligns your life with God's will, so that you can move from victory to victory. This is our ultimate goal. This is walking out our salvation.

5. You must believe God's plans for you are good, and are not to harm you

Choose to believe that God is good. Regardless of circumstances, seasons, or how things may appear — God is always good. He cannot deny His own nature which is love. *"And so we know and rely on the love God has for us. God is love. Whoever lives in love lives in God, and God in them" 1 Jn. 4:16 NIV.* Because God loves you as a father loves his child, He wants to be close to you and to give you good things. *"And we know that in all things **God works for the good** of those who love Him, who have been called* *according to His purpose" Rom. 8:28 NIV.* He is actively working for the good of those who love Him. When you let this truth sink in, you will realize how powerful it is, and how you can live with confidence and courage, no matter what you are going through. The declaration of God's goodness becomes your armor when difficulty strikes. Standing on the Word and refusing to entertain thoughts that speak otherwise, makes you strong in battle. Own the truth that God is always good, and defend it.

6. Stay connected to God's heart

Jesus lives within us. That means we can have constant connection with Him. Our hearts are one. When was the last time you asked, "Jesus, what's on Your heart? What do You want to do here?" It's a two-way relationship. He wants an intimate relationship with us. We need to maintain this heart connection.

Once you anchor your lifestyle in close communion with God, there are so many benefits. You'll find it is so much easier to enter into that secret place. Your heart-to-heart talks with God will open the door to revelation, and He will share His secrets with you. He'll tell you what's coming. This means when you're in the secret place, you're safe, because you know the mind and heart of God for you and your situation. Imagine sitting beside the Lord, being able to laugh at the enemy because you feel so unthreatened.

Remaining connected to God's heart makes you less vulnerable to the enemy's attacks, because you've been warned ahead of time, and are prepared. So, nourish your relationship with Jesus. Bask in His presence. As you hunger to know His heart, you will find your connection growing stronger and stronger.

SEVEN FAITH INTERFERENCES

When our relationship with God gains strength, Satan's influence weakens. When we mature in our faith and spiritual understanding, we stand taller in the Spirit. We have confidence and authority when we pray. We know who we are and we know who our God is. Satan can't mess with us the same way he used to. Therefore, he will do anything in his power to disrupt our progression into spiritual maturity. One of his primary strategies is distraction. It seems simple, but it is powerful. Building ourselves up in the Lord takes time, attention, and commitment. We've learned, as a people, to follow the world's systems and priorities. Now, we have to unlearn that. God doesn't want you to be distracted with the things of this world. The things of this world are temporary, but the things of the Spirit are eternal. God designed you to be focused on your God-given purpose.

"And what do you benefit if you gain the whole world but lose your soul? Is anything worth more than your soul?" Matthew 16:26 NLT.

There are seven common things that can interfere with our relationship with God. As you read through this list, prayerfully examine your own life and become aware of any ways the enemy might be wanting to sabotage you.

1. **The Love of Money** - Be on guard if you find yourself driven to make more money. Your priorities reveal what your heart loves. If money comes first, you are actually worshipping money. You are letting it take leadership over the rest of your life.

   "Don't store up treasures on earth where moths eat them and rust destroys them and thieves break in and steal them. Store your treasures in heaven where moths and rust and thieves don't break

in and steal" Matthew 6:19-20 NLT.

This Scripture is about where your treasure is. There's nothing wrong with having money, we need it to live, but don't make it an idol. There are much more important things, eternal things, to be pursuing. Remember the story of the rich young ruler? Jesus said to him, *"If you want to be perfect, go, sell what you have and give to the poor, and you will have treasure in heaven; and come, follow Me." But when the young man heard that saying, he went away sorrowful, for he had great possessions" Matt. 19:21-22 NIV.* Jesus was giving him wise advice about the true meaning of life. It's not about money at all! But despite the young man's claim to love God by obeying the commandments, his unwillingness to let go of his wealth revealed the true attitude of his heart. Make sure you can give money away freely, and joyfully. Developing a generous heart is key to being able to receive freely from heaven.

2. **Religion** - Participating in religion is different from participating in faith. Religion refers to a rule-based system where one can become holier than thou and develop self-righteous attitudes (as opposed to the faith described in the Bible where we are not saved by works but by grace, which we receive with humility Ephes. 2:8-9). The Pharisees were the leaders of the people of God, and they put their faith in the system. They were so boxed in by religion, they couldn't let God be God! This same pharisaical

spirit still exists today. Christians get caught up with following the rules of the community, fearful of how they appear to others, aiming for public esteem in the church more than their personal walk with Jesus Christ. They seem to do the right things, and can quote Scripture, but have no depth of revelation about what it really means. It was the same in Jesus' ministry when He spoke in parables, and only those enlightened by the Holy Spirit would gain revelation. The meaning of the parables were hidden from the religious. Jesus said to them, *"These people honor me with their lips but their hearts are far from me" (Mark 7:6 NLT).* Be wary! Religion can actually separate you from God. He is looking for an authentic relationship, based on faith, full of grace and love, grounded in the Word, and inspired by Spirit-led revelation.

3. **Our Hobbies** - Hobbies can be expressions of your personality and sources of joy, but God will become jealous for your attention if your passion for entertainment takes over your schedule and you have minimal time for God. Exodus 34:14 says, *"You must worship no other gods, for the LORD, whose very name is Jealous, is a God who is jealous about His relationship with you" (NLT).* Hobbies can become idols — whether skiing, or knitting, or cooking or playing scrabble — hobbies can distract you from the true reason God put you on earth. Jesus says, *"If you cling to your life, you will lose it, but if you give up your life for Me you will find it" Matt. 10:39 NLT.*

4. **Media** - What is it about media that is so addictive? Binge watching and scrolling through social media are quicksands of entertainment. Video games and late night movies can affect your dreams. Pleasure and enjoyment are gifts from God, just keep them in balance or they will tear your eyes away from what He wants to show you. The things of this world crowd out God's voice, and creating enough space in your thought-life to listen to Him and abide with Him is necessary for spiritual maturity. We must use our free time wisely. The whole idea is for God's children who belong to him to be less connected to these worldly things. Instead of turning on the TV, open up the Word of God, and let it minister to you. As you do it more and more, you'll be

developing a relationship and you'll begin to hear Him speak to you.

5. **Relationships** - Family can be all-consuming. Romantic relationships and even friendships can be demanding. God created us for connection with others. God created Eve because He saw it was not good for man to be alone. But, we need to remember that there is a Divine relationship that keeps the rest working well. Not having clear boundaries with the people in your life, including your spouse or your children, can interfere with your relationship with God. God expects that you put Him first. There is always time to make God a priority. And as you put Him first, God will take care of those you care for.

6. **Work** - We tend to push ourselves to work, work, work. Whether at the office, or over-committing ourselves elsewhere. Becoming a workaholic can rob you of the life God designed for you to live. The problem is that we don't know how to talk with God, to hear His response, and to trust that He's leading. Get off the hamster wheel and talk to God about this: "Help me with this God! Help me to prioritize my time. Teach me how to listen to your guidance." He always has a solution, but we forget to invite Him in. He could have an entirely different job planned for you. One that frees you up for more time with family, etc. God always has His best in mind for you so don't get so busy that you miss out on what could have been.

7. **Self-serving prayers** - You know those prayers that focus on getting blessings from God more than just loving Him? When 90 percent of the conversation is about me, me, me? These are self-serving prayers. God doesn't exist to serve us — we exist to serve Him, and our prayer life should reflect that. The two most important commandments are love God, and love others; is that demonstrated in what you discuss with Him? Selfishness is a quality of the enemy, and we don't want to be made in his image. Changing the focus of our prayer life is a significant step in spiritual maturity and spiritual intimacy.

If you have discovered any of these areas interfering in your walk with

God, identify them, but don't wallow in shame or guilt. *"There is now no condemnation for those who are in Christ Jesus" Rom. 8:1 NIV.* The kindness of the Lord leads us to repentance (Rom. 2:4). Simply acknowledge the wrong done and make a change. Turn your attention back to God and receive His abundant and unconditional love once more. He is eager to meet with you and restore you.

You were created for relationship with God. He put mankind in the Garden of Eden to dwell with, and to walk among them. He loves you and wants to spend time with you. Will you share that desire with Him? Will you do battle in your inner life to protect significant time with Him? Will you invest in this most important relationship, and allow it to form an unshakeable Rock under your feet? Don't wait till you are on your deathbed to look back and realize that it was the eternal things that were the most important things.

And remember, your walk with God has a direct influence on the spiritual atmosphere in your nation. Where light refuses to shine, where lanterns lack spiritual oil and can only shine dimly, the darkness dominates. But, as the resilient army of God's children rises with God-given authority, there is still hope. The stakes couldn't be higher. Rise into your destiny and let's take back the land!

CHAPTER 16
YOUR TRUE SPIRITUAL IDENTITY

The biggest question we all ask is, "Why am I here? What is my purpose?" Let me tell you today: there is a purpose behind your birth! You are not an accident, for it was God who ordained you to be born. How do I know you have a purpose? Because God's word says:

> *"For you formed my inward parts;*
> *you knitted me together in my mother's womb.*
> *I praise you, for I am fearfully and wonderfully made"*
> *Psalm 139:13-14 ESV.*

You were "formed" by the Father's hands. This verse speaks of intention and design. God knit you together. He knows you. And you were made "wonderfully." You are truly an incredible creation.

Ephesians 2:10 says, *"For we are God's masterpiece. He has created us anew in Christ Jesus, so we can do the good things He planned for us long ago" (NLT).*

You are a masterpiece — an incredible piece of art! Not only did God design you, but He has made specific plans for you. We see this in Genesis when God created Adam and Eve, He gave mankind (that includes you!) dominion over the earth *"Then God blessed them and said, "Be fruitful and multiply. Fill the earth and govern it. Reign over the fish in the sea, the birds in the sky, and all the animals that scurry along the ground" Genesis 1:28 NLT.* We have a job to do on this earth. We have been given authority to rule.

In addition, Jesus says, *"I am the vine; you are the branches. If you remain in me and I in you, you will bear much fruit; <u>apart from Me you can do nothing</u>" John 15:5 NIV.* A part of our purpose is to bear fruit. We have been designed to live closely with God and produce something through our lives. Not on our own strength, and not by man's understanding.

But, sometimes it can be difficult to figure out how to live out our spiritual purpose. We might know we have a destiny, but feel we are living short of it.

BORN FOR MORE

Maybe you can relate to my story. I became a doctor because my mom told me I should. Looking back it's funny how I thought my destiny could be determined by a human, instead of the God who created me! My mom was focused on career choices that could make a lot of money, so that my sister and I could become self-sufficient. We didn't know any better, so we just followed her advice. I thank God that He blessed me with the ability to get into a highly competitive grad program following dental school. This allowed me to build a career where I could make a decent living, but I always knew this was not my passion. I was never truly satisfied with my career choice and direction of my life; something was missing. I always believed I was born for so much more. I just got stuck under human expectations and in the system of the world.

One day, the Lord told me I was like the wicked servant who buried his talent (Matthew 25:25). I argued with Him, "what do you mean? I tithe, I give offerings and I help out at church — how am I like the wicked servant who hid his talents?" He showed me that I was keeping my money in the bank, making very little interest, and not multiplying it for the Kingdom. I was following the ways of the world. I was a slave to the system. When you're in the system, you feel you can never make enough money; when you do make it, it leaks out like you have holes in your pocket (Haggai 1:6), so you go back to making more. It's a monotonous rhythm of slavery: "Keep making those bricks, keep making those bricks," as we labor in the systems of the world.

My stress, poor eating and bad habits seemed to go hand in hand with a career-driven life, leading me to a place of having to fight for my own health. This was a very formative part of my life and the time I began to discover what my passion actually was. God was guiding me toward my destiny through the trial! He took me on a path through difficult times, and step by step, my heart learned to long more and more, for God's predestined plan for my life. God's ways of doing things are incredibly wise — even when we don't understand where He is leading us.

I think it is so sad that many people, like myself, can waste their lives, buried in busyness, chasing someone else's dream for their life, blinded by addiction, lost in distraction, avoiding what matters most; meanwhile, God has already written a beautiful and powerful purpose for them to fulfill. Do you remember the parable of the ten virgins (Matthew 25:1-13)? Ten women went out to meet the bridegroom (Jesus) as they waited for His coming. They all took lamps, but five of them neglected to bring oil to sustain the flame, so when the bridegroom approached, they had to go find oil, and missed His arrival! They missed the purpose completely. They were too preoccupied to remember what was most important.

Your purpose goes far beyond what job you choose. My career in dentistry was not my true identity. Looking back now, I can see with the mind of Christ that my life story has given me a testimony. Through my trials, I have discovered a clear passion for health and wellness. The more I learned, the more passion bubbled up inside of me until I had to share it with others. We're never fully happy unless we are fulfilling our destiny. **Don't get stuck living a life you don't really want. Redesign it!** When we don't live according to our divine design, it must grieve the heart of our loving Father. He created us to experience life in abundance (John 10:10)! Not a life of boredom or disappointment, a life without hope — that is not our portion. If that's you right now, I urge you not to give up. Believe me, I know the frustration of feeling like you're not where you should be. Wondering why you even exist. The battle can be intense, but God's plan is so much bigger and better than you can imagine. Use your dissatisfaction as motivation to press deeper into God. Begin knocking on His heavenly door and asking Him to align you with your true purpose and calling.

JACOB'S CHANGE OF IDENTITY

Jacob was a man who didn't know his calling. His grandfather Abraham and father Isaac may have spoken about faith in God, but Jacob didn't seem to know Him in the same way. He was always trying to outwit those around him for his own gain. I think Jacob was fearful about not being blessed, not having enough money or favor to secure a good future for himself. Afterall, he deceived his father into giving him his older brother's inheritance. Many times in Jacob's life, he tricked and deceived others to get ahead. In fact his name even means, "the supplanter," or one who circumvents. But God met with Jacob in a powerful way to realign him onto the path of his destiny.

Jacob was travelling, and one night when he lay down to sleep, he had a dream of a heavenly ladder. This was the moment his life radically changed. In Genesis 28:12-15 it says: *"He had a dream in which he saw a stairway resting on the earth, with its top reaching to heaven, and the angels of God were ascending and descending on it. There above it stood the Lord, and He said: 'I am the Lord, the God of your father Abraham and the God of Isaac. I will give you and your descendants the land on which you are lying. Your descendants will be like the dust of the earth, and you will spread out to the west and to the east, to the north and to the south. All peoples on earth will be blessed through you and your offspring. I am with you and will watch over you wherever you go, and I will bring you back to this land. I will not leave you until I have done what I have promised you'"* (NIV).

Wow! This was an "encounter moment"! God revealed Himself, and Jacob's heart began to shift. As he began to connect with God he became aligned with God's destiny for him.

"When Jacob awoke from his sleep, he thought,'Surely the Lord is in this place, and I was not aware of it.' He was afraid and said, 'How awesome is this place! This is none other than the house of God; this is the gate of heaven.' Early the next morning Jacob took the stone he had placed under his head and set it up as a pillar and poured oil on top of it. He called that place Bethel, though the city used to be called Luz. Then Jacob made a vow, saying, 'If God will be with me and will watch over me on this journey I am taking and will give me food to eat and clothes to wear so that I return safely to my father's household, then the Lord will be my God and this stone that I have set up as a pillar will be God's house, and of all that You give me I will give you a tenth' (Genesis 28:16-22 NLT).

The shift began in the area of his greatest fear: Provision. It is as if he said, "If God will take care of me, I'll let go of my money and give a tenth back to Him." This is a sign that Jacob was ready to change. He was ready to release that which he had clung tightly to. You've got to be ready to make personal sacrifice in order to shift into living a divine lifestyle. To go on God's grand adventure into the unknown, listen to Him and trust Him; it will require a ready heart and a ready mind. When we begin to release the false securities we cling to, we take the first step of freeing ourselves into the lives we are meant to live.

But Jacob's shift had only begun. As Jacob travelled from Bethel, he came to a place where he would once again meet his elder brother whom he had betrayed by stealing his inheritance. Once again, Jacob's old fears rose up: "What if he asks for all my possessions? What if he wants to kill me? Will my family be safe? Will we be provided for?" The enemy comes to steal the good works that God has done in our hearts. The enemy always wants to take us back to our old nature. Jacob had met with God and heard God's promises over his life, however he was being tested. **A test means that God wants to grow us spiritually.** Jacob had to fight for his new identity! He prays, *"Save me, I pray, from the hand of my brother Esau, for I am afraid he will come and attack me, and also the mothers with their children. But You have said, 'I will surely make you prosper and will make your descendants like the sand of the sea, which cannot be counted'" Gen. 32:11-12 NIV*. He was upholding the word of God over his emotions, fighting for his new identity to take root.

It is a war to become who you are called to be. It is a war to get to the land of promise. But you can't reach your destiny if you don't become who you are called to be! So, Jacob had to wrestle it out with God declaring, *"I will not let You go unless You bless me" Gen. 32:26 NIV*. And at the end of the battle, God confirmed Jacob's new spiritual identity. He was no longer Jacob, the deceiver but was now the one who "overcame." God's angel said, *"Your name will no longer be Jacob, but Israel, because you have struggled with God and with humans and have overcome" Gen. 32:28 NIV*.

DIVINE DNA

Have you ever felt like Jacob? Struggling to become who God has designed you to become, having your own priorities, going your own way, but God keeps breaking in to get your attention? No matter how far you feel from your calling, or how wayward you think you are, or how many times you've stumbled, God is devoted to transforming you, and enabling you to live a divine lifestyle, one that trusts and follows Him. He will do whatever it takes to get through to you, and to help you become who you were made to be. What a patient God we serve!

When I was going through my own transformation, whenever I deviated from His path, He would lovingly place me back on track whenever I needed it; and through this, I learned the love of Father God. He never gave up on me! I slowly began to define myself by what He thought of me, and not what the world expected of me. Coming into my calling was a journey of letting go of how others defined me. I was always trying to live up to the expectations of my parents, my work, my colleagues, or the worldly culture around me, but it didn't fit God's design for me, so it never felt quite right! God had to move me out of that mindset, and teach me something I had never learned before. **The more time I spent with Him, the more He showed me who I was really created to be.** Now, when I look back and see how much I have matured in the things of God, and how much He has transformed me, I can confidently declare: **it is possible to become a new creation!**

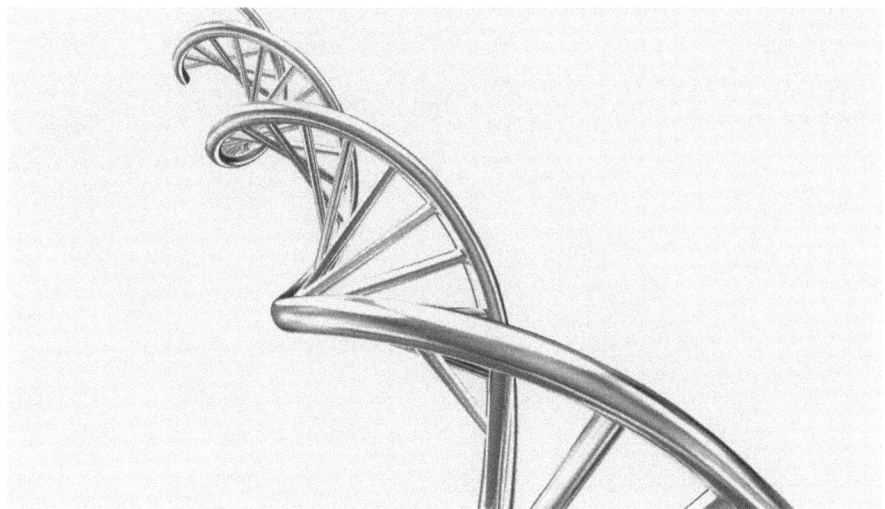

Have you ever noticed that the double helix DNA strand (the symbol of our unique identity) looks like a ladder? It was at Bethel, the place of Jacob's spiritual calling, that a heavenly ladder appeared to him, dynamically charged with angels going up and down between heaven and earth. It was like a DNA strand appearing right over Jacob's head while God spoke to Him about his identity. From the top of this ladder God revealed Himself and downloaded promises over Jacob's life and all his descendants. And Jacob responded by vowing to put his life in God's hands. He set up a memorial of remembrance and established the principle of tithing. It was from Bethel that Jacob's spiritual DNA began to change. From there, he had to choose to walk out the truth of what God had spoken, refusing the enemy's temptation to go back to where he had come from, and move into new territory. With God's help along the way, Jacob became a new creation!

Jacob's dream points to Jesus, who also alludes to this heavenly ladder, telling His disciples that they would see heaven open and angels ascending and descending over the Son of Man (Jn. 1:51). This models for us the key to obtaining our spiritual DNA. Jesus was always in connection with the Father, fully accessing the heavenly realm. He was the God-man, living on earth, operating with divine DNA, walking with power and performing miracles. Jesus showed us what divine living looks like. Just like heaven opened over Jacob, it can open over you too. **The more we commune with the Lord, and live in the power of the Spirit of God, the more we can access that heavenly exchange and walk in the divine provision of the Father.** And Jesus said, *"I tell you for certain that if you have faith in me, you will do the same things that I am doing. You will do even greater things, now that I am going back to the Father" John 14:12 NLT.* This is our true spiritual identity: accessing heaven, through Jesus Christ, to receive from the Father, and bring heaven to earth.

YOUR HEAVENLY BOOK

What if I told you that God wrote a book about you? Would you believe me? God's Word says:

> *"You saw me before I was born.*
> ***Every day of my life was recorded in your book.***
> *Every moment was laid out*
> *before a single day had passed" Psalm 139:16 NLT.*

The book of Daniel confirms this when God reveals to Daniel what is written about the future. He describes a time of *"terrible suffering, the worst in all of history. And your people who have their names written in The Book will be protected... Daniel, I now command you to keep the message of this book secret until the end of time, even though many people will go everywhere, searching for the knowledge to be found in it" Daniel 12:1,4 CEV.*

The books in heaven contain all the days of history — pre-written. What do you think He has written about you? Use your imagination, and picture God seeing everything that you would be doing on earth even before it was spoken into existence. God has thought out every detail of your life. Isn't that exciting! It is actually in a book in heaven! I don't know about you, but that makes me want to discover God's plan for my life more than ever!

When I found out that I had a book written about me in heaven, I knew I was special in the eyes of God. This is true for you too! In that book is our prophetic destiny and our purpose for being alive on this earth. In that book is the length of our life and what we are to accomplish with the days we've been given. What's even more interesting, is that God has hidden clues in our hearts to discover what He has written. What are your interests, desires, longings, and dreams? Many times, our lives become so cluttered and busy that we lose touch with these parts of ourselves. We need the Holy Spirit to unveil what is in our hearts. When we discover what we are truly passionate about, we will begin to understand what is written in our book in Heaven.[231] God has such a great passion for His children, and likewise, He has placed passion within our hearts. I have observed that **God's passion or destiny for us is always way larger than we could ever imagine.** So dream big! And know that your God is even bigger!

2 Timothy 1:9 confirms that our calling began before we were born: *"who has saved us and called us with a holy calling, not according to our works, but according to His purpose and grace **which was given to us in Christ Jesus before time began"** (NKJV).*

Did you catch that? Purpose and grace have been given to you and have been waiting for you to discover them before time began. **Purpose is your destination, and grace is the empowerment you'll need to bring it into reality on Earth.**[232] This means there is hope for your life! Even if you don't feel you are walking in any great purpose yet, it has been assigned to you, and you have been awarded grace to empower you when the season comes for you to step into it. God wants to see His words come to life as you activate them by living them out on earth. You will become His word made flesh![233] The battles you face, are really a part of a war to have whatever is in the book, manifest through your life on Earth. But take heart - God is fighting for you (Rom. 8:31). The great cloud of witnesses are cheering you on (Heb. 12:1)! Each battle won moves your destiny forward. God will provide everything you need to fulfill it, and your body, soul and spirit will prosper under His wisdom. This is how God will establish His Kingdom on earth. So, put your faith in Him, and joyously live out the victorious story He has written for you.

ENDNOTES

231   Robert Henderson, Unlocking Destinies from the Courts of Heaven (Shippensburg, PA: Destiny Image Incorporated, 2016), 10.

232   Ibid.

233   Ibid.

CONCLUSION

You were made to experience divine health in your body, soul, and spirit.

Your body was meant to function with a strong immune system, digesting nutrients from whole foods, with a healthy lymphatic system clearing out toxins. You are meant to have a clear mind that is receptive to wisdom, a strong heart that is free from disease, healthy muscles to help you endure, and self-control to keep you alert against all that would rob life from you.

You were made to function with the mind of Christ; to think the way God thinks. Not to determine reality based only on what you see, following the opinions of the world. This only leads to hopeless complaining! Your mind is meant to be filled with the Word of God, discerning the thoughts of the Spirit.

You were made to experience divine emotions, overflowing with the fruits of the spirit: love, joy, peace, patience, kindness, goodness, faithfulness, gentleness and self-control (Gal. 5:22-23); uprooting bitterness, cleansing out pain, and applying forgiveness as your medicine. Practicing a spirit of thankfulness elevates your body's frequency, keeping your whole system in perfect well-being.

Your spirit has been made new in Christ. Through the blood of Jesus, with access to Father God, guided and empowered by the Holy Spirit, you are a spiritual being with a spiritual purpose: to release heaven on earth. You have a unique destiny, written in your heavenly book. You were designed to live a lifestyle of obedience, in humble reverence and repentance. You were meant to rise and take dominion over your environment and circumstances. You have been given authority to defeat the enemy, and hold all his schemes at bay. You are God's hands and feet on earth.

Divine health is your inheritance unto Jesus' return. Don't listen to man's story of death and hopelessness, of viruses and disease. Don't get caught up in the deception of depending on prescription medications. No! There's a better way! God says, "Seek me and You will find me! Ask and I will answer. I will help you. I have made you to experience abundant life! This is My earth. I commission you to take it back! I am the same God yesterday today and forever. Trust me! You've already won. I've died for this victory! Rise up and live victoriously for my name's sake. I created you. I believe in you. I love you."

AFTERWORD

First of all, I want to thank you for taking time to read this book. I hope my testimony has encouraged you to speak with God and get answers about your health. The enemy may scheme against us, but we have a relationship with the Almighty God! My prayer is that you will be filled with hope, knowing that you have a purpose. You have an amazing life ahead of you yet to be discovered. Just think, Almighty God thought of you before He formed you in your mother's womb. You are uniquely handcrafted by Creator God Himself! You've been given special gifts that were planned for you before the beginning of time for His purposes on this earth. These gifts may still need to be discovered, but He will lead you into them. So, hold fast to the truth, take any fear or lies that the enemy whispers in your ear out of the equation, and BELIEVE what Almighty God says about you! You are the apple of His eye and He wants your body, soul, and spirit healed and whole.

No matter what trials you face, this amazing destiny set before you is possible because of what Jesus did on the cross. A transaction happened. His life was sacrificed for your sins, so you are now able to walk in wholeness, righteousness, prosperity, and freedom. God is not mad at you! He isn't counting your sins and holding them against you! God wants so much to have a personal relationship with you that He sent Jesus His only Son, to shed His blood and die on the cross and then be raised from the dead. This transaction puts us in right standing before Father God. We can come boldly into His presence (Hebrews 4:16), and when we pray, we can be sure that He hears us!

Romans 10:13 says: *"Whoever calls on the name of the Lord shall be saved" (NKJV).*

Romans 10:9-10 *"If you declare with your mouth, "Jesus is Lord," and believe in your heart that God raised him from the dead, you will be saved. For it is with your heart that you believe and are justified, and it is with your mouth that you profess your faith and are saved" (NIV).*

If you want to have this personal relationship with the Lord, or to renew your relationship with the Lord, here is a simple prayer:

Dear God in heaven, I come to you in the name of Jesus. I acknowledge that I am a sinner, and I am sorry for my sins and the life that I have lived; I need your forgiveness.

I believe that your only begotten Son, Jesus Christ, shed His precious blood on the cross at Calvary and died for my sins, and I am now willing to turn from my sin. You said in the Bible that if we confess faith in the Lord our God and believe in our hearts that God raised Jesus from the dead, we shall be saved. Right now, I confess Jesus as my Lord. With my heart, I believe that God raised Jesus from the dead. I accept Jesus Christ as my personal Savior, and according to His Word, right now, I am saved.

Amen.

What a blessing to know that you, dear reader, are my brother or sister in Christ! We're family! And we are family with a purpose. We are co-laborers with Christ, to see His Kingdom established on the earth as it is in heaven. We are more than conquerors through Christ who loves us (Rom 8:37). And as we partner with Him, we will win the war on health. Satan may have an agenda, but God has the victory.

www.ingramcontent.com/pod-product-compliance
Lightning Source LLC
Chambersburg PA
CBHW051609120626
46551CB00014B/1736